Praise for *Summer of '68*

"*Summer of '68* captivated me from the get-go . . . Cheers to Tim Wendel for bringing it all back so vividly."
—David Maraniss, author of *Clemente*
and *When Pride Still Mattered*

"No book better captures how in 1968 sports changed America . . . *Summer of '68* reads like a novel brimming with surprising action, colorful characters, and fresh insights. I enjoyed every page."
—Tom Stanton, author of
The Final Season and *Ty and The Babe*

"*Summer of '68* brilliantly evokes the glories and the grim realities of that time, when America and baseball came to a crossroads."
—John Thorn, Official Historian of Major League Baseball
and author of *Baseball in the Garden of Eden*

"[Wendel] astutely marks this summer as a landmark year for baseball—the game, like the country, would be forever changed."—*Cleveland Plain Dealer*

"Wendel engagingly presents the facts of what was a game-changing year in American history for baseball, but most importantly for the citizens of America."   —*New York Journal of Books*

"The story of one baseball season and the players that made it fantastic, even as the world seemed to be falling apart around the field."
—*Savannah Morning News*

"This riveting account masterfully weaves the social turbulence of 1968 into a narrative of one of the game's most memorable seasons."
—*American Profile*

"Wendel consistently gets to the heart of a changing world."
—*Charleston Post and Courier*

"An appealing mix of baseball and cultural history."   —*Kirkus Reviews*

"An engaging, well-researched book"   —*San Antonio Express News*

"Bring[s] the season alive."   —*Milwaukee Sunday Journal Sentinel*

"Wendel . . . brings this crucial year to life."   —*Library Journal*

SUMMER OF '68

Also by Tim Wendel

SUMMER OF '68

THE SEASON THAT CHANGED BASEBALL—AND AMERICA—FOREVER

Tim Wendel

Da Capo Press

A MEMBER OF THE PERSEUS BOOKS GROUP

Designed by Timm Bryson
Set in 11.5 point Arno Pro by the Perseus Books Group

First Da Capo Press edition 2012
First Da Capo Press paperback edition 2013

Library of Congress Cataloging-in-Publication Data
  Wendel, Tim.
  Summer of '68 : the season that changed baseball—and America—forever / Tim Wendel.
    p. cm.
  Includes bibliographical references and index.
  ISBN 978-0-306-82018-2 (hardcover)—ISBN 978-0-306-82105-9 (e-book) 1. Baseball—United States—History—20th century. I. Title. II. Title: Summer of 1968. III. Title: Summer of nineteen sixty-eight.
  GV863.A1W446 2012
  796.3570973'09046—dc23

                                                        2011047084

ISBN 978-0-306-82183-7 (paperback)
ISBN 978-0-306-82248-3 (paperback e-book)

Published by Da Capo Press
A Member of the Perseus Books Group
www.dacapopress.com

Da Capo Press books are available at special discounts for bulk purchases in the U.S. by corporations, institutions, and other organizations. For more information, please contact the Special Markets Department at the Perseus Books Group, 2300 Chestnut Street, Suite 200, Philadelphia, PA 19103, or call (800) 810-4145, ext. 5000, or e-mail special.markets@perseusbooks.com.

10 9 8 7 6 5 4 3

In memory of Eric Wendel, John Douglas, and Bill Glavin.
For Jacqueline, Sarah, and Chris, my heart of the order.

CONTENTS

So often we look to sports for an escape. We prefer to imagine it inhabiting a place that's cordoned off from the fractured and complex world outside the lines. And in many ways it is. It's a place where well-defined rules govern the action and outcomes are resolute; where the drama plays out in familiar ways we can easily understand and appreciate (if not always predict); and where we can celebrate victories vicariously, but still keep the pain of failures at arm's length.

But what happens when events in the outside world become so chaotic, so divisive, that it's no longer possible to fully escape them? When larger issues begin to permeate sports in such a way that it impacts our ability as fans to follow the action and the story lines in the usual way? In such a situation the games we watch and play cease to be merely diversions, but perhaps that's also when they matter to us most, and when the potential is there for their outcomes to mean something more.

How does such added pressure impact players? What happens when even they are no longer able to stay above the fray, and when it becomes impossible for them to isolate themselves by focusing on single moments—one game, one at-bat, one pitch at a time?

Time and again throughout the remarkable, turbulent year of 1968, the best in sports had to fall back on something else and find other ways to persevere. In the case of World Series champion Bob Gibson, the St.

Louis Cardinals ace channeled his anger into one of the most dominant pitching performances of all time. Detroit's Denny McLain, his counterpart in that season's World Series, found it best to embrace celebrity and fame in an effort to assure things never cut too close to the heart. For Tigers' slugger Willie Horton, he had to expand his definition of home to include something more than Detroit, the divided city he had grown up in. For Luis Tiant, who was about to have his break-out season pitching for the Cleveland Indians, it was finding the personal strength to be a witness to the sea changes in everything from politics to music to sports. And for Cardinals center fielder Curt Flood, perhaps it was realizing that the boundaries between sports and the outside world weren't so impermeable after all; that he could be a catalyst for change, too.

And yet it also remained true that sometimes all it takes to propel an athlete is the chance to win with everything on the line. That was the fervent hope that kept Detroit pitcher Mickey Lolich going: that he would one day have the opportunity to succeed when few believed he could ever rise to the occasion.

Today we often place our sports heroes beyond arm's length. Maybe it's a natural result of a day and age when professional athletes make so much money and no longer live in our neighborhoods that our closest glimpses of them are captured through fleeting images on the JumboTron or our TVs at home. They are regarded as celebrities, perhaps more so than at any other time in history. Yet it didn't use to be this way. In '68, for better or for worse, we were often in it together—even when we rallied to different sides of the political argument and allowed the storms of protest to wash over everything. The idea for this book came one night when I was channel surfing, bouncing between the talking heads on cable television and thinking to myself, "Could we be any more divided?" The great thing about history and our nation's narrative is that we can take Mr. Peabody's WABAC Machine back to a previous era or moment when things were seemingly just as difficult in order to gain perspective and maybe even glean a few lessons. In looking back at times in which we struggled and yet somehow carried on perhaps we can find a way to move ahead again.

In 1968, the gods were angry. It's been called "the year that rocked the world," and it rarely showed any mercy. How else to describe a single year in which Dr. Martin Luther King Jr. was killed by an assassin's bullet and weeks later Robert Kennedy met the same fate? In which riots broke out in the streets in cities across the country, and millions gathered to protest the issues surrounding the Vietnam War and civil rights, often to be met with resistance and in some cases brutality. In which everything boiled over late that summer in the streets of Chicago. Thanks to television, our world in 1968 was shrink-wrapped forever. We were able to view all this on a nightly basis, with much of it cued up for instant replay. Seemingly overnight we had become Marshall McLuhan's "global village," and what we saw was that things everywhere were unraveling, being pulled apart at the seams, often with unbearable force.

And yet, through it all, juxtaposed against the turmoil, there was sports. In 1968, baseball was still regarded as the national pastime, but the barbarians were at the gate, so to speak. Only a few weeks into the new year, Vince Lombardi's Green Bay Packers won their second consecutive Super Bowl. From this point on, empty seats at the Super Bowl were unheard of, and football would soon surpass baseball in popularity, with Joe Namath and the upstart American Football League poised to "guarantee" victory in the next championship game.

Much has been written about the impact of this tumultuous year on politics, music and our culture in general. But in our discussions of '68, the glories and struggles that occurred in sports during that time are too often cast aside. Bill Russell, the legendary player-coach for the Boston Celtics, once said that sports favor the short view. Little in this realm lasts longer than a season, regardless of how epic the team or contest may be. And yet, while scores fade and names and even outcomes may recede in our memory, select moments—so fully representative of larger forces and events that we refer to them as iconic—remain. And once pieced together, these moments can form a narrative that still speaks to us to this day.

TIM WENDEL
Vienna, Virginia

PART
I

A Bad Moon Rising

*The image was so overwhelming, so unforgettable, that
people's common sense ended up somewhere else. . . .
The shape of their world changed.*
—TOMAS ELOY MARTINEZ, *SANTA EVITA*

Back before times became so chaotic and turbulent, contentious, and even dangerous, Willie Horton made it his mission to ask Bob Gibson for his autograph. The Tigers' slugger doesn't recall when this curious quest began. Was it 1963 or maybe 1964? To this day, Horton isn't exactly sure. What is certain is that his first real chance came during spring training. As Horton recalled, he could have opted out of a particular Grapefruit League swing, which saw the Tigers' split squad stopping by Winter Haven to play the Red Sox, then heading another seventy miles west for a contest against the Cardinals at their spring training home at old Al Lang Field in St. Petersburg, Florida. Instead, he signed up for the trip, with a purpose in mind.

"My father had been a big Bob Gibson fan," said Horton, whose parents died in a car crash in 1965. "My father knew that he was a great basketball player, too, so I thought why not? I'll make this trip. I'll get him to sign."

Little did Horton realize how difficult it would be. After taking batting practice at Al Lang, Horton waited, pen and paper in hand, for the rest of the home team to appear. As Gibson strode out to shag balls with the other St. Louis pitchers in the outfield, Horton approached and asked if the right-hander would be kind enough to sign.

"What position do you play?" Gibson replied curtly.

Horton told him outfield.

"Outfield?" Gibson answered. With that he turned away, wanting nothing to do with an opposing player.

Crestfallen, Horton slunk back to the visiting dugout, where his friend and teammate Gates Brown waited for him. Brown had seen the snub and knew exactly what had happened. "You're a damn fool for making this trip," Brown said. "Anybody could have told you that guy is all business, all the time."

Indeed, the Cardinals' ace rarely smiled and always seemed to play with a chip on his shoulder. "The basis of intimidation, as I practiced it, was mystery," Gibson later explained. "I wanted the hitter to know nothing about me—about my wife, my children, my religion, my politics, my hobbies, my tastes, my feelings, nothing. I figured the more they knew about me, the more they knew what I might do in a certain situation. That was why, in large part, I never talked to players on other teams. That was why I never apologized for hitting anybody. That was why I seemed like such an asshole to so many people."

Sometimes things start from a long way off, build and build over the seasons without anybody really noticing or being any the wiser. That's how it seemed to Willie Horton years later, on a bright autumn day in St. Louis in 1968. The stands at old Busch Stadium were filled to overflowing with fans wearing straw hats with either a cotton tiger or cardinal stapled to them. The color of that afternoon—many games, even World Series contests, still began before sunset back then—stood out as firehouse red. Of course, that was the respondent hue of the hometown team, the St. Louis Cardinals. At stake was something far bigger than a spring training contest between two split-squad teams. This was Game One of the 1968

World Series, and as Willie Horton watched starter Bob Gibson warm up, he couldn't help thinking back to that day in Florida and whether the Cardinals' ace was about to give him a hard time all over again.

Anybody who had picked up a bat that year could have identified with Horton's trepidation. It had been a season that would be forever known as the "Year of the Pitcher," a time when hitting streaks were usually measured in days rather than weeks. Early on in '68, Jim "Catfish" Hunter of the Oakland Athletics pitched a perfect game, the first tossed in the American League regular season in forty-six years. Meanwhile, in the senior circuit, two no-hitters were thrown on back-to-back days in the same ballpark for the first time in major-league history. Don Drysdale of the Los Angeles Dodgers kept the opposition off the scoreboard for a record 58 2/3 innings, while Luis Tiant of the Cleveland Indians held hitters to a paltry .168 average. Both were new standards. In every ballpark across the country hitters, even the best in the game, struggled. Carl Yastrezemski of the Boston Red Sox, the previous season's Triple Crown winner, hit just .301 for the year, but that was enough to win the batting title in the American League. In fact, the junior circuit's collective slugging average of .340 stood as the lowest since 1915 and the dead-ball era.

"No hitter had an easy time of it that year," said Cardinals' first baseman Orlando Cepeda. "You might put together a string, get hot for a week or two, but anything more was asking too much in '68."

It was no surprise then that in the "Year of the Pitcher," the two starters for the first game of the World Series stood front and center. While Gibson's record was a modest 22–9, he finished the regular season with a 1.12 earned run average, the lowest ever for anyone pitching as many as 300 innings in a season. His counterpart for Game One, Denny McLain of the Detroit Tigers, had compiled an amazing 31–6 record, the first pitcher to reach the thirty-victory plateau since Dizzy Dean in 1934.

By the time the two were set to take the mound that afternoon on October 2, the teams themselves had been eyeing each other for almost two months. In 1968, the last year before additional teams were added to postseason play, the Tigers won the American League pennant by twelve games and the Cardinals by nine. Everyone, including both ballclubs, their fans in each city, and the national press, had eagerly been awaiting this Fall Classic for some time.

Certainly there had been bumps in the road along the way for both teams, however. Built on speed and defense, the Cardinals sometimes fell into a swoon at the plate and in fact had been no-hit by the Giants' Gaylord Perry only a few weeks before. Many believed Detroit, rather than the Boston Red Sox, should have won the pennant in 1967. So it didn't surprise many when the Tigers kept the Baltimore Orioles, Cleveland Indians, and Red Sox at arm's length this time around. Yet some still questioned Detroit's ability to win under pressure.

If St. Louis captured the 1968 Fall Classic, the franchise would be recognized as a dynasty, the top ballclub of the sixties after winning in 1964 and 1967. If Detroit triumphed, the championship would be the city's first in twenty-three years, and perhaps a psychic balm for a locale ravaged by rioting and racial division.

While few realized it at the time, the game of baseball was fast approaching a crossroads in 1968. In fact, the game's first century of existence was about to go down in the history books. The first pro team, the Cincinnati Red Stockings, had come into existence in 1869, nearly a century before, posting a 65–0–1 record while barnstorming 11,877 miles. Along the way, the game had authorized such advances as the curveball (in 1872), turnstiles (1878), and night baseball (1935). During this sweep of history, Cy Young retired with 511 career victories (1911), Babe Ruth walloped 60 home runs in a season (1927), and Sandy Koufax pitched a perfect game, his fourth no-hitter in four years (1965). Looking ahead, a divisional format and play-offs were on the horizon—changes that were about to alter the national pastime forever. "People forget how honest and pure things used to be," Willie Horton said. "Back then we played the whole season so the best team in the American League could play the best team in the National League. You cut right to the World Series. I always kind of appreciated that."

On this day in October 1968, and at this time in U.S. sports history, baseball had everything going for it. Not only did the sport offer fans an epic pitching showdown in Game One, what some scribes called "The Great Confrontation," the game itself reigned as king throughout the American sports landscape. In '68 the national pastime was as popular as it had ever been. Soon it would fall from this lofty perch, thanks in large part to many events that took place during this watershed year. For now, however, the game was ready for another turn on center stage.

As Game One began, Cardinals catcher Tim McCarver settled in behind home plate. Tom Gorman, the home-plate umpire, took up his position behind him, and out on the mound stood Gibson, glaring in at both of them as if they were strangers, even adversaries. Even though the intimidating right-hander struggled somewhat early on, needing seventeen pitches to get through a scoreless first inning, it soon became apparent that Gibson was in rare form. His fastball displayed great movement, hissing like a snake as it flew through the strike zone. After gaining a touch more control, Gibson struck out seven of the first ten Tigers batters he faced. On this afternoon, the heart of the Detroit batting order—Al Kaline, Norm Cash and Horton—was overmatched, registering the lion's share of Detroit's strikeouts.

"That day was trouble all over again for me, for my ballclub, for anybody from Detroit," Horton said, "In that game, Bob Gibson was the toughest pitcher I ever faced in my career. Ever."

When it came to pitching in 1968, neither league was truly able to gain the upper hand. Nearly every team could roll out a quality ace, or at least one in the making. In the National League, the top arms included Gibson, Juan Marichal, Tom Seaver, Gaylord Perry, Mike McCormick and Ferguson Jenkins, not to mention such promising youngsters as Gary Nolan, Larry Dierker, and Steve Carlton. "Against studs like Gibson and Marichal," Drysdale wrote in his memoir, "you knew damn well that you could give up three runs or less in a game and lose."

Undoubtedly, everyone in the American League knew the stakes had been raised as well, with McLain and Mickey Lolich in Detroit, Luis Tiant and "Sudden" Sam McDowell in Cleveland, Dean Chance and Jim Kaat in Minnesota, and Jim Lonborg coming off his Cy Young season in Boston. Throughout 1968, this chord became the clarion call, sounded time and again. Sometimes it would be the game's top stars that delivered this refrain. In other moments, unknown arms, at least at the time, would underscore this trend. While professional football, especially the upstart American Football League, strove for explosive offense and points, the more the better, in baseball that year teams often struggled to put a few runs on the board. Early on, veteran hitters could tell there was a bad moon rising for them in '68. One needed only to look at the daily headlines to realize that pitching ruled the national pastime.

"You could see that the pitching was going to be something that season," Gates Brown said. "Anybody with eyes knew that even as early as the first weeks of spring training. My God, the arms that were out there. As that '68 season began all I was thinking was put the damn ball in play and see what happens. That's about all a man could do some days."

In the Pirates' fourth game of the season, Jim Bunning picked up his first win with the Pittsburgh Pirates, a 3–0 victory at Dodgers Stadium. The shutout was the fortieth of his career and included his one-thousandth strikeout in the National League. That made him the first pitcher since Cy Young with one thousand in each league.

A day later, the Houston Astros defeated the New York Mets, 1–0, in twenty-four innings. The game lasted six hours and six minutes.

Of course, one could rationalize Bunning's star turn was the culmination of a Hall of Fame career, and indeed, the no-nonsense right-hander was inducted into Cooperstown in 1996. As for the marathon in the Astrodome? Just a fluke, right? Maybe, maybe not.

The following week, on April 19, Nolan Ryan, in his season debut for the New York Mets, struck out eleven, including three batters on ten pitches in the first inning. Afterward, announcer Ralph Kiner compared the soft-spoken Texan with Bob Feller when it came to sheer velocity. But as was Ryan's luck during his years with the Mets, things didn't turn out well. The Texan lost 3–2 when Rocky Colavito, who was a last-minute addition to the Dodgers' lineup, drove in the winning run. Jim Fairey was supposed to start in the Los Angeles outfield, but mistakenly thought the game was a night affair and overslept. That put Colavito in the starting lineup and his single in the eighth inning decided it.

"Strikeouts weren't the problem for me back then," Ryan said. "Getting wins was another matter."

By the time the Orioles' Tom Phoebus no-hit the Boston Red Sox on April 27 in Baltimore little doubt remained that a trend was apparent. Brooks Robinson not only drove in three runs but saved the no-no with a diving grab, to rob Rico Petrocelli of a hit in the eighth inning.

"The evidence mounted quickly," said William Mead, author of *Two Spectacular Seasons*, "that this was going to be a great time for the pitchers."

On May 8, 1968, Catfish Hunter of the Oakland Athletics hurled a perfect game against the visiting Minnesota Twins. It was the A's first year in Oakland, after moving to town from Kansas City. Only 6,298 fans were in the stands that evening for what was just the eleventh game ever played at the new Oakland-Alameda County Coliseum. But what the privileged few in the stands witnessed was the first regular-season perfect game—no hits, no walks, no errors—in the American League since 1922.

For baseball insiders, Hunter's "perfecto" came down to a precious moment or two. In the seventh inning, the twenty-two-year-old faced Twins slugger Harmon Killebrew. The count ran to 3–2, and just about everyone, including Killebrew, figured the baby-faced right-hander would throw a fastball. But Hunter crossed up the future Hall of Famer, going with a changeup that Killebrew swung at and missed.

From there, things quickly moved to the game's final batter, Rich Reese. The Twins' pinch hitter fouled off four pitches with a 3–2 count before a called third strike. "For a while there I thought I was never going to get him out," Hunter said afterward. "That boy kept on fouling off everything I threw up there. I sure was glad to see him strike out."

At the time of Hunter's perfect game, the chances of a no-hitter were calculated at 1,300 to 1. The chances of a perfect game stood at 28,000 to 1. In the Oakland clubhouse, Hunter told representatives of the Hall of Fame they were welcome to anything they wanted, uniform, cap, even the bat he used to help his own effort by driving in three runs, everything except the ball that struck out Reese. "That last one belongs to me," the pitcher said. "I'll keep it as long as I live because it sure took me a long time to get that final out."

Afterward, Athletics' owner Charlie Finley promised Hunter a $5,000 raise—a princely sum in these days before free agency—in honor of the accomplishment. When Hunter called his father back in North Carolina, the old man cautioned his son, "Tell me all about that five thousand when you get it." After all, Finley already had the reputation for being a notorious skinflint. In the end, though, Hunter got his money. Perhaps because of all the great players the Athletics owner employed over the years, this pitcher was his favorite.

In high school, Hunter pitched five no-hitters, including a perfect game. But before signing a professional contract, he was involved in a hunting accident, which blew off a toe and left thirty shotgun pellets in his right foot. He was winged by his older brother, who stumbled, the gun accidentally going off, while the two were duck hunting. Upon seeing Hunter's bleeding foot, the brother promptly fainted, leaving the wounded pitching prospect on his own.

Hunter crawled on his belly to a nearby creek, where he soaked his sweater in the cool running water. Then he scrambled back, wringing the garment over his brother's face. Thankfully that was enough to revive the sibling and soon Hunter was in the bed of the family pickup truck, hightailing it to the local hospital. There doctors told him that he would never play baseball or football again.

"I could see he was handicapped," said Finley, who visited the Hunter family's sharecropper shack in Hertford, North Carolina. "Yet he still played baseball. His determination grabbed me, and after I heard the story of his accident, I was convinced that I wanted him."

Other teams hadn't gone above $50,000 for Hunter's services, due to the damaged foot. But Finley made a preemptive bid of $75,000 "because the Catfish had character."

Early on, Hunter needed a good foot more than an admirable character. An operation to remove the shotgun pellets slowed his progress and many in the A's organization urged Finley to drop him from the roster. Yet four years after the signing, Finley's gamble paid off as Hunter was carried off the field on his teammates' shoulders. In pitching the first perfect game in the American League since Don Larsen's in the 1956 World Series, Hunter threw just 107 pitches, and only four balls were well hit. Left fielder Joe Rudi, making his first start in left field after being called up from Vancouver of the Pacific Coast League, tracked down two of them, including Rod Carew's line drive in the seventh inning. Afterward, Hunter said the latter was the only one that really concerned him.

"He probably threw no more than five curves all night," said A's catcher Jim Pagliaroni, who had caught Bill Monbouquette's no-hitter in 1962. "He shook off only two of my signs. He made my job easy."

With Hunter's perfect game, it was apparent to sports fans that—to paraphrase the Buffalo Springfield hit song of the time—something was happening here. Pitchers, young and old, had the fever, and looking back on it, Hunter's perfect game ushered in a season of excellence that we may never witness again. "It was the times," said Jon Warden, a rookie reliever with the Tigers in '68. "Everybody knew it. We were witnessing one of the great eras in pitching, and I, like anybody who threw a baseball back then, wanted to be a part of it in the worst way."

Ken (Hawk) Harrelson, who would go on to lead the American League with 109 RBI, remembered Hunter's perfecto as a sign of what was to come. "There were a lot of amazing pitchers in that season and folks will ask me, 'Who was the best?'" Harrelson said. "And I'll ask them, are we talking about best stuff or best pitcher? If we're talking stuff, it would have to be somebody like Luis Tiant or 'Sudden' Sam McDowell. I mean nobody had four pitches as good as McDowell in his prime.

"But if we're talking best pitcher, I'd go with Catfish Hunter. He didn't have the stuff of the guys we're talking about and I'd had glimpses of Bob Gibson or Juan Marichal or Don Drysdale, too. We'd go up against those NL guys in spring training and I'd faced Gibson in the '67 World Series.

"Catfish didn't have that kind of stuff. His fastball was kind of sneaky and he had a spinner of a breaking ball. Maybe not much. But what he did have was the biggest heart and more balls than anybody I ever faced. I mean the man was a competitor. If you're asking me who's the guy to win me a game when my family's lives are at stake, I'm going with Catfish."

No landmark event or epic confrontation caused the United States to go to war in Vietnam. No Pearl Harbor. No September 11th. The Gulf of Tonkin Resolution in 1964 pales in comparison. Yet by the spring of 1968, United States troop levels were at their highest, with more than 536,000 troops committed to the venture in Southeast Asia.

Early in the year, U.S. forces were rocked by the Tet offensive, a wide-ranging series of attacks by the Vietcong. To better assess the war effort and the United States' expectations for eventual success, CBS anchorman Walter Cronkite traveled to Vietnam for a series of special reports. The culmination was an analysis he gave at the end of his nightly network broadcast on February 27, 1968: "We have been too often disappointed by the optimism of the American leaders, both in Vietnam and Washington, to have faith any longer in the silver linings they find in the darkest clouds," Cronkite told his audience of 100 million or more—a stunning number that underscores how powerful network television was before the advent of cable and satellite TV. Cronkite declared that the United States was "mired in stalemate . . . and with each escalation, the world comes closer to the brink of cosmic disaster." He closed his commentary by saying, "it is increasingly clear to this reporter that the only rational way out then will be to negotiate, not as victors, but as an honorable people who lived up to their pledge to defend democracy, and did the best they could."

Cronkite's speech to the American people, which was very much out of character for what he felt a nightly news broadcast should be, resonated throughout America. Already polls showed that a majority of Americans thought the war was a mistake. In large part that was due to the fact that so many citizens were directly impacted by Vietnam. The draft fueled the military machine. Even for those who were never sent to Vietnam, who had made other arrangements, the war was often on their minds.

During this period, one way to gauge a team's chances, which was rarely even mentioned in any annual previews or scouting reports, was to determine how many players a ballclub had serving in the military reserve. While being in the National Guard or a similar organization kept a player out of the draft and away from the front lines in Vietnam, it played havoc with one's professional career and personal life. Reservists usually left the team to be with their military unit for one weekend a month throughout the year and often were required to put in another two weeks of continuous service for training exercises during the season. Nolan Ryan was one of the players whose baseball development was severely hampered during '68.

"I experienced so much frustration that particular season," said Ryan, who was then with the New York Mets, "in large part because I couldn't focus on my game. I was juggling two worlds, two commitments, all the time."

For a time, Ryan needed to fly back to Houston several weekends a month to be with his reserve unit. Its specialty was constructing landing strips, and for a time Ryan thought his unit would actually have to go to Southeast Asia. Yet after the Tet offensive any such plans were ratcheted down.

On the Detroit Tigers, left-hander Mickey Lolich found himself in a similar situation. He was a member of the 191st Michigan National Guard unit, which ran a motor pool based out of Alpena, Michigan, about 200 miles north of Detroit. Unlike Ryan, he was close enough to often head down to Tiger Stadium to be with the team, even pitch in a game, before returning to his unit. What drove him to distraction, though, was the lack of quality training partners. Away from the team, Lolich contacted local high school coaches and threw to whoever was game enough to play catch with his lively stuff. Once his batterymate was a local priest who said, "Heavens to mercy, I never saw a ball move so much." In that particular training session, Lolich's offerings ricocheted off the man of the cloth's shin guards and chest protector, with a curveball finally bouncing off the priest's toe. "Let's just say it wasn't the best of circumstances," Lolich said.

In the spring of '68, Lolich worked out for a week at the Tigers' camp in Lakeland, Florida, before heading on to Savannah for fifteen days of active training. It could have been worse. The season before, during the Detroit riots, the left-hander had been thrust into the action due to his role with the reserve. After being in uniform with the Tigers one afternoon, he was in combat fatigues that evening, rifle in hand, helping to guard a supply depot and then a radio tower that also served as a police relay station in downtown Detroit.

As the city burned around him, the situation pinwheeled between the tragic and the comical. The *Detroit Free Press* commandeered an armored vehicle for its reporters to cover the event, while the National Guard established a machine gun nest atop a JCPenney store in suburban Grosse Pointe until more rational minds realized such firepower was better served six miles west in Detroit proper.

"People hit the streets, looking for anything they could grab—a side of beef, something out of the freezer at the supermarket," said William Mead, who was bureau chief for United Press International at the time. "What aggravated the situation was that the parts of Detroit that rioted were mostly black and the troops they sent in to settle things down were mostly white guys."

One of Lolich's assignments was to accompany the ranking commander through the city, which was by now under curfew and on fire in several areas. Despite the danger, Lolich tried to stay upbeat. When the ranking major stopped at a red light, the Tigers' pitcher asked, "Sir, why are we stopping?"

"It's a red light," the major replied.

"But, sir, we're the only truck in downtown Detroit tonight," Lolich said. "We're not going to get a ticket if we go through that red light."

The major pondered this for a moment before stomping on the accelerator.

The rioting that spread throughout the city and caused Detroit to burn in 1967 would prove to be a harbinger of things to come. As the new year began a number of U.S. cities, including the nation's capital, were poised to explode. "There was no getting around it," recalled Frank Howard, the top slugger on the Washington Senators. "Everywhere you went, you sensed it. The whole thing could go up at any minute."

With tension and turmoil spreading increasingly throughout the nation, the start of the '68 baseball season was marked not by celebration, but by a somber note of tragedy, delayed by a day of mourning for Dr. Martin Luther King. Afterward, Howard struggled as much as anybody with a bat in his hand. Yet Howard had always been a streak hitter and he told himself to hang in. At six foot seven, Howard towered over nearly everybody else in the game. He had played basketball at Ohio State University and anyone could see that he had loads of athletic potential, regardless of the sport. In 1958 he signed with the Dodgers for the princely sum of $75,000. The organization promptly hailed him as the next Babe Ruth.

"To me, Frank Howard was the hitter's version of [the Indians' Sam] McDowell," Bob Gibson said in a conversation with Reggie Jackson in *Sixty Feet, Six Inches: A Hall of Fame Pitcher & A Hall of Fame Hitter Talk About How the Game Is Played*. "He was a big, strong guy who swung hard, and every once in a while he was going to hit one eighteen miles. But he wasn't a good hitter in the way that the really good hitters were."

Despite the occasional long ball, Howard never hit better than .300 and, more importantly, cracked the thirty-home run plateau only once in his first five full seasons in the majors. Word had it he would be better off as a platoon player. Before the 1965 season, the Dodgers traded him as part of multiplayer deal to Washington. While Howard knew he wouldn't come close to winning a championship in the nation's capital (the ballclub was rarely any good), he did secure a regular spot in the Senators' lineup. Along with the playing time, Howard arguably received better coaching in D.C., as well. There coaches urged him to open up his batting stance and cut down on his stride length. His large step toward the pitcher caused the big man to bob his head and lose sight of the ball as it was traveling to the plate. In the spring of '68, Washington manager Jim Lemon told Howard to move closer to the plate. That way the big man could crush the outside curveballs and sliders that had sometimes bedeviled him. Other than that Howard's approach remained pretty basic. "I just go up to the plate and try to get my three rips," he once told the *Washington Post*. "I try not to take too many good pitches or swing at too many bad ones."

A few weeks into the '68 season, however, Howard had a revelation. When he had two strikes on him, he realized most pitchers would invariably throw him a fastball. A few others might try a changeup and most of them often tipped that pitch anyway. Despite the pitching excellence that ran throughout the game, only a few hurlers had full confidence in their curve, slider, or other breaking stuff. Hence, with two strikes in the count, he decided to keep an eye peeled for the fastball.

"That's as true then as it's ever been," Howard said years later. "But nobody really ever explained it to me. So when I discovered that I was able to lock in better at the plate. It was a real jump forward for me."

Sure enough Howard began to pummel the ball. In late April and into early May, most of his hard knocks went for doubles instead of home runs. That was about to change in hurry, though.

On Sunday, May 12, 1968, Howard hit two home runs against the visiting Detroit Tigers at D.C. Stadium. The first was "a routine one" off Mickey Lolich—part of a bad stretch for the Tigers' southpaw that would soon land him in the bullpen. The second was off Fred Lasher and soared well into the upper deck.

"I've always been a streaky hitter and those two homers were enough for me to get locked in," Howard said. "Now the best hitters ever in the game, guys like Hank Aaron, Ted Williams, Barry Bonds, can really concentrate. They can get in this state of mind for weeks and weeks. I never had that ability. It's so hard to do. But I could get locked in for a week or so, even in that crazy year."

In the Senators' next game, a Tuesday night contest in Boston, Howard hit two more home runs. The first one was a blast into the netting atop the Green Monster. The second was eight rows deep in the centerfield bleachers. During the next game, he hit another, this time off Red Sox ace Jose Santiago. As the *Washington Post* later pointed out, this homer was perhaps the only cheap one of the bunch as it barely made it over the left-field wall and would have been an out in most ballparks.

About this time Howard began to wonder why some pitcher didn't "flip" him, or in other words, throw at him deliberately. That's how things were done back in 1968. An Old Testament god still ruled in baseball, where it was very much an eye for an eye, a tooth for a tooth. But even though Howard would be flipped plenty as the season continued, during his hot streak nobody dared topple the big man.

From Boston, Howard's traveling home run show headed to the old stadium in Cleveland, where nearly every long ball needed to be legit. Howard did his part by driving one a dozen rows into the left-field stands and a second into the alley between the grandstand and the bleachers. The second dinger came within ten feet of being the first hit into the un-covered seats in Cleveland, sailing nearly 525 feet. By now Howard was one better than Babe Ruth and a few others who had hit seven home runs in five consecutive games. Ruth had done it in 1921, Jim Bottomley in 1929 and Vic Wertz in 1950. Howard blew by them all on a Friday night in Detroit as he hit yet another homer in the ninth inning off the Tigers' Joe Sparma. That set up a final round of fireworks for Saturday afternoon.

Once again Howard homered twice and once again Lolich was the pitcher. "Don't talk to me about Mr. Howard," the Tigers' southpaw said years later. "That guy wore me out to begin that season."

Of course, Lolich was the guy on the mound when the streak started the previous Sunday. As was the pattern, Howard's first home run was "routine," while the second blast bordered upon the unbelievable. This time, Howard hit one that landed atop the left-field grandstand, which rose ninety feet above the field at Tiger Stadium. The ball then bounced completely out of the ballpark.

Howard didn't homer in the next day's doubleheader. Still, his ten home runs in six games was a record. Decades later, Howard said he can remember every long ball from that epic run.

"I was certainly in the zone or whatever you want to call it," he said. "It was like I'd gone someplace where nobody could touch me, where I could do no wrong.

"In looking back on that time in our country, things were as screwed up as they can ever be. As a ballplayer, you try to protect yourself by wrapping yourself up in the game and paying attention to nothing else. Of course, it rarely works that way. Things worm their way inside you and how that didn't happen to just about everybody back then I don't know. My goodness, you think of all the crap that was happening. But for a week or so, I felt like I was safe from all that. For a while, I was somehow flying above it all."

PART
II

On the Brink
of a Dynasty

*St. Louis is the best baseball town (in America)
because fans are as enthusiastic as in other places but
are probably more fair-minded. You can get booed here
some, but you're not going to get embarrassed.*

—TONY LA RUSSA

When *Sports Illustrated*'s Neil Leifer photographed the St. Louis Cardinals' starting nine, sitting in front of their individual lockers, the more conventional shot would have been to have each of the 1967 world champions in uniform, ready to take the field for another game. But for the final takes, only manager Red Schoendienst was in uniform, holding his red Cardinals cap loosely in his hand.

Fanned back alongside of him, each astride a red-and-white stool, were the players who made up the best team in baseball. Their civilian threads were bright hues of blue, red, yellow, and even an off-pink. The scene would have held its own with any of the day's fashion shoots. The Cardinals' ranks included Roger Maris (the single-season home-run leader), catcher Tim McCarver, pitcher Bob Gibson (the reigning World Series MVP), third baseman Mike Shannon, outfielders Curt Flood and Lou Brock (the top base-stealer in the game) and first baseman Orlando Cepeda (one of the top Latino players of the day).

At this point in history, they were also considered the best team that money could buy. *Sports Illustrated* had no reservations about hanging a price tag on each of the stars: Maris, $75,000; McCarver, $60,000; Gibson, $85,000; Shannon, $40,000; Flood, $72,500; Brock, $70,000; and Cepeda, $80,000. Of course, such figures seem like a pittance today. As Gibson later remarked, today one would be hard-pressed to sign a utility infielder for the team's total payroll of $607,000. Yet in '68 this was considered an unprecedented chunk of coin. At the same time, there was no arguing the fact that the investment had certainly yielded results. The Cardinals were a budding dynasty, the world champs in 1964 and 1967, and many expected them to repeat in 1968. But the team was also perceived by some fans and certainly some sportswriters as enjoying the spotlight, the fancy threads, and the big money a bit too much.

Among the everyday players, the flamboyant Cepeda had established himself as one of the team leaders. Nineteen games into the 1966 season, the Puerto Rican star had been traded away from his adopted city, San Francisco. At first he dreaded leaving the Giants for St. Louis, a city that he considered to be as segregated as any in America's heartland. Then he met his new teammates and quickly became one of their most vocal clubhouse personalities.

"When I was traded from the Giants to the Cardinals in '66, it was a complete shock to me. A real heartbreaker," Cepeda said. "I grew up with the Giants' organization. While I'd had my differences with them before the trade, you always thought you'd be with the team you came up with. I was a Giants player, first and foremost, and then to be shown the door was difficult.

"People need to remember it was a different time back then. Almost everybody thought they'd begin and end their careers with the ballclub that signed them. It's not like today when you go from one team to another. Back then you were proud to play with the same team your whole career. But I have this gift—I never look back. And that's what I did after I was traded to St. Louis."

When Cepeda joined the team, he was surprised by how fast his new teammates made him feel welcome. It soon became apparent to the slugger that the Cardinals were "a bunch of great personalities, great teammates, and we knew how to play the game."

Cepeda added, "Each and every one of them went out of their way to tell me how much I was going to like playing in St. Louis, how we were going to win a World Series together. You couldn't have asked for more. I'll be honest—it took me awhile to get over that trade. But soon I realized what a good situation I was in. Soon I was beginning to look at those guys as my brothers."

Cepeda became so at home with the team that he helped with a pregame ritual that the old Cardinals still love to talk about. Before big games, Cepeda would stand atop the money truck, the place where the team's rings, watches and wallets, were locked away and stored during games. From his perch, he would lead the group in a round of cheers.

"All right, El Birdos," Cepeda began. It was Cepeda who made sure the mangled Spanish nickname, originally authored by coach Joe Schultz, stuck with the team. "Who made the great play out there tonight? Was it Heinie Manush?"

(For those scoring at home, Hall of Famer Henry Emmett Manush was a left fielder for a half-dozen teams in the majors.)

"No," the team would chant.

"Was it Toulouse-Lautrec?"

"Was it Curt Flood?"

"Yes!"

And so it would go, with Cepeda playing cheerleader, highlighting the efforts of as many of his teammates as he could until the entire clubhouse was chanting, "El Birdos, El Birdos."

"That team was a group of guys who knew how to get along," Cardinals pitcher Nellie Briles said. "Orlando had no problem fitting in with us. He brought a real passion to the game."

In '67, the Cardinals won the pennant by ten and a half games over the second-place Giants, Cepeda's old team. Then they defeated the Boston Red Sox in that season's Fall Classic. "The whole thing was as satisfying a season as I've ever had as a player," said Cepeda, who hit twenty-five home runs and a league-leading 111 RBI (runs batted in) that year.

As the *Sports Illustrated* cover showcased, this was one confident, aggressive bunch, more than willing to stick up for each other. And no incident better illustrated that than the famed brawl against the Cincinnati Reds.

On a hot day in July of 1967, the Cardinals got off to a quick start against Milt Pappas and the Reds. They batted around in the first inning, opening up a 7–0 lead. When Lou Brock reached base after his second bat in the inning, he tried to steal second. Even though he was thrown out, the Reds were infuriated by the attempt. Some in baseball consider stealing bases when your team is already staked to a big lead to be rubbing it in. The gambit would later upset the Tigers' Mickey Lolich in Game Two of the '68 World Series, ending with Lolich yelling a few choice words at Brock. In the game against the Reds, things escalated into a far more serious situation.

"Much of my reputation as a badass pitcher resulted from the fact that Lou Brock was on my side," Bob Gibson explained in his candid memoir with Lonnie Wheeler, *Stranger to the Game.* "There was no other player who irritated the other team as Brock did, and consequently no other who was knocked down quite as often. When somebody on the other team threw at Brock, I considered it my duty to throw at somebody on the other team. That's simply how the game was played—at least in my book."

In the fourth inning against Cincinnati, Brock was hit by Don Nottebart, the Reds' new pitcher. That resulted in Gibson buzzing Reds slugger Tony Perez, high and tight.

After flying out, Perez shouted at Gibson as he trotted past the pitcher's mound. Gibson stared him down as Cepeda moved in from first base to get between the two. In quick order, the benches emptied. Things further escalated when Reds reliever Bob "Man Mountain" Lee raced in from bull pen, wanting a piece of Cepeda. Instead of waiting for the mountain to come to him, the Cardinals' first baseman decided to go to the mountain. As the players jostled and yelled at each other, Cepeda tapped Lee on the shoulder. When Man Mountain turned around, Cepeda decked him with a single punch and the fight was on in earnest.

Eventually, twenty policemen came on to the field, but they couldn't immediately stop the wide-ranging brawl, which soon spread to both dugouts. Gibson ended up in the Cincinnati bench, wrestling Perez, Tommy Helms, and Pete Rose. "I'll never forget the sight," Cardinals announcer Jack Buck said. "There was Gibson in the Reds' dugout, visibly manhandling about three Reds and tossing them bodily out of the dugout and onto the field. That was just a sample of something you saw from Gibson every time he went out there."

Putting such loyalty, money, and success aside, what's startling about the *Sports Illustrated* cover shot remains the racial makeup. Even today, with the rise of Latinos in the game, where they make up roughly 25 percent of major league rosters, ballclubs often break along ethnic and racial lines. Yet the 1968 Cardinals, in this iconic photograph, were represented by five white players (Maris, McCarver, Shannon, infielder Dal Maxvill, and manager Schoendienst), three black players (Gibson, Brock, and Flood), and two Latinos (Cepeda and infielder Julian Javier). Long before Jesse Jackson, the Cardinals "were the rainbow coalition of baseball," Gibson said.

A pitcher, even an ace, isn't necessarily one of the leaders of ballclub. After all, he plays only every fourth or fifth day. No matter how memorable his performance, the impact has usually finished rippling through the clubhouse long before he takes the mound again. Yet in 1968, there were several exceptions to this rule. Nobody made more headlines in Motown, good and bad, than Denny McLain. Like it or not, many considered him the face of the franchise. For McLain embraced the glitz and the glamour of celebrity wholeheartedly, becoming the jokester, the trickster, the life of the party. He realized that if somebody was a superstar, the normal rules didn't really apply.

In comparison, Gibson was all business. "I'll never forget the look he gave me. It scared me to death," Reggie Smith said after the 1967 World Series. "He sent a stare right through me, like, 'Who do you think you are?' I thought for sure there was a knockdown coming, but he fooled me with a slider that I tapped out in front of the plate. McCarver picked it up and tagged me out."

Gibson knew full well how his public persona and the sight of a no-nonsense black man on a big-league mound worked for and against him back in the mid-1960s. "There's no way to gloss over the fact that racial perception contributed a great deal to my reputation," he wrote. "I pitched in a period of civil unrest, of black power and clenched fists and burning buildings and assassinations and riots in the street. There was a country full of angry black people in those days, and by extension—and by my demeanor on the mound—I was perceived to be one of them.

"There was some truth to that, but it had little, if anything to do with the way I worked a batter. I didn't see a hitter's color. I saw his stance, his strike zone, his bat speed, his power, and his weakness."

Still, Gibson knew as well as anybody that perception often becomes reality, especially in a year like 1968. "As a black man, I was member of a race that had been intimidated by the white man for more than two hundred years, in which we learned something about the process," he added. "When one is intimidated, he resigns himself to the backseat. He defers to his so-called superior, having no other legitimate choice, and allows himself to be dominated. As a major-league pitcher, I had the opportunity, at least, to push off the mound in the other man's shoes."

The Cardinals' home, Busch Memorial Stadium, had opened in 1966 and was the first multipurpose concrete bowl in the National League. (San Diego's Jack Murphy, Pittsburgh's Three Rivers, Cincinnati's Riverfront, and Philadelphia's Veterans soon followed.) Busch II, which the locals called the new digs to distinguish it from its predecessor, Sportsman's Park, was arguably the best of the cookie-cutter stadiums. Designed by architect Edward Durrell Stone, whose credits include the Kennedy Center in Washington, D.C., the stadium sported a distinctive circular roof and was within a short walk of the new Gateway Arch and, ironically, the Old Courthouse, site of the infamous Dred Scott trial in 1846.

Early on, certainly in 1968, Busch II was a pretty good place to watch and play baseball. Back then the field was still natural grass. However, even here, in a longtime baseball town, football eventually gained the upper hand. In 1970, the outfield at Busch was ripped up for football as the stadium was also home to the St. Louis Cardinals of the National Football League. The infield was replaced by Astroturf seven years later and an unforeseen consequence was that the man-made stuff caused the temperature on the field to soar past 100 degrees Fahrenheit. (Lou Brock resorted to putting aluminum foil inside his cleats to beat the heat.) In addition, the change in turf at times made the game unrecognizable to the way the Cardinals played in the mid-1960s. Manager Whitey Herzog loaded up with speedsters (Vince Coleman, Willie McGee. and Ozzie Smith), who could turn bouncing hits to the outfield into doubles and triples. Such a brand of baseball took St. Louis to the World Series in 1982, 1985, and 1987.

That last ballclub brought me to St. Louis for the first time. I was covering the San Francisco Giants, my first year of big-league ball, and that divisional series went seven games, with the Cardinals taking the last two to upend Roger Craig's "Humm Babies." It was my first experience in being drenched with cheap champagne. As I was covering the winner's clubhouse, Tommy Herr, whom I'd pestered for quotes throughout the series, got me. I didn't think about it until I returned later that evening to my hotel, changed into a new shirt, and wrote away as the sun came up over the Mississippi River. But when I went to run a hand through my hair, the fingertips became stuck. The bubbly had dried into a shellac-like dome-do.

––––––––––

The same week Catfish Hunter pitched his perfect game, Jim Ryun ran the trails under a dormant volcano outside of Flagstaff, Arizona. The best miler in the world ran alone, gasping for breath.

Two years before, at the age of nineteen, Ryun had set world records in the half-mile and mile. *Sports Illustrated* named him its "Sportsman of the Year" and he won the James E. Sullivan Award as the nation's top amateur athlete. But in the spring of 1968, everything went seriously off track. Three days after announcing his engagement to Anne Snider, it was confirmed that Ryun had mononucleosis. As a result, he missed the first round of the U.S. Olympic Trials.

After three weeks of prescribed rest, he traveled to northern Arizona to train at seven thousand feet, the approximate height of the Mexico City Games. With the Olympics less than five months away, Ryun and the powers that be feared he wouldn't be ready. One night Ryun made a single entry in his training journal. "Worried," it read. In June, America's top track star planned to run a 3:50 mile. Now he was pressed to break four minutes in his specialty. After years of training for the Olympic Games, he feared that he might "not even get a chance to try out."

Ryun's struggles, however, went well beyond one man trying to make the Olympic team. ABC Sports' Roone Arledge had paid $4.5 million, three times the amount NBC laid out for the Tokyo Games four years earlier, for the rights to broadcast the Mexico City Games. Using his popular *ABC's Wide World of Sports* as a media springboard, Arledge planned to offer live coverage of the Olympics to the American audience. Four years earlier, in the Winter Games from Innsbruck, Austria, the action was taped and flown back to New York before being aired. Ultimately, Arledge's goal was to one day have the Olympics become as popular as the World Series. But he realized that could happen only if the best-known athletes—and in the track world nobody was more famous than Ryun—found their way to the starting line.

No sport cast a bigger shadow in 1968 than major league baseball. The '68 World Series was on NBC and ranked among the first major sports events to be rated. Nobody was surprised when it drew a 50-plus percent market share—an amazing number compared with today's fragmented audience. If anything, people tuned in to the Fall Classic to be reassured. A drug scandal had tainted that year's Kentucky Derby and golfer Roberto De Vicenzo missed out on a play-off in the prestigious Masters tournament when he signed an inaccurate scorecard. "What a stupid I am to be wrong here," De Vicenzo said.

The Mexico City Summer Games were scheduled to begin days after the baseball season ended. Earlier in 1968, skier Jean-Claude Killy and American figure skater Peggy Fleming were gold medalists at the Winter Games in Grenoble, France. While their performances drew strong audiences in the United States, the Grenoble coverage paled in comparison to what Arledge was putting together for Mexico City. By employing personalized storytelling, augmented by satellite feeds, upgraded graphics, and videotaped highlights, Arledge planned to broadcast forty-four hours of coverage, three times as many hours as any previous Games. All of it would go a lot better with Ryun running in the 1,500 meters, the Olympics' equivalent of the mile and one of track's showcase events.

Among Ryun's advisors was Dr. Jack Daniels, who decades later would be named the world's best coach by *Runner's World* magazine. Back in 1968, however, Daniels had difficulty getting anybody to take him seriously. His program to better prepare athletes, especially distance runners, never had sufficient funds. In addition, U.S. track officials told Ryun to simply train, often by himself, and not worry about races right away. He would receive another chance to make the American team in mid-August.

Daniels contended such an approach would only set Ryun up for failure. Ryun might make the U.S. team, only to come apart in the high altitude at

Mexico City. "Racing at altitude is like changing events," Daniels said, "you need some races at the new distance."

Nobody in power took the time to listen.

Pack Robert Gibson was born during the Depression, November 9, 1935, in Omaha, Nebraska. His father, Pack Sr., died a few months before Gibson came into the world. While Gibson said he missed not having a father around when he was growing up, he so disliked the name Pack that he had it changed as soon as he was on his own.

Some philosophers contend that we accept our parents and even their particular worlds as part of the price for being born again, returned from whatever purgatory or state of spiritual limbo we may enter when we die. Before souls enter human life, they pass through the plain of Lethe (oblivion, forgetting). We agree to the circumstances and then we forget about such a contract when the higher power seals our lips, allowing us to also forget our previous lives, mistakes, and compromises.

"[The] evidence for this forgetting," psychologist James Hillman wrote, "of the soul's prenatal election, is pressed right into your upper lip. That little crevice below your nose is where the angel pressed its forefinger to seal your lips."

When one looks back upon Gibson's childhood, one wonders if he remembered more than he forgot after passing through the plain of Lethe. With his father gone before his birth, Gibson was raised by his brother, Josh, who was fifteen years older than him. It was Josh who wrapped him in a quilt and carried him to the local hospital when Gibson became "deathly sick" with pneumonia as a small boy. As Josh Gibson handed over his little brother to the doctors, he told the boy that he would buy him a baseball glove after he pulled through. That may have been the last warm and cuddly act ever performed by Josh Gibson on behalf of his little brother. When Bob was eleven, the two of them had a conversation that would shape the rest of the younger Gibson's life. Jackie Robinson had just broken baseball's color barrier, signing to play for the Brooklyn Dodgers. The door was now open for black men to play sports professionally.

"I decided on the spot to be a ballplayer," Gibson remembered. "I didn't know if the sport would be baseball or basketball, but I would play one of them professionally."

With that in mind, and with his big brother as the head coach for many of his youth sports teams, Gibson made the rounds of Iowa and Nebraska, playing local all-star teams. In some of those locales, it was difficult for a predominately black team from Omaha to catch a break from the officials. That's when Josh would call everyone out, from the umpires to the hostile crowds. Several times he strode out to the pitcher's mound and invited anybody who cared to take him on to settle things right there.

Bob sometimes feared for his big brother's life. Several times the entire team would be lucky to get out of some far-flung crossroads in one piece. But Gibson soon learned that one way, perhaps the best way, to battle adversity was head-on.

In 1951, the Gibsons' Y Monarchs won the Nebraska state baseball championship. This was American Legion ball and Bob Gibson was fifteen years old. Sometimes there's a misconception that Gibson, especially in those early years, was more comfortable playing with blacks, and that his world broke down into black versus white, Us versus Them, perhaps at the urging of his big brother. But the common denominators for Gibson's youth teams had more to do with location and class than race. In fact, his catcher at one point was a white kid, Andy Sommer.

In high school, Gibson starred in basketball and his coach wrote to Indiana University about his interest in playing hoops there. The Hoosiers replied that they had filled their quota of black players—one was already on the roster. From there Gibson broke the color line at Creighton University's basketball team. He held the school scoring record until Paul Silas, who would go on to play for the Boston Celtics, surpassed it six years later. For a time, it appeared that professional basketball would be Gibson's career path. He was an exceptional guard, able to score and set up his teammates, as well. Yet at the time there was no clear-cut path to making a living in professional sports. After finishing college in 1957, Gibson signed a pair of $4,000 contracts. One was with the Cardinals' baseball farm team in Omaha. The other was to play basketball for the Harlem Globetrotters, whom he joined after the baseball season was over.

While Gibson liked the money and travel, he never really embraced the clowning that is so much a part of the Globetrotters' act. His favorite moments came in the second and third quarters when the Globetrotters played things more or less straight up. For a time Gibson roomed with the legendary Meadowlark Lemon, whom he discovered was "a sincere, serious guy." It fell to Gibson to break the squad's warm-up circle (when they spun the ball on their fingers) and begin the dunking parade. Despite such highlights, when Cardinals general manager Bing Devine offered him an additional $4,000 the following season to concentrate on baseball, Gibson quit the Globetrotters. "It was the best deal I ever made," he told friends years later. "For the first time, I was headed in one and only one direction."

Bob Gibson, like most athletes, often tried to insulate himself from the so-called real world. The goal was to keep the focus on the next game, the next pitch. But in 1968 that soon proved to be impossible. Early that year, a few weeks before spring training, Gibson passed the Reverend Martin Luther King Jr. in the Atlanta airport. "He'd looked at me as though he recognized me," Gibson wrote in his memoir, "but wasn't sure who I was."

That's unlikely. At that moment, Gibson was one of the most famous pitchers in the game, the staff ace whom the Cardinals turned to to win the deciding games of the 1964 and 1967 World Series. King, of course, had many other focuses and priorities, but sports, its makeup and impact, played a part in his concerns, as well.

"Many of us in the movement were sports fans," recalled Rev. Samuel "Billy" Kyles. "Martin enjoyed sports and he really championed Jackie

Robinson after his playing career was over. But remember this was '68 and we couldn't help but watch how things played out with what I would call an historical eye. For example, what teams had a person of color as their top pitcher, their quarterback? That's what the question was more often than not in our world at that time."

Gibson later confirmed that he and King did nod at each other. Years later, he declined to elaborate on what he would have told the civil rights leader if a conversation, no matter how fleeting, had taken place.

Kyles, who was a part of King's inner leadership circle, along with Andrew Young, Ralph Abernathy and Jesse Jackson, has no doubt that the civil rights leader recognized the Cardinals' pitching star. Decades later, he and I discuss this forgotten moment in Kyles's office at the Monumental Baptist Church in south Memphis, where he has been the pastor since 1959. Unlike some who were irreparably hurt by how the year 1968 played out, Kyles somehow rose above it all. The walls of his offices remain a testament to his faith and his conviction in bringing King's message to the world. Photographs of the Dalai Lama, Harry Belafonte, Lena Horne, Al Gore, Bill Clinton, and Nelson Mandela, most personally addressed to the pastor, adorn the walls.

"I was there when Dr. King was killed. I was one of the last to see him alive," Kyles said. "And I was deeply saddened by what happened. But soon afterward I realized that I had a new role, a job to do.

"Some are destined to be our leaders. Others are meant to be witnesses, to make sure that the message is still carried out. After what happened in April 1968, I saw I was put upon this earth to be a witness—to tell people about Dr. King and what he stood for."

With that in mind, Reverend Kyles ponders my question: What would King have told Gibson, if they had stopped and exchanged words.

"I have no doubt that Martin would have known of Mr. Gibson, would have recognized him," Kyles said. "Knowing Martin as well as I did, he would have probably told him to 'keep going.' And certainly congratulations for what [Gibson] had already accomplished in 1967 and before.

Martin was more of a sports fan than me. He would have known what to say. I have no doubt about that."

In his memoir, Gibson wrote that while he "greatly admired" Dr. Martin Luther King, he simply "couldn't do as he said. . . . The Gibson clan, as nearly as I can figure, has consisted over the years of two basic types—those who practice passive resistance and those who don't."

Although King hadn't been much of an athlete growing up (billiards was his game), he certainly understood the power of sports. Early on, King realized what a crucial role it played in America. As a teenager in 1947, he too watched Jackie Robinson break the color barrier in baseball. In the early 1960s, King supported the baseball legend's right to speak out about civil rights, comparing Robinson to "a pilgrim that walked the lonesome byways toward the high road of freedom."

Throughout the sixties, King was a supporter of boxer Cassius Clay, aka Muhammad Ali. In 1968, soon after he crossed paths with Gibson, King met with Tommie Smith, Lee Evans, and John Carlos. The track athletes' grievances included Ali being stripped of his heavyweight title due to his protest of the Vietnam War, as well as South Africa, then an apartheid nation, being allowed to compete in the upcoming Mexico City Games. In 1968, activist Harry Edwards advocated an Olympic boycott, especially by the top American sprinters. While talk of an outright boycott eventually dissipated, a strong belief remained that something needed to be done, like public demonstration of some kind at the Mexico City Games in October, once the World Series was over.

"I can't really say what I'd do if I were in their shoes, but I admire the guys who are involved in the Olympic boycott," Bob Gibson told Dwight Chapin of the *Los Angeles Times* in 1968. "They're taking a terrific chance—risking an awful lot. I don't know what their goals are. But if they feel that the country has been kicking them in the rears for fifty years, then I agree with them."

As the meeting at the Americana Hotel in New York drew to a close, Carlos asked King why he was intent upon returning to Memphis later that spring. After all, the civil rights leader had received death threats if he set foot back in the city. "I've got to stand up for those who won't stand," King replied, "and I've got to stand up for those who can't."

The comment left the normally loquacious Carlos speechless.

While the baseball players prepared for the new 1968 season in sunny Florida, King and his movement were embroiled in a bitter dispute involving the sanitation workers in Memphis. At issue was King's message and whether he could effectively deliver it anymore. For King believed that nothing was gained if such demonstrations turned violent. But that's exactly what had happened earlier in Memphis. A march led by King had been essentially taken over by local vigilantes, the so-called Invaders gangs. After briefly going home to Atlanta, where he asked himself serious questions about his movement and his approach, King decided to return to Memphis, determined to lead an orderly, nonviolent march.

On April 3, 1968, King gave his last speech. The setting was the Mason Temple in Memphis, a vast concrete building built between 1940 and 1945. At dusk, a violent storm hit the city. Kyles remembered sirens going off, warning of possible tornadoes, and lightning filling the sky. The rain was so hard that King decided nobody would be out on such a night and decided to stay back at the Lorraine Hotel, sending Kyles and Abernathy in his stead. When the leaders of the Southern Christian Leadership Conference reached the Mason Temple, though, they found a crowd of three thousand waiting for King, and only King, to speak. Abernathy called the civil rights leader back at the hotel, telling him to hurry over. The people would only be satisfied by his presence.

For what became such a memorable, often-quoted speech, King initially got off to a rocky start that evening. The winds outside buffeted the shutters of the Mason Temple, causing loud creaks to echo through the vast two-level interior, followed by loud bangs of the shutters slamming back against the walls. With almost every outburst, King would flinch, sometimes glancing over his shoulder. "Martin had been under so many death threats at the time," said Kyles, who asked a custodian to secure the shutters, quieting them. "His plane out of Atlanta had been under guard."

Speaking without notes, King told his listeners that there would be "difficult days ahead." But he soon added that such things didn't "matter with me now. Because I've been to the mountaintop."

With that King had found his rhythm and the speech's cadence began to accelerate and flow through the crowd that was now hanging on his every word.

"Like anybody, I would like to live a long life," King told them. "Longevity has its place. But I'm not concerned about that now. I just want to do God's will. And he's allowed me to go up to the mountain, and I've looked over and I've seen the Promised Land. I may not get there with you."

That last line got Kyles's attention. Years later, he believes that King "smoothed it out" for everyone in attendance that evening. "In looking back at that time, I realize he knew that his time on earth was growing short," Kyles said. "He said, 'I may not get there with you' when he knew full well that he would not. He talked more about death that night than he had in a long time. . . . That evening at the Mason Temple he somehow found a way to preach his way past those fears, the fear of dying."

King's closing flourish brought the crowd to its feet: "But I want you to know tonight that we as a people will get to the Promised Land. So I'm happy tonight. I'm not worried about anything. I'm not fearing any man. Mine eyes have seen the glory of the coming of the Lord."

To loud applause, King stepped down from the pulpit and collapsed into Abernathy's arms.

The next afternoon, King and his entourage gathered at the Lorraine Hotel. During the day, Andrew Young, another member of King's inner circle, had been in court, seeing to it that an injunction was lifted so another march could be held in Memphis. The route was planned to go by the downtown State Theater, where the marquee boasted Elvis Presley's newest film, *Stay Away, Joe.* When Young arrived at the room that King and Abernathy shared, Room 306, he found a lighthearted King, who was so happy the march could now go ahead that he started a pillow fight with Young and others. "It was sort of like after you make a touchdown and everybody piles on everybody," Young said. "It was just throwing pillows at each other, piling atop each other and laughing."

Dinner that evening was at Kyles's home. He had just bought a new house nearby and King's group gathered at the Lorraine to drive over. Dinner was scheduled for five, but earlier in the afternoon King had called to the Kyles's residence and talked with another family member, who told him that dinner was at six. So it made no difference when Kyles arrived to drive King and Abernathy over. The civil rights leader believed he had an extra hour and, as was his wont, he wasn't in any hurry.

Kyles waited with King and Abernathy in Room 306 as they dressed. Any time Kyles tried to hurry things along, King told him he had been told dinner was at six. Several times Kyles began to argue the point—after all the dinner was at his house, he would know—and King simply replied, "Six."

"I was frustrated at the time," Kyles said, "because I wanted to get going. But in looking back on it, I realize what a blessing it was. I was able to spend that last hour of his life with him."

About six that evening, King and Kyles went out on to the balcony that still overlooks a small parking lot. Back in the room Abernathy was finishing shaving. As King waited for his friend, he lingered on the balcony outside the room, resting his arms on the balcony rail. Kyles, Young, and others had noticed that King appeared more at peace, even teasing coworkers, after his speech at the Mason Temple. Back in the room, Abernathy was about ready. King called out to Jesse Jackson and others in the parking lot and Kyles began to walk down the stairs to his car. Finally, as Young later remembered, the group was prepared to "have us a dinner."

A moment later, a blast echoed through the Lorraine Hotel courtyard. Kyles and Abernathy found King lying on the balcony landing, the right side of his face ripped open and his head beginning to rest in a halo of blood. He had been stuck down by a .30–06 caliber bullet.

Kyles ran back inside Room 306 and tried to call an ambulance—an attempt that was stymied when the hotel switchboard went dead because the operator had raced into the courtyard to see what had happened. Amid the chaos, Abernathy attempted to speak with King but received no answer. Kyles remembered there was so much blood. He found a sheet to cover his friend's body.

King died hours later and across the country cities began to burn in protest, with more than one hundred American cities soon erupting in flame. In Washington, D.C., smoke could be seen only a few blocks from the White House. Just days before, President Lyndon Johnson had announced that he wouldn't run for reelection. The move seemingly gained him traction for ongoing efforts to end the war in Vietnam and settling things on the domestic front. Yet as the reports of rioting came in, the president realized that any political momentum he had gained in recent days was now lost forever.

In Indianapolis, presidential candidate Robert Kennedy was about to speak from the back of a flatbed truck to a predominately black crowd at a campaign stop when he received the news that King had been assassinated. In what would later be looked back on as the second of two extraordinary speeches in as many days, and a stunning example of the healing power that words can offer, Kennedy told his audience about King's death. For most of them it was the first they had heard of the tragic news.

After asking many in the crowd to lower their signs, Kennedy said, "I have some very sad news for all of you and I think some sad news for all our fellow citizens and people who love peace all over the world. And that is that Martin Luther King was shot and killed tonight in Memphis, Tennessee."

A gasp ran through the crowd, followed by shouts of "No!" and "Black Power!" Indianapolis, like so many cities across the nation, seemed ready to come apart at the seams. But here Kennedy, speaking only from a few scribbled notes, and beginning in a trembling, halting voice, slowly brought the people back around and somehow held them together.

"Martin Luther King dedicated his life to love and to justice between fellow human beings," Kennedy said. "He died in the cause of that effort . . . "

Listening to the speech decades later, you can hear the crowd soon become still, ready to hear the candidate out. Speaking from the heart, Kennedy told the crowd how he "had a member of my family killed"—a reference to his brother, of course, who had been assassinated less than five years before.

"But we have to make an effort in the United States," the younger Kennedy continued, "we have to make an effort to understand, to get beyond, or go beyond these rather difficult times.

"My favorite poem, my favorite poet was Aeschylus. And he once wrote: 'Even in our sleep, pain which cannot forget/ falls drop by drop upon the heart,/ until, in our own despair,/ against our will,/ comes wisdom/ through the awful grace of God.'"

A few minutes later, Kennedy closed by telling the crowd, "Let us dedicate ourselves to what the Greeks wrote so many years ago: to tame the savageness of man and make gentle the life of this world. Let us dedicate ourselves to that, and say a prayer for our country and for our people."

Indianapolis was one of the few cities that didn't burn that evening in April 1968, or in the days ahead.

Memphis didn't burn that night, either. Hours after King's death, Kyles, Abernathy, Young and many of their group were back at the Lorraine Hotel, counseling their followers not to fall into violence. "As you can imagine, it was a very, very difficult evening," Kyles said. "I have never felt so sad, so angry, so lonely in all of my life. But we found a way to carry on. We knew it was important to carry on Dr. King's message to the world. We decided that night that you can kill the dreamer, but you cannot kill the dream."

Back at Kyle's home, the home-cooked food that had been laid out for that evening's dinner still sat on the table. Kyles's youngest son, Dwain, couldn't bring himself to eat any of it. He made himself a peanut butter and jelly sandwich instead.

———————

The next morning, in St. Petersburg, Florida, the Cardinals' spring training camp was like most places in America: the King assassination the
major topic of conversation. Gibson was devastated by the news and got
into a heated exchange with his catcher, Tim McCarver. After telling Mc-
Carver that he couldn't possibly comprehend what it was like to be a black
person on this morning, and that it was impossible for whites, no matter
how well intentioned, to totally overcome prejudice, Gibson turned his
back on his batterymate.

To McCarver's credit, he didn't let the situation go. Undoubtedly, he
realized that the last person Gibson wanted to hear from at that moment
was a white man, who had grown up in Memphis of all places. Yet Mc-
Carver told Gibson that it was possible for people to change. If anything,
he was Exhibit A. Back when McCarver was new to the team, Gibson and
Curt Flood had ribbed him about his reluctance to share a sip of soda offered by a black man. McCarver had seen a lot of truth in their teasing.
Perhaps that's why he wouldn't let things drop after King's death. In talking with Gibson, McCarver found himself in "the unfamiliar position of
arguing that the races were equal and that we were all the same."

Years later, McCarver wrote that "Bob and I reached a meeting of
the minds that morning. That was the kind of talk we often had on the
Cardinals."

Of course, baseball wasn't the only sport in America reeling after King's
assassination. The civil rights leader's death occurred just before the opening of the National Basketball Association's Eastern Division Finals between the Philadelphia 76ers and the Boston Celtics. The year before,
Philadelphia had eliminated the Celtics, who had won nine titles in the
past ten seasons. In 1968, the 76ers continued their newfound dominance, winning a league-best sixty-two games and finishing eight games
ahead of Boston in the Eastern Division. Philadelphia center Wilt Cham-

berlain was the league's MVP, averaging an astounding 24.3 points and 23.8 rebounds per game.

"Everywhere we went, especially in Philadelphia, they had a chant, 'Boston's Dead. Boston's Dead.' The dynasty is over," recalled John Havlicek, the Celtics' Hall of Fame forward. "You'd hear it at the airport when you got off the plane in Philadelphia. The cab drivers would be on you, riding you a little. Everywhere you went, the fans were real vocal."

After King's death, Chamberlain and Bill Russell, the Celtics' player-coach and the only African American coach in U.S. sports that year, met before Game One of that best-of-seven series. The decision was made to play on, with the second contest delayed from Sunday to the following Wednesday. Not that it seemed to matter, at least for Boston's chances.

Even though the Celtics took the opener, the 76ers proceeded to run off with the series, winning three consecutive victories to take a 3–1 lead. Indeed, the chant appeared to be correct: it was the end of Boston's epic run. Even Celtics' general manager Red Auerbach sensed the series was perhaps over. Before the next game in Philadelphia, he nodded at Russell, saying, "There are some people who have already forgotten how great that man really was."

Despite being down three games to one, Russell and the Celtics battled back to deadlock the series. The Celtics' Larry Siegfried remembered Russell as a man of few words. But when the player-coach spoke, he was "direct and precise." When the team fell behind to Wilt Chamberlain and the 76ers, Russell simply told his team, "We've come so far and I don't want to go home now."

The Celtics rallied to take Game Five in Philadelphia, 122–104, and Game Six back home in Boston, 114–106.

Before the 1967–1968 regular season began, Russell had gathered together a half-dozen of the team's veterans during an exhibition tour in Puerto Rico. "He wanted our help—he wanted to tap that knowledge," John Havlicek later told George Plimpton of *Sports Illustrated*. "Of course he told us that his would be the final decision. It helped a lot. He told us to criticize him if we felt he warranted it."

In 1968, the Eastern Conference's seventh and deciding game returned to Philadelphia. Before the opening tip Russell strode to the jump circle with purpose. "Other players would be slapping each other and pumping themselves up," he wrote in his autobiography *Second Wind*, "but I'd always take my time and walk out slowly, my arms folded in front of me. I'd look at everybody disdainfully, like a sleepy dragon who can't be bothered to scare off another would-be hero. I wanted my look to say, 'Hey, the King's here tonight.'"

Sometimes Russell would take things even farther.

"'All right guys,' I'd say to the other team, 'Ain't no lay-ups out there tonight. I ain't gonna bother you with them fifteen-footers' cause I don't feel like it tonight, but I ain't gonna have no lay-ups!' Or I'd lean over to one of the forwards and say, 'If you come in to shoot a lay-up off me you'd better bring your salt and pepper because you'll be eating basketball.'"

Russell didn't say such things to Chamberlain, Oscar Robertson, or Jerry West. Those were all-stars and able to reply in kind. Just about anyone else, though, was fair game.

In the final seconds of Game Seven, Russell backed up his tough talk. Down 98–96, the 76ers controlled a jump ball, with Chet Walker driving for a shot that Russell blocked. Philadelphia's Hal Greer retrieved the loose ball, shot, and missed. Russell soared over Chamberlain for the pivotal rebound. Boston won 100–96, coming all the way back from a 3–1 deficit to take the series and advance to the finals against their bitter rivals, the Los Angeles Lakers.

While the Celtics' comeback against the favored 76ers certainly earned national headlines, baseball remained king of the mountain. And the national pastime was about to gain even more attention for what was about to begin in Los Angeles.

Don Drysdale's record-setting scoreless streak started convincingly enough with a 1–0 shutout over Ferguson Jenkins and the Chicago Cubs on May 14, 1968. On team after team, pitchers bemoaned the lack of timely hitting and runs, and Drysdale's Dodgers were no different. Even during its championship years, Los Angeles was known for its quality starting pitching—Drysdale, Bill Singer, Claude Osteen, Stan Williams, and Sandy Koufax—rather than any real firepower at the plate. The ballclub was still years away from fielding such hitters as Ron Cey, Rick Monday, or Steve Garvey. In fact, a few seasons earlier, when Drysdale was briefly away from the team, Koufax pitched a no-hitter against the Phillies and Drysdale's first reaction was, "Did he win?"

As '68 began, the Dodgers were considered more pretender than contender. Koufax had retired after the 1966 season. In '67, Drysdale had labored to a 13–16 record, with a respectable 2.74 ERA (earned run average). In spring training, he hurt his right arm while covering third base in an exhibition game at the Houston Astrodome. Even the big right-hander himself admitted he "was on the downside of the baseball mountain."

Still, four days later, on May 18, 1968, Drysdale defeated Dave Giusti and the Houston Astros. Again, the final score was 1–0. Several trends were apparent to everyone, especially Drysdale. Not only were the Dodgers scoring few runs, but more likely than not, Drysdale was matching up with the opposing team's ace. "You'd better think about pitching a shutout," Drysdale later explained, "or giving up at most one or two runs, if you had any ideas of winning."

That was certainly true for the third game of the shutout streak. The Dodgers were on the road facing the Cardinals, and Drysdale's opponent was none other than Bob Gibson. It had rained much of the day in St. Louis and some wondered if the contest would be called. Yet Drysdale knew that Gibson "always meant box office." In fact, the Cardinals had a big advance sale for the showdown, so the game was played despite the subpar conditions. St. Louis out-hit the Dodgers, five to three, but Drysdale won the game, 2–0, over Gibson. To this point, Drysdale had pitched twenty-seven scoreless innings—three consecutive shutouts.

On May 26, the Dodgers were back in Houston and Drysdale had to pinch himself to make sure the five runs his teammates put up for him were real. Still, the Dodgers' ace was unable to rest easy. Astros manager Grady Hatton was convinced that Drysdale was using petroleum jelly or some other foreign substance to make the ball dive or soar. Reluctantly, home plate Al Barlick came to the mound to check the pitcher.

"I've got to look around here," he told Drysdale. "Don't worry about anything."

Shrugging off the incident, the Dodgers' ace shut out the Astros' and Houston starter Larry Dierker, 5–0. "I was a kid back then, not quite twenty-two," Dierker said. "But anybody could see that this was perhaps a once-in-a-generation thing. That guys like Drysdale and Gibson were setting a new standard. When you're in the same profession, trying to do the same job, you're just trying to keep up with it all."

Ironically, the home-plate umpire would play the biggest role in Drysdale's next start—May 31 at home against the rival San Francisco Giants. By this time the media was on the case, determining that Drysdale's scoreless streak was the longest since Guy Harris "Doc" White pitched five consecutive shutouts for the Chicago White Sox in 1904. (During his playing career, White would combine with sportswriter Ring Lardner to write several popular songs, with "Little Puff of Smoke, Good Night" the most popular.) The all-time scoreless innings streak was held by Hall of Famer Walter "Big Train" Johnson, who pitched fifty-five and two-thirds scoreless innings in 1913.

Against the Giants, Drysdale was sailing along, holding a 3–0 lead into the top of the ninth. That's when Willie McCovey walked, Jim Ray Hart singled, and then Drysdale walked Dave Marshall to load the bases with none out. (Marshall would break up Drysdale's bid for a no-hitter later in the summer at Candlestick Park.)

Seizing the opportunity to end Drysdale's scoreless string and perhaps even pull out a victory, Giants manager Herman Franks inserted Nate

Oliver to be McCovey's pinch runner at first. San Francisco catcher Dick Dietz, who was next up, worked the count to 2–2. Drysdale went with a slider, but the pitch didn't have much bite and it grazed Dietz on the left elbow. The Giants' batter began to jog toward first base, which would have brought in Oliver from third. Pretty much everyone in the ballpark, including Dodgers catcher Jeff Torborg and Drysdale, thought the streak was over. The hit-by-pitch had forced in a run. Yet home-plate umpire Harry Wendelstedt surprised everyone by ruling that Dietz hadn't tried to get out of the way of the pitch. Instead of allowing him to head to first base, the ump told him to get back in the batter's box. Wendelstedt ruled the pitch a ball, making the count 3–2.

The Giants' protest was long and loud. Third-base coach Peanuts Lowrey argued the call, as did Franks, halting the game for nearly a half-hour. Dodgers announcer Vin Scully filled the time by reading the rulebook on the air to listeners. The infielders stayed warm by throwing the ball around as Drysdale stood on the mound, watching Dietz, Lowrey, and Franks plead their case to Wendelstedt.

When play finally resumed, Dietz fouled off the next pitch. Then Drysdale got him to hit a shallow fly to left field. It wasn't deep enough to score Oliver, so it was one out and the bases still loaded.

Next up was pinch hitter Ty Cline. He hit a line drive toward first base, where the Dodgers' Wes Parker dug it out of the dirt and fired home in time for the out. Two down and the bases were still loaded.

Drysdale then induced pinch hitter Jack Hiatt to pop out to Parker at first. Somehow the Dodgers' ace had gotten out of the jam and his scoreless string was intact. Drysdale had now pitched five consecutive shutouts.

"It took a lot of balls on Harry's part to make that call," Drysdale said, "but he was absolutely right. Dietz made no effort to avoid that pitch."

Juan Marichal, the Giants' Hall of Fame right-hander, later told Drysdale that Dietz had said he was eager to be hit by the pitch. If that's what it took to break up the scoreless streak, he'd pay the price.

Afterward, Franks called Wendelstedt "gutless," while Dodgers manager Walter Alston said he "never saw the play called before. But then, it's the first time I ever saw anyone get deliberately hit by a pitched ball."

In 1968, football was positioned to supersede baseball as the most popular game in the land. What seems incredible looking back on things is that few saw this sea change coming.

Unlike baseball, football could be played in almost any weather. The 1967 "Ice Bowl," the National Football League Championship game between the Dallas Cowboys and the host Green Bay Packers the previous December, solidified the game's status among sports fans. With the game-time temperature of thirteen degrees below zero, on a field that had literally frozen overnight into the famed tundra, the Packers drove for the game's deciding score. Despite the weather, a sellout crowd packed the stands at famed Lambeau Field. Public address announcer Gary Knafelc said it was like "seeing big buffaloes in an enormous herd on a winter plains. It was prehistoric." And great television.

But one game doesn't make a sport king of the hill. Other planets must fall into alignment and that's exactly what was afoot in 1968. An integral series of events was set into motion when, after leading the Packers to another Super Bowl championship, Vince Lombardi stepped down as Green Bay's coach.

"Historians should recognize that the first real superstar in modern professional football was not Jim Brown or Joe Namath, but a coach—Vince Lombardi," Bill Russell wrote. "He was much more of a celebrity across the country than any of his players—in fact, more than anybody who'd ever played pro football.

"Lombardi was the military commander, the dictator of the Green Bay Packers, and the players were useful only if they fit into the machine he designed. It was a winning one, and he drove his men to the limits of their endurance. Stories circulated about how he scoffed at injuries and expected his players to keep going. He demanded that they eat, drink and sleep football, in complete submission and loyalty to his discipline."

On the surface, losing a single coach, even a legend like Lombardi, doesn't seem like a deal-breaker. After all, the National Football League (NFL) had plenty of great teams left, starting with the Cleveland Browns and Baltimore Colts. Yet many in the rival American Football League, the upstarts who had been crushed in the first two Super Bowls by Lombardi's Packers, recognized that they now had an opening, perhaps a real opportunity to run for daylight. Even though discussions continued about making it possible for two NFL teams to meet in the Super Bowl—the insinuation being that this would ensure a matchup between better teams—the American Football League (AFL) had nonetheless gained a growing following. How large? Early in 1968 nobody was quite sure. But events would soon conspire to underscore that it was in fact far bigger and more national than many in the sport realized.

Football was a different kind of game in the AFL. Players on the Buffalo Bills, Oakland Raiders, Kansas City Chiefs, San Diego Chargers, and New York Jets usually weren't as big or as heavy as their counterparts in the more established NFL. The new league had more than its share of castoffs and misfits. It also emphasized offense, especially the long ball. While lacking at some positions, its cadre of quarterbacks—Joe Namath, Daryle Lamonica, Jack Kemp, John Hadl, Lenny Dawson—could throw the pigskin downfield.

"We knew we couldn't just duplicate what the NFL was doing," said Kansas City Chiefs owner Lamar Hunt. "At least in part, we had to go in a different direction. Often that meant throwing the ball, the quick-strike offense. We had to show we could put points on the board. That was our way to win over more fans."

Of course, any football owner would have loved to woo fans away from baseball. But as farfetched as it may sound now, baseball was often the front-page news in 1968. It was the sport that kept everybody talking.

With five consecutive shutouts, Drysdale had tied Doc White's record. Next up were the Pittsburgh Pirates on June 4 at Dodger Stadium. Before another capacity crowd at Chavez Ravine, Drysdale gave up only three hits, one to Maury Wills, the Dodgers' former shortstop who was now with Pittsburgh. The streak had now reached fifty-four innings and counting.

Later that same evening, Robert Kennedy made his way through the crowded Embassy Ballroom to the podium at the Ambassador Hotel. When he positioned himself at the two microphones, nobody could hear him at first.

"Can we get something that works," Kennedy asked, anxious for the technical difficulties to be ironed out.

Even when the problem was fixed, he asked several times, "Can you hear?" before going ahead. Only minutes earlier, the networks had named RFK the winner of the California primary. At this point in time, many believed he held the inside track to the Democratic Party nomination for president. With his wife, Ethel, at his side, Kennedy smiled again and ran his fingers through his hair. On either side, the media held out their microphones to capture every word, while others took photographs. Behind him, former professional football player Roosevelt Grier, who often traveled with Kennedy, broke into a wide grin, surveying the cheering crowd. To watch the scene decades later, on YouTube or elsewhere, is to be reminded how distant our heroes stand from us now, how wide the gap between the stage and the first row has become, and how much security is now in place. Of course, that's due, in large part, by what happened on this evening.

"I'd like to express my high regard to Don Drysdale," Kennedy said, and the packed ballroom broke into applause for the hometown pitcher. "Who pitched his sixth straight shutout tonight."

Here Kennedy paused, suppressing a smile. The more jaded among us would say that the candidate was doing what any good politician does: dropping the name of a hometown favorite. An easy applause line to break the ice. Yet Kennedy certainly knew of Drysdale's achievement. He, as much as anybody at that time, realized that politics had already become forever intertwined with sports.

"And I hope," Kennedy continued, not wanting to let go of the Drysdale thread quite yet, "we can have as good fortune in our campaign."

From there, he spoke for about fifteen minutes, a rambling address that was later compared to an Academy Awards acceptance speech rather than traditional political oratory. He concluded with a Churchill-like V-for-Victory sign and then, to the surprise of several of his handlers, he exited through the kitchen.

The networks had already cut away when the bad news began to filter through the ballroom at the Ambassador Hotel. Still, the cameras rolled as the rumor spread like a shadow and face after face dissolved into tears and anguish. Campaign workers began to hug each other out of nightmarish sadness rather than euphoric happiness. Later it was learned that Grier, along with Olympic gold medalist Rafer Johnson and writer George Plimpton, had wrestled Kennedy's assailant, Sirhan Sirhan, to the floor.

Kennedy's campaign held a genuine connection with the world of sports. The *New York Times* stated that "at least fifty star athletes, former athletes and coaches" had enlisted in his presidential bid. Their ranks included Vince Lombardi, Gale Sayers, Gary Beban, Stan Musial, Hank Aaron, Donald Dell, Bob Cousy, and Dave Bing. Oscar Robertson did advance work for the campaign in Indiana, while Bill Russell taped radio endorsements for Kennedy. The assassination devastated the nation, and sports, like any other group or institution in America, was unsure about how best to carry on.

After Kennedy's death, President Johnson declared a national day of mourning. But in response, baseball commissioner William "Spike" Eckert opted to postpone games only in New York, between the Yankees and Angels, and in Washington, between the Senators and the Twins. He told the other ballclubs that their particular contests could go ahead, as long as they didn't start until after Kennedy's funeral services were concluded. "From here on," the *Sporting News* noted, "the confusion got out of hand."

In Houston, the Astros were supposed to host the Pittsburgh Pirates on Sunday, but players on both teams didn't really want to play. Three of them took matters into their own hands. The Pirates' Maury Wills stayed in the training room, reading Kennedy's book *To Seek a Newer World*. The franchise looked the other way and didn't discipline its player representative for what others deemed as insubordination.

"I was out of uniform when Dr. King died," Wills said, "and if I didn't respect Senator Kennedy's memory, too, I felt I would be hypocritical.

Roberto Clemente was also ready to sit out the Sunday game but changed his mind after meeting with Pittsburgh manager Larry Shepard. That didn't mean the Pirates future Hall of Famer was on board with matters. "I preferred not to play," Clemente said. "The disturbing thing to me was the indifferent attitudes of some of our players. Some didn't take a stand either way, just said they didn't care whether they played or not."

He added, "This is one of things wrong with our country—too much indifference. I didn't want to play but I did. I also voiced my opinion."

Voicing one's opinion and even taking a stand proved to be costly for players in other dugouts, however. The Astros' Rusty Staub and Bob Aspromonte joined Wills in refusing to take the field. For their actions, they were fined a day's pay by Houston general manager Spec Richardson. The GM wanted the game to go on and reportedly was ready to fine anybody else who threatened to sit it out. "Among all the mealy-mouthed statements, it remained for Richardson to come up with the nauseating prize," Red Smith wrote. "The games would go on, he said, because 'Senator Kennedy would have wanted it that way.'"

In San Francisco, the Mets' were scheduled to play the Giants at Candlestick Park. It was Bat Day for the home team, with an estimated 40,000 tickets sold. Unlike some ballclubs, the Mets stuck together and decided, as a squad, not to play. Even under threat of forfeiting the game, management told players to stay at the team hotel and not show up at the ballpark.

The issue became the most contentious in Cincinnati, where Reds pitcher Milt Pappas, the ballclub's player representative, pleaded with his teammates not to take the field against the visiting St. Louis Cardinals. An initial vote among the players settled nothing, as it was deadlocked at twelve to twelve, with one player abstaining. That's when manager Dave Bristol did some arm-twisting and a second vote was thirteen to twelve in favor of playing, with Tommy Helms, Jim Maloney, and Pete Rose among those opting to play.

"You guys are wrong," Pappas shouted as his teammates prepared to take the field. "I'm telling you you're all wrong."

Reds' assistant general manager Dick Wagner tried to intimidate Pappas, with little effect. "[He] stopped me on the field in front of the St. Louis dugout and started to put his finger on my shoulder as if he were some kind of tough guy," Pappas later wrote. "He was one of those short guys who was mad at God for making him short, so he had this enormous chip on his shoulder. I looked him in the eye and said, 'If that finger reaches my shoulder, I'm going to break it.' I meant it, and he knew it."

Soon afterward Pappas resigned as his team's player rep.

Robert Kennedy's press secretary, Frank Mankiewicz, sent telegrams to Pappas, Wills, Staub and Aspromonte, and manager Gil Hodges on behalf of the entire Mets team. "Please accept my personal admiration for your actions," it read. "Senator Kennedy indeed enjoyed competitive sports, but I doubt that he would have put box-office receipts ahead of national mourning."

Less than seventy-two hours later, Pappas was traded as part of a six-player deal to Atlanta. Reds general manager Bob Howsam denied that the move was linked to Pappas's position on the Kennedy funeral and the day of mourning. "We had been working on a trade of this kind since May 17," Howsam said. "We wanted to strengthen our pitching staff, and we had made it known then that Pappas was among those we would consider trading."

Meanwhile, the confusion and disjoined action by the commissioner's office resulted in criticism from many quarters.

"Baseball again returned to normalcy—confusion," wrote Les Bieder-man, sports editor for the *Pittsburgh Press*.

"Baseball's observance of Senator Kennedy's death was disorganized, illogical and thoroughly shabby," added Bob August in the *Cleveland Press*.

Dick Young, columnist for the *New York Daily News*, went further, calling for commissioner Eckert to resign. "This is the portrait of a commissioner trying to please everyone," Young wrote. "I have funny, old-fashioned notions that students should not run universities, inmates should not run asylums, and ballplayers should not tell owners when they will play. . . . When that happens, the commissioner looks bad. When that happens, baseball looks bad."

With his teammates wearing black armbands on their uniforms' left sleeve to honor Robert Kennedy, Don Drysdale's next start took place at Chavez Ravine against the visiting Philadelphia Phillies. The practice of wearing such memorial markings in baseball dated back to 1876, the first year of the National League, and ballplayers Ray Chapman and Ed Delehanty, and President Franklin Roosevelt were among those so honored. The Dodgers would wear the armbands in honor of Kennedy through the remaining games of the homestand on June 12.

In the top of the third, Los Angeles third baseman Ken Boyer made a great play on a hard-hit smash by Roberto Pena, assuring that the inning stayed scoreless and that Drysdale would break Walter Johnson's major league scoreless record.

In the fifth inning, the streak ended as quickly as it began. The Phillies' Tony Taylor singled and went to third on Clay Dalrymple's hit. With one out, Howie Bedell stepped up to the plate as a pinch hitter for pitcher Larry Jackson. He had appeared in fifty-eight games for Milwaukee back in 1962 and was now up for a cup of coffee with the Phillies. He hardly seemed like a dragon slayer. Yet Bedell, who would have only seven at-bats that season, collecting one hit in the process, lofted a high fly ball to left-center field. Even though Dodgers outfielder Len Gabrielson easily caught it, the drive was deep enough to score Taylor. With that, Drysdale's streak was over.

Moments later, after Drysdale got the third out of the inning, Philadelphia manager Gene Mauch requested that home-plate umpire, Augie Donatelli, check Drysdale for foreign substances. The umpire took Drysdale's hat and then ran his fingers through Drysdale's hair.

"Usually when someone runs their fingers through my hair," the pitcher said, "she gives me a kiss, too."

With that Drysdale pursed his lips.

"Get out of here," Donatelli said. "Go back to the dugout. You're OK. There's nothing wrong with you."

Later, Drysdale decided that Mauch had instigated the whole thing. The Phillies manager bided his time until the streak was over before insisting that the men in blue pat down the pitcher one more time. "That's baseball, folks," Drysdale wrote in his memoir *Once A Bum, Always A Dodger.* "I probably had stretches when I actually threw the ball as well or had just as much stuff. To go 58 2/3 innings without yielding a single run, you have to be doing something right, true. But you have to have some luck, too. There has to be a combination of both, and I had it."

Nearly every athlete believes that if you think too much about what's going on in the surrounding world, you'll lose your focus. Yet early in the '68 season, Bob Gibson decided that "there was no escaping the pervasive realities of 1968—the assassinations, the cities burning, the social revolution."

While Martin Luther King's death had greatly saddened him, Gibson found that Kennedy's assassination affected him as no event ever had. Whether or not it was coincidence, Gibson pitched his first shutout of the season the day after Robert Kennedy died. At that point in the '68 season, Gibson considered himself a mediocre pitcher, who hadn't done much yet to warrant any accolades. It bugged him that Drysdale "was hogging the headlines." After Kennedy's assassination he felt he had so much rage he might as well try to utilize it to raise his game. Some of what he was feeling had to do with what was going on in the country around him. Another aspect was the embarrassment he felt when comparing himself with his peers early in the 1968 season. In any event, Gibson decided that the only thing he could do was outpitch his situation.

"The answer, clearly, was to take a cue from Drysdale," he later wrote, "and throw some damn shutouts, which was something that appeared to be within my power at the time. My fastball was boring into [Tim] McCarver's mitt and my sliders were behaving like smart missiles. I was definitely settling into what would be referred today as a zone. . . .

"I really can't say, in retrospect, whether Robert Kennedy's assassination is what got me going or not. Without a doubt, it was an angry point in American history for black people—Dr. King's killing had jolted me; Kennedy's infuriated me—and without a doubt, I pitched better angry."

After blanking the Houston Astros, Gibson shut out the Atlanta Braves. In short order, his performances caught on with the rest of the Cardinals' rotation—Nellie Briles, Steve Carlton, and Ray Washburn. As a staff, they were considered the best in the National League and they eventually carried St. Louis into first place. "Bob pitched with such intensity that it rippled through an entire staff," Briles said years later. "All you had to do was watch him, as a teammate, and you felt yourself getting excited about your next turn on the mound. If you could emulate him, even just a little bit, you'd probably win, too."

Gibson's third consecutive shutout was an epic affair against Cincinnati's Gary Nolan. The Cardinals' ace struck out thirteen and allowed four hits in dropping his ERA to an impressive 1.30.

Next up was the Cubs and Ferguson Jenkins, and it took a 1–0 shutout for Gibson to win that game. After throwing a four-hitter against the Pirates June 26 in St. Louis, Gibson's shutout streak stood at five. Only a few weeks after Drysdale had established a new standard, supposedly one for the ages, Gibson was now in his rearview mirror, with forty-seven consecutive scoreless innings and counting.

To a large extent, Gibson excelled by becoming caught up in the incongruity, even the mayhem that defined 1968. In fact, when asked about the pressure of the mounting shutout streak, Gibson replied that he felt more pressure being a black man in America at the time.

His next start was July 1, 1968, a Monday night in Los Angeles, against none other than Drysdale and the Dodgers. More than 42,000 fans were in attendance, knowing that another shutout would put Gibson within just three innings of surpassing Drysdale's new mark. But in the first inning, with two out, Gibson gave up a single to the Dodgers' Len Gabrielson. Tom Haller then hit a hard groundball that Julian Javier couldn't corral and Los Angeles had men at the corners.

Next up was Ron Fairly, who usually hit well against Gibson. Johnny Edwards, the Cardinals' backup catcher, who was giving McCarver a rest that night, decided to stay away from Fairly's power. Edwards set up on the outside corner, signaling for a fastball. Even though it was early in the game, Gibson had exhibited good control, so Edwards wasn't prepared when the next pitch sailed inside, handcuffing him.

The ball glanced off the tip of Edwards' glove and bounced toward the backstop. That enabled Gabrielson to sprint home, where he raised both fists in the air as he crossed home plate.

Now it was up to the official scorer to decide if Gibson's scoreless streak would remain intact. If the play was ruled a passed ball, the run would be unearned and the streak would be safe. But if it was ruled a wild pitch—in other words Gibson's fault—the scoreless string would be over.

As the Cardinals' ace stood on the mound, his initial thought was that the pitch would be recorded as a passed ball. After all, it had hit Edwards' glove. But then he realized where he was—in enemy territory, at Dodger Stadium, where Drysdale's record was still fresh in so many minds. That's when it hit him that the play would be ruled a wild pitch, ending his run at Drysdale's epic streak. And that's exactly what happened.

The strange way in which the world sometimes worked wasn't lost on Gibson. It had taken a controversial call to preserve Drysdale's streak. Now another controversial call had ended his attempt to surpass it.

Gibson tried his best to have the last laugh—defeating Drysdale 5–1 that evening for his seventh consecutive victory. In addition, it was his 135th career win, moving him past Dizzy Dean on St. Louis's all-time list.

Still, this one stung—plenty. Afterward, in the visiting clubhouse, the press asked Gibson about the only run he had allowed.

"You saw it," the winning pitcher replied. "[He] missed the ball."

The room grew quiet until Gibson added, "Hey, that's the way it goes."

PART
III

Eager for a
Second Chance

What does a town that's been to hell and back know about the finer things in life? Well, I'll tell you. More than most. You see, it's the hottest fires that make the hardest steel. Now we're from America. But this isn't New York City. Or the Windy City. Or Sin City. And we're certainly no one's Emerald City. . . . This is the Motor City.

—"IMPORTED FROM DETROIT,"
CHRYSLER COMMERCIAL

To a man, the Detroit Tigers arrived in Lakeland, Florida, in the spring of 1968, believing they had been robbed the season before.

"We had a strong belief, shared by just about everyone on that ballclub, that we should have won the pennant in 1967," second baseman Dick McAuliffe recalled. "Not doing it when it's right there for you, to have it slip away is something you never forget."

The previous season had ended with four teams—the Boston Red Sox, Minnesota Twins, Chicago White Sox, and the Tigers—in contention for the American League pennant entering the final days. On October 1, 1967, the last day of the regular season, the Red Sox and Twins played each other at Fenway Park, with the winner clinching at least a tie for the title. The Tigers were a half-game back, needing a doubleheader sweep of the visiting California Angels to force a one-game play-off for the right to advance to the World Series.

The Red Sox edged the Twins 5–3 that day with Carl Yastrzemski going four for four and staff ace Jim Lonborg on the mound. In Detroit, the Tigers took the first game 6–4, thanks to seven strong innings by Joe Sparma. But with the season on the line, Detroit's pitching, considered by many to be the strength of the team, didn't come through. Due to rain-outs earlier in the week, the Tigers and Angels had played a doubleheader the day before, too, splitting that affair. Now for its fourth game in two days, Detroit went with its would-be ace, Denny McLain.

Early on, the Tigers held a 3–1 lead in the second inning. But McLain, who would go 0–2 in five starts in September, was tagged for three runs and was soon out of the game. The Tigers' starter gone, the Angels proceeded to hang crooked numbers on the scoreboard, building an 8–5 lead heading into the bottom of the ninth. Despite the deep hole, the Tigers fought back, putting two men on with none out. That brought up catcher Jim Price, the potential tying run, to the plate. But he flied out to left field. Dick McAuliffe followed him, setting up one of the cruel ironies sports often display. To that point in the '67 season, the Tigers' second baseman had hit into only one double play. Now with the crowd on its feet, the season on the line, McAuliffe laced a grounder to his counterpoint, the Angels' Bobby Knoop. While the two were among the best fielders at their position in the American League, Knoop won more Gold Gloves—something that still annoys McAuliffe to this day.

Knoop snared the grounder, beginning the double play that ended the game and the Tigers' season. The "Impossible Dream" Red Sox, a squad that finished second to last in 1966, edged the Tigers and Twins by one game and the White Sox by three to advance to the World Series against the powerful St. Louis Cardinals. The memory of coming up short was still fresh in the minds of the Tigers four months later as they arrived in Lakeland, their spring training home.

"In '67, we were really hurting for pitchers, especially guys coming out of the bullpen, in the final week," McAuliffe said. "Playing back-to-back doubleheaders didn't help us any. Our general manager, Jim Campbell, didn't swing a trade to help us. Even without the pitching, we still felt we'd win it and we didn't."

As camp opened, Tigers' manager Mayo Smith told the press, "I don't see anything to make me believe we won't have a strong team. I can't promise we'll win the pennant. But losing it last year on the last day has done something to this team. The team really grew up last year."

Lakeland, a sleepy and, for the most part, still racially segregated town located about fifty miles east of Tampa, appeared to be a curious place to start down the road to redemption. There was a black side of town and a white side of town, with the Tigers running a shuttle bus to and from the new Holiday Inn, where many of the players and their families made their home in February and March. Still, the locale, which had been the Tigers' spring home since 1934, oddly fit the organization. The Tigers, along with the Red Sox and Yankees, had been one of the last big-league teams to integrate. Of course, those days were over with Willie Horton, Earl Wilson, and Gates Brown now on the Detroit roster. But perhaps being off the beaten track in Florida, in a place that reminded them of how things used to be, helped the team come together. Of the twenty-five players on the 1968 ballclub, fifteen had spent time in Tiger Town. Many in that group had gone on to play Triple-A ball in Syracuse, with most reaching the big leagues within a season or two of each other. Overall, the Tigers were a focused veteran ballclub in 1968, almost loyal to a fault, whose pride had been stung by how the previous pennant drive played out. The core group was intent upon making amends.

As the 1968 season began, the consensus was that the bullpen had let the team down the season before. That opened the door for a few new faces to make the team. Among them was a hard-throwing left-hander from southwest Ohio—Jonathan Edgar Warden.

Raised by a single mom, Warden had starred in baseball, football, and basketball at Pleasant View High School in Grove City, Ohio, outside of Columbus. He had attended the University of Georgia, pitching a no-hitter and several shutouts, and drawing the Tigers' attention. The organization drafted him in the fourth round in 1966. Now, after a year in the Florida State League and a year in the Carolina League, he had an outside chance to make the big-league team, in large part because the front office remembered what happened last October when they ran out of arms when it mattered most. "The door was open for me," Warden said. "I knew it. So did pretty much everybody else in camp that spring. But sometimes that doesn't make it any easier. If anything it might be tougher when everybody is expecting it from you."

Nobody was more certain about the Tigers' chances of success in '68 than right-handed pitcher Denny McLain. Upon arriving in Lakeland, he told the press that Detroit would "win by six to seven games if we get off to a good start and nobody falls off any couch."

The last was a tongue-in-cheek reference to how McLain had hurt himself toward the end of the previous season. Somehow he had severely bruised two toes on his left foot. At first he'd claimed that the incident happened at home when he awoke blurry-eyed from a nap on the family couch. "People think there's something funny about the couch story," he added.

In 1967, McLain posted a so-so 17–16 record. What grated on teammates and fans alike was his inability to pitch effectively down the stretch. Exactly how McLain injured his toes remained open to debate in the spring of 1968. At first, McLain stuck to the couch story—that he had fallen asleep while watching television and stubbed his toes after standing up. Subsequently, the star pitcher said he had hurt himself chasing raccoons away from his garbage cans. Teammate Mickey Lolich chimed in by saying he saw McLain kick a water cooler after being yanked from a game. Another account had McLain kicking lockers in the clubhouse after another lackluster outing.

What wasn't in dispute was how poorly McLain finished: 0–2, allowing nearly a run an inning his last five starts. (A few years later, *Sports Illustrated* reported that McLain had contact with the mob during that time. A crime boss had reportedly dislocated McLain's toes in a disagreement over a horseracing bet—a story that McLain vehemently denied.) Whatever the case, McLain was eager to move on and, besides, there was always plenty to talk about when he was around.

McLain arrived at the Tigers' spring camp sporting orange-tinted hair ("I've been out in sun a lot," he said) and no eyeglasses. Instead he was wearing contact lens, detailing to the media how he had gotten used to them while bowling and playing his Hammond X-77 organ. McLain was a scratch bowler, averaging 190 to 200, and he talked about how he had assembled a team that finally beat a squad headed by Lou Boudreau, once a stellar shortstop for the Cleveland Indians, who also happened to be McLain's father-in-law. McLain explained that he pulled off the victory by employing "a couple of ringers."

As adept as McLain was at bowling, he was even better at music. After performing in clubs throughout the Midwest during previous off-seasons, he spent the months before the '68 season working for Grinnell Brothers, Michigan's largest musical retailer. He played at Detroit-area shopping centers and promotional events. As with everything he did, McLain dreamed big, really big. Musically, he wanted nothing less than to record an album and be a headliner in Las Vegas. But he knew such aspirations were linked to how well he did on the mound this season.

While McLain was the American League starter in the 1966 All-Star Game in St. Louis, as well as Detroit's youngest twenty-game winner since Schoolboy Rowe in 1934, he told anybody who would listen that he was ready to lead Detroit to the World Series. After all, he had added a side-arm delivery and maintained that bowling, of all things, had helped the arm action with this new "out pitch."

"I want to be in the position next month to tell the man what I want," said McLain, who was entering the last year of his contract.

Asked about a possible salary figure for his next deal, McLain replied, "I think $100,000 is a beautiful figure, but I'm not halfway there yet."

Heading into the '68 season, McLain's goals could be listed as follows: win plenty of ballgames, score a six-figure contract, land a gig performing his music in Las Vegas, and appear on the *Tonight Show* with Johnny Carson—and not necessarily in that order.

"Me? Revel in the media? Damn right," he later wrote in his memoir, *I Told You I Wasn't Perfect*. "Baseball was all show biz and that's why there were writers covering it in the first place. And nobody, including [Detroit columnist] Joe Falls, can imagine how much I craved the attention. Put me, a kid whose sense of worth came from playing baseball, in front of a bunch of attentive jock-sniffing men with pens and microphones, and you've got all the elements you need for headline-making quotes. . . .

"I wanted the attention of the writers so badly that I'd get depressed between starts because they weren't in front of my locker. I wanted to talk about anything and everything in grand fashion and be the center of attention.

"I've been in situations where a writer's pen ran out of ink and I've given the one out of my pocket."

Despite the hype, much of it self-inflicted, McLain remained a gamer between the lines. He played through pain, taking cortisone shots to ease up his right shoulder, and when he was on, few in the American League were better. But in addition to batters, on the mound (and perhaps even more so off of it) McLain also had his own demons to contend with. After all, his relationship with the game was forever clouded by his relationship with the man who introduced him to it—his deceased father. A no-nonsense guy who liked to drink, Tom McLain had often beaten his son. Spare the rod and spoil the child could have been rule number one in that household. The old man was an insurance adjuster who moon-lighted as a music instructor. Growing up, Denny was fascinated with his father's ability to play the organ. "He came to love music the way he came to love sports," McLain's mother, Betty, told the *Chicago Tribune*. Tom McLain also single-handedly brought Little League baseball to Markham, Illinois, the working-class suburb of Chicago where McLain grew up. He did it so his son could play.

"I loved baseball and felt safe around my dad when we practiced and played," McLain later wrote. "Baseball was my refuge, where I could avoid the fear and crushing discipline that was enforced at home. It was only on the ball field that my dad and I could truly enjoy each other's company. We embraced the competition and loved winning. Playing baseball—and to a somewhat lesser degree, playing piano—were the only ways I got approval and a sense of importance.

"Dad wasn't a cheerleader. He'd never jump up and down or shower me with superlatives. I never remember getting a hug, a kiss, or even a handshake. But for him to just come up to me after the game and say, 'Nice goin', good game' meant the world. I lived for that."

On May 5, 1959, Tom McLain was driving to one of his son's games for Mount Carmel High School in Chicago when he had a heart attack that killed him. "It was only two days after Tom's thirty-seventh birthday," Betty McLain said. "He was on Thirty-Fifth Street, right within the shadows of White Sox park, when he had the attack. He died right there."

As important as Denny McLain was to the Tigers' chances in 1968, everyone on the ballclub knew they weren't going anywhere without a good season from another starting pitcher, Mickey Lolich. McLain and Lolich couldn't have been more different in personality. McLain was the kind of guy who sucked the oxygen out of room, while Lolich was the kind who often hung back in a crowd. If the two had been blood brothers, McLain would have been the oldest—the one who enjoyed the spotlight and demanded the lion's share of attention. Lolich was like the little brother in so many families, rarely earning the applause despite trying so hard.

Lolich grew up in Portland, Oregon, the son of the city's parks director and a batboy for the hometown team, the Beavers. Despite hailing from the Pacific Northwest, Lolich was a Yankees fan as a kid, with another left-hander, Whitey Ford, as his boyhood hero. Through high school, Lolich wore number sixteen, the same as Ford. Yet when Lolich blossomed into a top prospect, taking his Babe Ruth team to the national championship (where he was co-MVP with New Jersey's Al Downing), he turned his back on the Yankees at the eleventh hour. Instead, Lolich signed with Detroit because the Tigers' offer was higher—$30,000 over three years—and he had learned that the Tigers "didn't have a lot of good left-handers in their system."

Early on, Lolich won only a handful of games, pitching for Durham and Knoxville, two of Detroit's lower-rung farm teams. Still, his stuff remained impressive and he started the first game of the 1962 season with the Denver Bears, Detroit's Triple-A affiliate. The first batter he faced that season was Louisville's Bobby Boyd, who was nicknamed "The Rope" because of the line drives he regularly hit. True to form, Boyd roped Lolich's first pitch of the season right back at the mound, where it struck the pitcher near the left eye. The ball hit Lolich with such force that it bounced into the right-field corner for a triple.

"I was clobbered pretty good," Lolich remembered years later. "Something like that takes it out of you, no matter how many people are telling you to forget about it, to just move on."

Indeed, his eye swelled shut and he later lost several teeth due to the blow. While no bones were broken, Lolich wasn't in any hurry to pitch again. Fearful that he would become another Herb Score, a once promising fireballer for the Cleveland Indians who was never the same after being struck by a batted ball, the Tigers pushed Lolich to return to the mound—the sooner the better. Lolich would pitch four games for Denver and his heart obviously wasn't in it. He lasted just twelve innings, giving up twenty-four runs. When Jim Campbell, then the team's farm director, issued him a plane ticket for Single-A Knoxville, Lolich cashed it in for a flight home to Portland. Once he was there, he told the Tigers that he was quitting the game. At the age of twenty-two, he had retired.

In Portland word soon spread that Lolich was back in town. A semi-pro team in Portland's City League, Archer Blower, invited him to work with its pitchers, to be on the bench and advise them. In Lolich's first game as unpaid coach, Archer Blower got off to 7–0 lead, only to see the opposing team rally in the middle innings. That's when the manager asked Lolich's father, who was in the stands, if his son would be interested in pitching. Initially, Lolich said he would only play first base. But his father, somewhat uncharacteristically, persisted. "Son, why don't you pitch?" he asked.

Decades later, Lolich still finds that discussion so out of character for his father. "He never really pushed me to do much of anything," Lolich said. "He pretty much left me alone. But on that day, for some reason, he did. He really wanted me to try and pitch again."

The left-hander entered the game and he struck out all twelve batters he faced. A story in the next day's *Oregonian* read that Lolich had joined Archer "after severing ties with Denver of the American Association. He is the property of the Detroit Tigers."

The next morning Campbell called Lolich. Thrilled by the southpaw's performance, he urged Lolich to finally travel to Knoxville, and once again Lolich refused. Soon afterward the Detroit front office worked out an arrangement in which Lolich would remain under contract with the Tigers but could play the 1962 season for the Portland Beavers. There he fell under the wing of Gerry Staley, a former major leaguer, who was the Beavers' pitching coach.

"He asked if I'd give him ten days to let him try and turn me into a pitcher," Lolich said. "All I was then was a thrower really. I'd stand out there and throw it as hard as I could."

After a week or so, Lolich caught on to what Staley was trying to teach him. How it was better to be a sinker-ball pitcher, with control, than a kid trying to throw one hundred miles per hour on every pitch. The new goal was to keep the ball low, often away from the hitter, consistently hitting the outside corner. "Gerry Staley changed my whole life," Lolich said. "It's as simple as that."

In 1968, few outside of the ballclub realized how complete a pitcher Lolich could be. Instead it was more fun to focus on the lefty's idiosyncrasies. On days he pitched, Lolich often drove one of his five Kawasaki motorcycles to the ballpark. The high speed and wind in his face helped him unwind, he said. Besides, his home didn't have air-conditioning, so a motorcycle ride allowed him to cool off. Often after the game, Lolich and his wife, Joyce, loaded the Kawasaki onto a trailer and rode the forty miles back home together. All in all, it seemed a curious hobby considering that as a two-year-old Lolich had in fact driven his tricycle off the curb outside the family home in Portland and plowed it right into a parked motorcycle. The rig fell atop him, pinning Lolich to the ground. After his mother couldn't free him, a passerby helped roll the motorcycle away. Lolich was left with a broken collarbone. While the right arm was in a sling, he began to throw left-handed. After he healed, Lolich returned to doing almost everything else right-handed again—eating, writing, batting—but with a ball in his hand he was forever a southpaw. And he often loved to carry on like one.

"Sometimes when I lean too far to the left on the mound," he said, "I find myself thinking sideways."

The Detroit press considered him a good quote, yet on a deep pitching staff and a colorful team Lolich was sometimes overlooked.

"Denny McLain was Denny McLain," McAuliffe explained. "Larger than life and well-spoken. Everybody got a daily report of what was on his mind and what he was doing. But we knew Mickey was as important to our ballclub that season as anybody. He had led the league with six shutouts in '67. We knew weren't going anywhere without him."

That's why McAuliffe and others were reassured when the first pitches from Lolich in Lakeland that spring of 1968 had plenty of zip, with the great sinking movement he was known for. Even though the portly left-hander was often a slow starter, dating back to his days in the minor leagues, this time Lolich appeared ready. "We smiled when we saw how well he was throwing that spring," McAuliffe said. "A lot of us believed that it was finally going to be our time."

When ballclubs report to spring training in today's world, one of the major topics of conversation is invariably the recent Super Bowl. The sports seasons overlap to such a degree now that the big game is some-times played only weeks before pitchers and catchers report. Of course, nothing stands taller on the sports landscape than the Super Bowl, one of today's cultural icons. It's a game now watched as much for the com-mercials as for the teams that play in it.

Yet in 1968, football was still going through plenty of growing pains. The year before, Super Bowl I had been played at the Los Angeles Coli-seum, where there were 30,000 empty seats. "Nobody cared," Green Bay Packers receiver Max McGee later told HBO.

As part of the merger agreement between the National Football League and its upstart rival, the American Football League, Commis-sioner Pete Rozelle had only a month to put the event together. The stitch marks sure showed. NFL and AFL owners mixed about as well as oil and water at a pregame cocktail party, with their wives on a verge of a catfight.

When Kansas City Chiefs' owner Lamar Hunt called the event the Super Bowl (after a popular toy at the time) instead of its official name, the AFL-NFL World Championship Game, the nickname stuck. When CBS, which carried the NFL games, and NBC, which had the AFL con-tests, each claimed first dibs to the inaugural Super Bowl, Rozelle let both of them broadcast it. Back then a sixty-second commercial for Super Bowl

I cost $85,000. (Four decades later, that price tag would balloon to $2.5 million for thirty seconds of airtime.)

Super Bowl I proved to be competitive for almost two quarters. After halftime, Vince Lombardi's Packers took control and trounced the Kansas City Chiefs, 35–10. No network footage of Super Bowl I exists today. Legend has it that the game, at the network level, was taped over for a soap opera. During that era tape units were as big as refrigerators, and one of the few who owned such a rig was *Playboy*'s Hugh Hefner. But even though Hefner said he's been "hooked on football" since his college days at the University of Illinois, he didn't bother to tape the early Super Bowls.

The outcome of Super Bowl II, held early in 1968, was remarkably similar—once again demonstrating that Green Bay was the best team in the land. This time the contest was played at Miami's Orange Bowl, and the Packers opened up an early 13–0 lead. Their AFL opponent, the Oakland Raiders, did trim the lead to 13–7. But in the second half Green Bay took a 26–7 lead and cornerback Herb Adderley sealed the victory with a sixty-yard interception return.

The game drew the first $3 million gate in football history and marked the last time Lombardi would coach the Packers. During his nine-year reign in Green Bay, the legendary coach won six division championships, five NFL championships, and two Super Bowls. Despite the record gate, however, serious questions remained about the Super Bowl's long-term success in 1968. Sports commentator Haywood Hale Broun dubbed the event "too predictable to be memorable." Especially when most experts and even fans considered the AFL inferior to the more established NFL.

Through it all, Rozelle was determined to turn his championship into the world's biggest sports event. "He consciously positioned it as bigger, grander, more concentrated event than baseball's World Series," says Michael MacCambridge, author of *America's Game: The Epic Story of How Pro Football Captured a Nation.*

But to do so, Rozelle knew he needed a few breaks to come his way. Most notably he needed the AFL teams to show a lot more spunk, to be more competitive in the Super Bowl itself. After Lombardi's teams handily defeated the AFL teams in the first two championships, serious discussion began about employing tournament bracketing and play-in games. This could result in two teams from the older league, the NFL, playing in the Super Bowl. Early in 1968, many wondered if the AFL, despite its high-powered offenses led by such quarterbacks as the Oakland Raiders' Daryle Lamonica and the New York Jets' Joe Namath could compete against the more established league.

In the spring of '68, the St. Louis Cardinals were favored to repeat as National League champions and return to the World Series. Over in the junior circuit, the Detroit Tigers were determined not to be caught short again in the bullpen as they invited twenty-five pitchers to camp. As the weeks went by and that total was whittled down to the ten-man pitching staff expected to travel north for the regular season, rookie Jon Warden noticed that manager Mayo Smith often informed the next player to be released or sent down to the minors during batting practice. The Tigers' skipper walked around the outfield, a fungo bat in hand. Acting nonchalant, Smith would sidle up alongside the next poor soul and give him the bad news. That's when Warden decided to stay as far away as he could from the manager.

When Warden survived the first round of cuts, a week or so into camp, he moved into the main clubhouse, alongside such stars as Lolich, McAuliffe, Al Kaline, Willie Horton, and Norm Cash. He fought the temptation to ask them for their autographs. Instead he kept his mouth shut, to the point that he became known as the quiet kid.

"Warden, we couldn't get you to say a thing in '68," Kaline told the pitcher decades later. "Now we can't get you to shut up."

In 1968, players came to camp to actually work themselves into shape. Playing professional ball wasn't a year-round job and most players couldn't afford to work out at a local club or at home. Many needed a second job to make ends meet. That was especially true for a newcomer like Warden, who helped unload produce trucks at the local supermarket back home in Ohio.

In the 1960s, ballplayers had only a short period of time to get up to game-speed and perform, and if they didn't they were often sent packing.

On March 31, Warden got his chance—and he made the most of it. Against the St. Louis Cardinals, the defending World Series champions, the rookie was brought into a tie game in the ninth inning. Warden proceeded to shut down the Cards for four innings—the ninth, tenth, eleventh, and twelfth. He struck out six and walked just one.

That evening Warden ran into Wally Moses, one of the Tigers' coaches, in the Holiday Inn lobby at Lakeland. "You didn't hear it from me," Moses told the rookie, "but you just made the ballclub today."

Warden ran up to his room and called his mother collect. At first she didn't realize what he was trying to tell her: that her son had leaped past Triple-A and the lower rungs of the minor leagues and would open the '68 season with the big-league club. But soon enough the two of them were laughing and crying, yelling and screaming over the phone.

"That's the greatest feeling that a twenty-one-year-old pitcher could ever have," Warden said. "That I was heading north with a ballclub that had only lost the pennant the year before by a single game in the final game of the season. Everybody in baseball knew they were the favorites to win it all in the American League. That they were that good and somehow I was now a part of it all."

A few days later, the Detroit team bus pulled up to the corner of Michigan and Trumbull, the site of old Tiger Stadium. It was Monday, April 8, 1968—a mild spring evening in the Motor City. Despite the pleasant weather, the city streets were already deserted by six o'clock at night—a scene that Warden found disappointing, even a bit disturbing.

After pitching for Class A Rocky Mount in the Carolina League, following the Tigers' pennant chase from afar, Warden had made the most of his opportunities during spring training. Always a hard-thrower, he had gained some control, even the ability to pitch out of jams on occasion.

Yet making the big-league club had come as such a surprise he still needed to buy a blazer or suit jacket for road trips and team functions.

The regular season had been delayed due to Martin Luther King's assassination in Memphis. The funeral for the civil rights leader was scheduled for the next day, April 9, with the season to begin a day later, at home against the Boston Red Sox. The ballclub had stayed in Florida through the weekend, with Warden praying that the coaches didn't change their minds about him making the team. But somehow here he was, along with Daryl Patterson, another rookie, standing outside the regal, old-style ballpark, ready for the season to start.

Gear shuttled from the bus into the ballpark, and Warden and Patterson were able to catch a glimpse of the emerald-green grass and the distinctive two-story pavilion that rose behind home plate. Tiger Stadium wasn't considered a pitcher's ballpark but on that late afternoon the two rookies couldn't have cared less. While the design of Tiger Stadium remained as iconic as any in the land, the ballpark sported plenty of obstructed seats, thanks to a plethora of support columns, and the bleacher seats were uncomfortable and often a distance from the action. "Watching a game in Detroit is a graduate course in capturing the magic of the old-time ballparks," *Time* magazine said decades later. "Unlike the ivy-clad perfection of Wrigley Field or the self-congratulatory ugliness of Fenway Park, Tiger Stadium represents the last remaining link with baseball before it became too self-conscious."

Too soon, the gathering broke up. Cars driven by family or friends pulled up to take the veteran players and team officials home. Soon enough the two rookies, two white guys from the sticks, were the only ones left standing at the corner of Michigan and Trumbull. That's when Warden and Patterson realized that in the hubbub, they had been totally forgotten. Perhaps an easy thing to have happen, what with the disruption accompanying the news of King's shooting, the pending funeral, and the season opener being pushed back. Nobody had thought to reserve a room for them or make sure they were taken care of.

"We had fallen through the cracks," Warden recalled. "It wasn't like these days when I could call anybody up on my cell phone. That night still remains one of the eeriest sights I've ever seen. There was simply nobody around in this big city. Simply nobody. Detroit, the place where I was so determined to pitch, had become a ghost town."

With hanging bags slung over a shoulder, a suitcase in the other hand, the pair began to walk down the street until a police cruiser pulled alongside. The officer asked who they were. When Warden and Patterson replied that they were with the Tigers, the baseball team, the cop didn't recognize their names, even though he said he was a lifelong fan. "Of course, he wouldn't have heard of us," Warden said. "We were about the only new guys on a really experienced club. Household names? Well, we weren't exactly that."

The officer told them that Detroit was under curfew, with nobody allowed on the streets after dusk.

After some discussion, the officer dropped them off at the Leland Hotel, a twenty-two-story Beaux Arts building on Bagley Street, a few blocks from the stadium. There the rookies took an efficiency apartment for the night that eventually became their home for the rest of season.

That evening Warden recalled the stories that Willie Horton and the other African Americans on the team had told him during spring training. How last year had broken their hearts on almost every level. Not only had they lost the pennant to the Red Sox on the final day of the season; as they played on, the city literally went up in flames around them.

The summer before, President Lyndon Baines Johnson had ordered the Eighty-Second Airborne to Detroit after the rioting became so bad that the Michigan National Guard couldn't contain it. During the long hot summer of 1967, just about anything attempted by authority had struck the wrong chord. Tensions had finally come to a head in the early morning hours of July 23, 1967, when the police raided an illegal bar, also called a "blind pig," where a celebration for two black servicemen returning home from Vietnam was underway. When Detroit's finest, mostly white, began to load everybody into a paddy wagon, an angry mob, predominately black, had formed on the street outside. Outnumbered, the police retreated and rioting soon spread throughout the city.

Now, less than nine months later, it occurred to Warden as he gazed down the city's deserted streets that the quiet could well just be the calm before the storm. One could imagine that the cinders from the previous summer's fires were in fact still smoldering, merely waiting for the right spark to set them off. By now he knew the stories. How the afternoon after the police raid on the blind pig, the Tigers had taken the field for a doubleheader against the New York Yankees. After losing the first game that evening Mickey Lolich had reported to active duty with his Guard unit. Meanwhile, Horton, who had lived near the site of the police raid, hurried to that section of town still in his game jersey. There he climbed atop a car and spoke to the crowd, trying to calm them down. But it was no good. It took five days to restore order in Detroit, and when it was over, forty-three were dead, 7,200 had been arrested, and more than 2,000 buildings had burned, many to the ground.

Of course, that was last season, and one could say it was time to turn the page. Yet as Warden studied the city that was to be his new home, silent and dark now, cleared by curfew, he thought about what he had heard about King's assassination, and he couldn't help but wonder if it was inevitable, that Detroit was set to erupt all over again.

In sports, events can often solidify or dissolve in a heartbeat. Nobody knew that better in 1968 than Bill Russell. In fact, he explained that his philosophy of coaching was based as much upon moments—and what those moments would ultimately determine—as it was his play on the court. "All that is required to choreograph the action is the ball," he wrote in his autobiography, "just throw it out there and the moves will gather around the ball wherever it goes.

"This is true of many major sports: the ball provokes the art all by itself. A baseball player like Willie Mays can stand all night out in some deserted pasture called center field, but if nothing is hit near him, he doesn't really deserve watching. Once there's a fly to center field, however, the picture changes instantly. He runs in that pigeon-toed sprint, all concentration, with a hundred thousand eyes in the stadium glued to every step. Those eyes belong to people whose entire days are improved by the sight of what Willie does when he gets to the ball. What a catch!"

After rallying to defeat the Philadelphia 76ers in the Eastern Conference Finals, Russell's Boston Celtics faced a faster, more elusive opponent in the 1968 National Basketball Association finals. Instead of a dominating center like Philadelphia's Wilt Chamberlain, the Lakers alternated Mel Counts and Darrall Imhoff in the low post. Los Angeles' main weapons were guard Jerry West and forward Elgin Baylor, with quality guards Archie Clark, Freddie Crawford, and Gail Goodrich.

The championship series opened on April 21, 1968, less than three weeks after King's assassination. The teams split the first two games in Boston, with the Celtics taking the upper hand with a 127–119 victory in Game Three in Los Angeles. That's when West began to take things over. He scored thirty-eight points, with Baylor chipping in with thirty, as the Lakers squared the Series at two games apiece.

"If we can rebound, we can win," West said. "We're little, but we match up well against Boston. We're quick and we shoot well, and that can be enough in a seven-game series."

Through it all, Russell emphasized the little things with his teammates, the hustle plays that can turn the tide. Time and again he delivered them himself. Few realize what a well-rounded athlete Russell was in his prime. Track and field, not hoops, had been his first love at the University of San Francisco. Team members there received a spiffy buttoned sweater with S.F. stitched across the front. Funny what will motivate a guy at times, isn't it? To secure such duds, Russell high-jumped six feet, seven inches. For meets, he wore the sweater, track suit, silk scarf, and sunglasses.

"Track is really psychic," Russell once told *Sports Illustrated*. "There wasn't a guy I jumped against I couldn't beat if I had the chance to talk with him before beforehand."

Teammate and fellow Hall of Famer John Havlicek remembered Russell as "a fantastic athlete. He could have been a decathlon champion. He could broad-jump twenty-four feet. He did the hurdles in 13.4 (seconds). I've seen him in plays on a basketball court when he not only blocks a shot but controls the ball and feeds it to his forwards and then he's at the other end of the court trailing the fast break and if there's a rebound, he's ready for it. He just might be the fastest man on the Celtics."

Against the up-tempo Lakers, Russell had the opportunity to exhibit his athleticism. Several times in that final series, Los Angeles' Archie Clark stole the ball, with a wide open path to the basket, only to have Russell catch him from behind. "Each time Russell caught him and blocked the shot," Havlicek said. "Think of that. Think of being on the other team. There's got to be a funny feeling, going for the basket when Russell's around."

The NBA Finals soon became a battle of the all-stars: the Celtics' Russell and Havlicek against the Lakers' West and Baylor. In Game Five, despite playing on a badly twisted ankle, West scored thirty-five points, rallying Los Angeles from an eighteen-point deficit. The Lakers were down by four with less than a minute to play when West stole the ball and found Baylor for a layup. Then Los Angeles garnered another steal, the ball moving to West, who scored to send the game into overtime. In the extra session, though, Russell turned the tables again, blocking a pivotal shot by Baylor as Boston held on for the 120–117 victory and the series lead.

Heading into Game Six, Russell proved he was as adept when it came to X's and O's as any full-time coach. He moved Sam Jones to forward, where he could post up on Goodrich. That forced the Lakers to go with a taller yet slower lineup. The Lakers trailed by twenty at the half, and Boston held on to capture its tenth championship and its first with Russell as coach.

"He is an unbelievable man," West said of Russell. "To be frank, we gave them the championship. We gave them the first game, and we gave them the fifth. But I take nothing from them. There is something there, something special. For instance, twice tonight the ball went on the floor and Larry Siegfried dove for it. He didn't just go for it hard, he dove for it. They're all that way on the Celtics and you can't teach it."

Afterward Russell was asked what he had left to accomplish, as a player and a coach. "Well, I don't know," he replied, "because I never had a goal. To tell you the truth, it's been a long time since I tried to prove anything to anybody. I know who I am."

All in all, the loss to Boston left West bitterly disappointed. "It got to the point where Jerry hated anything (Celtic) green," Bill Sharman later said. "Jerry told me, 'I couldn't even wear a green sport coat or a green shirt for a lot of years.' Green really rubbed him the wrong way."

Soon after the series concluded, Lakers' owner Jack Kent Cooke received a phone call from 76ers' owner Irving Kosloff. Would Cooke be interested in trading for Wilt Chamberlain? Cooke jumped at the chance, signing the big man to a five-year deal at $250,000 a year. In exchange for Chamberlain, the 76ers received Darrall Imhoff, Archie Clark, and Jerry Chambers. Overnight, Cooke's team transformed itself from a small, run-and-gun outfit to a squad with a powerful frontcourt of Baylor and Chamberlain, with West heading up the backcourt. With that the NBA became defined as East versus West, the Boston Celtics versus the Los Angeles Lakers, Bill Russell versus Wilt Chamberlain.

"Don't be shy," says the heavy-set guy sitting behind a long table just inside the door to the luxury suites at Comerica Park. "C'mon, get your own autograph from 'The Gator.' Have something to take home and treasure forever."

Fans file past, heading for some of the most expensive seats in Detroit's new downtown ballpark and many at first don't give the smiling black man, with a Flair pen in hand, a second glance. But then something clicks and their gait slows and they turn, saying something like, "Gates, is that you?" Or, "Hey, I remember that game."

And just like that, William James "Gates" Brown has them in the palm of his hand once again. Not bad for a guy who learned to play baseball in prison of all places. Brown was arrested for breaking and entering at the age of eighteen and sentenced to a short stretch in Mansfield (Ohio) State Reformatory. Movie buffs may recognize Mansfield State as the setting for the film *The Shawshank Redemption*. Brown played on a team there and was visited by Pat Mullin, the Tigers' top scout. After Brown crushed a long home run with Mullin in attendance, the ballclub signed Brown to a $7,000 contract when he was paroled.

Once Brown was asked by somebody unaware of his background what he took in high school. "I took a little English," he replied, "a little mathematics, some science, some hubcaps, some wheel covers."

On this afternoon at Comerica Park, sitting alongside the longtime Tiger favorite can be like hanging with baseball royalty. Diligently Brown signs the black-and-white Xeroxed photographs as fans gather around.

"That home run against the Red Sox in 1968," one of the newcomers mentions.

Brown nodded his head, holding out the autograph sheet to the guy.

"That set the tone, didn't it?"

"Did it ever," the fan answers.

And just like that we're in Mr. Peabody's WABAC Machine, heading for 1968 and a season for the ages. Often people forget that the Tigers' epic year began with a 7–3 loss to the Red Sox. Earl Wilson, who had tied with the Red Sox's Jim Lonborg for the most victories in the American League the previous season, started the home opener (an honor that McLain felt he deserved). The attendance was 41,429—less than capacity. Carl Yastrzemski homered in the seventh and ninth innings and after the loss United Press International's Rich Shook wrote, "Detroit started 1968 the same way it ended 1967—one game behind Boston."

The following day, McLain got his shot, shutting out Boston for the first five innings. Yet he ran into trouble a frame later when the Red Sox tied the game at 3–3, setting the stage for the first set of improbable heroes of the Tigers' 1968 season.

After winning fifteen games the year before at Rocky Mount, Jon Warden improbably found himself on the mound at Tiger Stadium when McLain was lifted by manager Mayo Smith. Nearly a half-century later, Warden laughed when he recalled how badly his legs were shaking as he made his major-league debut.

"I kept wondering what I was doing out there," he said. "And how was I going to get out it? I mean I'm facing the Boston Red Sox. The defending American League champs."

The rookie proceeded to load the bases in the eighth inning but then escaped the jam without a run scoring. The next inning he fanned none other than Yastrzemski, the previous season's Triple Crown winner, for his first major-league strikeout.

"Carl Yastrzemski," Warden remembered. "Can you believe that?"

In the bottom of the ninth, with the score still knotted at three apiece, Brown came to the plate. The Gator had struggled in 1967 with a dislocated wrist and late in the season the ballclub obtained Eddie Mathews, one of the game's all-time home-run leaders, for pinch-hitting duties. The Tigers had been open to dealing Brown, eager to listen to any offer. Yet as the new season began, Brown was still on the roster.

"By the time '68 came around, [manager] Mayo Smith and I weren't the best of buddies, if you catch my drift," Brown said. "He didn't think I could do the job by then. He tried to trade my ass during the winter, but there weren't any takers. He wanted Eddie Mathews to be his prime pinch hitter and looking back on Eddie's career, who could blame him?

"But I'm not the kind of guy to take that kind of thing lying down. All I needed was a chance and I was going to make the most of it, and that's exactly what I did. Let's just say that when '68 began I was plenty pissed off."

In that second game of the season, Smith had already used Mathews as a pinch hitter. So it was left to Brown to do the job in the ninth inning. He indeed made the most of the opportunity by hitting the first pitch he saw for a game-winning home run off the Red Sox's John Wyatt.

In what would soon become known as the "Year of the Pitcher," Brown was one of the few batters who excelled. He would have an American

League record eighteen pinch-hits, and six of his first ten pinch-hits would be home runs.

"Being a pinch hitter isn't easy work," Brown said, between shaking hands at Comerica Park. "You're sitting on the bench for what seems to be forever and then you're up there with the game often on the line, often against a guy looking to strike you out just like that. Like he's got a car waiting for him outside, ready to hit the town. Everything can speed up in a hurry, so as much as you can, you try to slow things down. Slow it down so you can think. And what's pretty important, at least it was for me, you can't be afraid to enjoy the moment."

Sometimes Brown took that approach to extremes. Once he was called on to pinch-hit earlier than anticipated. Brown hurried up to the plate, drove one of the first pitches he saw into the outfield for a hit, and hustled around the bases, sliding head-first into second. As he stood up, the crowd gasped. The front of his jersey was covered with bright colors and pieces of squashed meat. The explanation was that Brown had been eating hot dogs while on the bench. When Smith called for him to pinch-hit, Brown had quickly jammed the snack down the front of his jersey (food in the dugout was against team rules) only to have it burst into a big mess in his slide to safety. "That's the only time I ever wished I'd struck out," he said.

While a few fans bring up that incident on this day at Comerica Park, Brown prefers to steer the conversation back to the '68 team and the camaraderie of that bunch, how everybody looked out for each other. He recalls how manager Mayo Smith once called Brown's room after the midnight curfew and Gates's roommate, Willie Horton, answered. Brown wasn't there and Horton realized that if he told the manager that piece of news his roommate would be fined for sure. So Horton did his best to stall. He walked around the hotel room, trying to decide what to do, before picking up the phone again.

"Well," Horton told the manager, "I couldn't find him in the bedroom, so I looked in the bathroom, and he wasn't there. And then I looked in the closet, and he wasn't there. And then, Skip, I found a note. It says Gates just stepped out to the ice machine and he'll be right back. Don't worry, Skip, he'll be right back."

With that Horton hung up and Brown somehow wasn't fined.

When things aren't going well in baseball, players talk about how it's only a game. The proverbial, "We play them one at a time." Still, memorable victories, say a game-winning homer in the bottom of the ninth, can ripple throughout a team, perhaps even a community.

"I'll never forget that first victory in '68," said Warden, the winning pitcher that day. "Not only was it huge for me, but it was something big for a lot of people. Soon enough our ballclub was on a roll and people really started coming back out to the ballpark again.

"The city of Detroit was still in the worst way. There was no denying that. But we began to feed off each other. Everybody in town began to rally around the team. Soon those of us in uniform began to feel like we were fighting for something bigger than just another ballgame. That somehow an entire city, the future of Detroit, was at stake, too."

"Will you stop Godding up those ballplayers?"

That's the advice sports editor Stanley Woodward once wired to his columnist Red Smith.

Smith later explained, "I've tried not to exaggerate the glory of athletes. I'd rather, if I could, preserve a sense of proportion, to write about them as excellent ballplayers, first-rate players."

Bob Broeg, the legendary sportswriter for the *St. Louis Post-Dispatch*, had similar concerns late in his career, wondering if David Halberstam and others perhaps made the Cardinals of the mid-1960s out to be "too noble." Yet throughout sports in 1968 even the most jaded scribes couldn't turn away from what they were watching. And those in Detroit certainly had the opportunity to take a long vacation from the game. The two local newspapers—the *News* and the *Free Press*—went on strike November 18, 1967. The work stoppage would last 267 days—until August

9, 1968. Despite being out of full-time work, Joe Falls, Jerry Green, and George Cantor doggedly continued to follow the team. Like so many, they knew something interesting, perhaps memorable, was going down. The last two would later pen books documenting the season—*Year of the Tiger* and *The Tigers of '68.*

Without a daily newspaper, well before the Internet and ESPN highlights, Detroit fans tuned in to broadcaster Ernie Harwell to keep up with much of the epic season. Born in 1918 in rural Georgia, Harwell suffered from a speech impediment growing up. He took weekly elocution lessons and among the pieces his teacher had him read aloud was a poem called "The House by the Side of the Road." Years later, it would work into Harwell's regular play-by-play when he said a batter who struck out had "stood there like the house by the side of the road."

Harwell began his broadcasting career at the age of twenty-two, as a student at Emory University in Atlanta. During World War II, he called a handful of Crackers' games while still a Marine and stationed in Atlanta. After the war, he caught the attention of Brooklyn Dodgers' executive Branch Rickey. Ever the creative thinker, Rickey traded catcher Cliff Dapper to Atlanta for Harwell, perhaps the only broadcaster-player trade in baseball history.

After a season in Brooklyn, Harwell jumped to the crosstown New York Giants. (The Dodgers hired Vin Scully to replace him.) After four seasons with the Giants, Harwell then moved to Baltimore for the Orioles' inaugural season. By 1960, he was in Detroit, where his Southern voice brought a distinctive flavor to the Tigers' broadcasts. During home games, he would often say a foul ball had been caught by a fan from Ypsilanti or Muskegon or Traverse City. Of course, Harwell had no idea where the lucky spectator was really from, but his listeners loved such flourishes.

Harwell, perhaps more than many at the time, realized what was at stake in 1968. "In baseball, democracy shines its clearest," he later wrote. "The only race that matters is the race to the bat. The creed is the rulebook; color merely something to distinguish one team's uniform from another."

PART
IV

The Fire Down Below

The only way to truly understand Detroit, then and now, is to drive its streets. With that in mind, Willie Horton has given us a road map to follow. Granted it remained a touch vague in spots. After all, streets can change names over the years. We didn't exactly get the Rand McNally out, although I wished that we had. Instead Horton rattled off a list of landmarks and must-sees off the top of his head. Easy for him to do as he grew up in the Jeffries neighborhood, the housing project that once dominated the city's western horizon. The worst riots in 1967 erupted nearby, and Horton will be forever remembered as the ballplayer who tried to make a difference at that time.

Soon enough we were on the road, with me riding shotgun and my friend Tom Stanton behind the wheel. Since we met fifteen years ago at the University of Michigan in Ann Arbor—both of us on a Knight-Wallace journalism fellowship—Tom has written a half-dozen books, including *The Final Season,* a haunting memoir about the last year in the life of Tiger Stadium.

From Comerica Park, the team's home since the old ballpark closed in 1999, we passed the refurbished Fox Theatre, where the Chrysler commercial ends with rapper Eminem on stage, and headed up the Midwestern-wide downtown boulevards. We crossed Interstate 75 and angled through the neighborhoods that line the John C. Lodge Freeway. Horton had a paper route in this part of town as a kid. He delivered the *Michigan Chronicle*, which has been reporting on the African American community since 1936. The *Chronicle* was one of the few papers still publishing in '68, as the *News* and the *Free Press* were on strike for much of the season.

"For the most part, fans had to follow us on the radio back then," pitcher Mickey Lolich remembered. "They'd get together and listen to Ernie Harwell do the play by play."

We were bound for Twelfth Street and Clairmont, where the worst of the rioting occurred back in 1967, and where Horton had shown up in full uniform. (He'd only changed out of his cleats.) With the fire and smoke billowing up around him, Horton climbed atop a car and pleaded with the mob to stop, to go home, to cease and desist.

"People knew immediately who I was," he said. "What I remember today is that they were so concerned for me, that I might get hurt. That's when they told me to go home. It looked like it was a war out there. I've never seen stuff like that—burning buildings, looting, smoke everywhere. They said, 'Willie, you best go home.'"

As we pulled away from the downtown, the cityscape opened up as if we were ready to barrel across the Great Plains, heading way out west. So much open space stands between the neighborhoods now that it can be difficult to comprehend what has happened to the Motor City. Census figures indicate that Detroit's population plunged 25 percent to approximately 713,000 people in the years 2001 to 2010. That's the lowest level since Henry Ford did business in 1910. According to the *Detroit Free Press*, the Motor City lost 238,270 residents during that period, or one every twenty-two minutes.

So many buildings have been deserted and then torn down that only great swaths of empty space remain. To paraphrase Gertrude Stein, that means there really is no there there. The result could be Mayor Dave Bing, who starred for the hometown Pistons basketball team in 1968, trying to convince people to move closer together so such city services as electricity, water, and sewer can be better utilized. Others have suggested more drastic measures extending to bringing farmers back in to plow the empty lots into productive fields.

Driving through Detroit that day, the sight bordered upon the bizarre. It was sort of like viewing a film that breaks off time after time, revealing a giant blank screen where the image should be. We were literally moving through a landscape with built-in pauses, giving anybody plenty of room for reflection and, dare we say, regret.

At Twelfth and Clairmont itself, we found more emptiness than commemoration. Of course, we are much more prone to erect a monument to our cities' zenith, than to their nadir. Perhaps with that in mind, Tom opted to check out another Motor City landmark. A few blocks away we came upon Boston-Edison, Henry Ford's old neighborhood. Tom told me that if you wanted to do business with the assembly-line king back in the day, you needed to live here, about four miles north of downtown. The stately homes still stand resolute and immense, a testament to when Detroit ruled the industrial world. Named for the neighborhood's two main streets, the Boston-Edison's residents once included labor leader Walter Reuther and Motown Records mogul Berry Gordy Jr. Somehow it survived the riots and white flight to the suburbs. Lately it has been coping less well with the threat of foreclosure. Thieves flock to the area looking to pilfer "doorknobs, light fixtures, doors, radiators (attractive as scrap metal) and especially, copper pipes and wiring" from the homes, according to The *Wall Street Journal*.

Gazing upon it all, I understood why Horton risked his life that evening the riots flared up. In Detroit, one can easily picture the best and worst of times. Often they stand within a few blocks of each other.

From Boston-Edison, we turned south, returning to the downtown sector. After a while, Tom pulled over and asked, "Know where you are?"

Not really. Even though I pride myself on having a good sense of direction, by then my head was spinning. Out the right window lay another empty lot, bigger than most that we'd seen on our tour.

I craned my neck to read the street sign and it dawned on me—the corner of Michigan and Trumbull.

"This is where the old Tiger Stadium was?"

"That's right," Tom replied. "They've fenced it off because too many people were playing pickup games on the old site. See the sign?"

Somebody had hung a piece of cardboard with handwritten letters on the chain-link fence that surrounds this piece of property, shielding it from what? Itself? The memory of 1968? City officials have remained adamant that even though Tiger Stadium itself is long gone, nobody can play ball on the land where it once stood.

The homemade sign read, Ernie Harwell Field.

Without a word, we looked out on the open field. The site of the hometown team's biggest accomplishment. Then the light at the corner changed, and we pulled away.

So what kind of ballplayer can string together a series of civic landmarks, some still standing, others leveled by the wrecking ball, right off the top of his head? Perhaps a guy who will always consider Detroit home. After all, Willie Horton worked as a clubhouse kid at the old ballpark. Still, when you get right down to it, he can feel at home just about anywhere.

Some mornings Horton parks on Woolworth Avenue, talking with folks as he walks the remaining blocks to his office at Comerica Park. Once at the ballpark, he often starts at the top level on game days, looping around the main concourse, where his statue is one of the six immortalized Tigers, saying hello to the ushers and the concession workers. It seems everybody knows Willie Horton.

"I never really felt any pressure when I played here in Detroit," he said. "Some of the people I'll see going to the game I've known since Little League. When they were in the stands, I felt like I'd been playing for them all my life. Those faces are familiar, so why get so worked up about the pressure or whatever? I know a lot of them and they know me."

When Horton played, he went out of his way to meet fans and make good friends in every American League city. He often broke bread with them after the ballgames and even today there are few major league towns where he doesn't know at least somebody. To hear him explain it, this philosophy, this way of doing things, really took root in 1968.

"As a player you like to insulate yourself from the rest of the world," he said. "Just ignore it all and simply go about your job. But back then it was next to impossible to do that, so everybody coped in different ways."

Bob Gibson was so angry with the world around him that each start became an opportunity to rage against the injustice of what was going on in that world. Denny McLain fell in love with celebrity and all its trappings. In 1968, Willie Horton decided that he never wanted to leave home. That's how crazy everything had become.

When he first told me this, I didn't fully understand what he was saying. How can a ballplayer, in a profession that puts him on the road for eight to nine months out of the year, stay close to home?

"I had to do some thinking about it all, that's for sure," Horton said, smiling. "Be a little creative."

The way Horton managed it was by going out of his way to make friends, close friends, everywhere the team played. "When we came back to that town, I wanted to know there was somebody I could call, somebody I could talk to," he explained. "What I was doing was making sure that I had a home everywhere I went playing ball. In 1968 especially, that's how I got by."

Making every port of call home. In a way, Horton has been doing that his entire life. In 1962, soon after signing with Detroit, Horton arrived in Lakeland, Florida, for the first time. He found that he already knew some of the Tigers' other top-flight prospects there—Mickey Stanley, Jim Northrup, Bill Freehan. Horton and Freehan had played on the same youth team, winning the national championship in Altoona, Pennsylvania, where they beat a team from Ohio that had Boston Celtics legend John Havlicek on its roster. Of course, we're talking about the era of the three-sport letterman when a future Hall of Fame basketball player like Havlicek wasn't locked into one sport year-round.

Horton was eager to get to Tiger Town and begin his professional career. But nothing prepared him for the rude welcome at the local bus depot. After gathering up his luggage, which consisted of a duffel bag and not much else, Horton went to hail a cab. The town had Yellow and Checkered cabs. But none stopped for him. A local told him he needed to call Riggs Taxi. As the local put it, that was the wheels for the colored folk. At first, Horton thought "it was a rookie joke. Something they pull on the newcomers. They said I had to call Riggs. I said that sounds like a barbecue place to me."

Instead, Horton threw his duffel bag over his shoulder and walked to Tiger Town. Along the way, he realized this was perhaps similar to what Jackie Robinson, Larry Doby, and other baseball pioneers had done to clear the way for players like himself. Along that long walk to the team's spring training home, he decided one of his jobs had to be to make things better for people who came after him. And maybe the best place to start was right there in Lakeland.

This wasn't the first time Horton had chosen to confront his circumstances by carrying himself forward on his own two feet. Before moving to Detroit, the Horton family had lived in Arno and then Stonega—coalmining towns in southwest Virginia near the Kentucky border. By the age of eight, young Willie excelled on the ball diamond. But the field in Stonega was dug up and dusty, with the games pickup affairs at best. Word had it that Appalachia, a bigger town six miles away, had a legitimate field, and Willie began to wonder what it would be like to set foot on a ball diamond like that, perhaps even dare to run the bases. So, on a spring day in 1950, he began to walk along the railroad tracks connecting the two locales.

Along the way, he met another kid, a white boy about his age. Willie asked if he'd like to accompany him to Appalachia, to run the bases on a real ballfield. Larry Munsey thought Horton was crazy and told him so, but he soon fell into step alongside and the two of them walked the rest of the way together.

The small ballpark in Appalachia was everything Horton had imagined it would be: bona fide baselines and a well-manicured outfield. As the two boys came upon the place, rising like a vision out of the rolling hills, they saw that something was going on. In a twist that makes you believe in larger things, they realized that Little League tryouts were about to start. Both of them were invited to swing a bat, field a few grounders. In the end, both boys made the Appalachia Wolves, sponsored by a local furniture store.

"Something took ahold of me that day," Horton said. "God, providence, whatever . . . But something got me walking down that railroad track that day and being able to play ball for the Wolves."

Years later, in Lakeland, Horton once again determined to put one foot in front of the other and walk the walk. He made the big-league club in Detroit for good in 1965. Along the way his efforts in the team's spring training home helped integrate the local theater and parks. Jim Campbell, the Tigers' general manager, often asked Horton what he was trying to accomplish down in Lakeland. "I don't know," Horton replied, "but I think I should do it."

Even though Denny McLain didn't win his first game until almost two weeks into the season, soon everything fell into line for him. He had good stuff. Cortisone shots often allowed to him take his regular turn on the mound, and McLain had a team behind him that could hit and exhibited a genuine zeal for late-game rallies.

McLain had made it clear he loved an audience. The bigger the hubbub the better he felt about things. But his behavior also made him a bit of a sorcerer's apprentice: sometimes he orchestrated too big a storm for anybody's good. Even with Detroit in the midst of a newspaper strike, McLain could still find ways to create a stir. Even if that meant sounding off to the wire-service reporters and out-of-town writers. Such was the case when the pitcher blasted his own fans.

Certainly there were some bad apples in the thousands that regularly attended games at Tiger Stadium. The year before, when the ballclub gave away the pennant on the final day, spectators had stormed the field afterward. Management turned on the sprinklers in an attempt to scatter the hordes, and inside the Tigers' clubhouse the sound of bottles, thrown from the upper deck, could be heard breaking on the main concourse. Perhaps that's what was on McLain's mind when he was asked about the fans booing the team despite a 13–5 record a few weeks into the '68 season. Inevitably, the loquacious McLain, the guy who would loan a reporter a pen to make sure his every word was taken down, bit, and responded by calling Tigers followers "the biggest front-running fans in the world."

And he didn't stop there. After explaining how the abuse made life difficult for Norm Cash and Al Kaline, McLain couldn't resist closing with a zinger: "Detroit is a great town. I like it. I've bought a house and have roots. But the fans in this town are the worst in the league."

Mayo Smith dressed down his ace in a closed-door meeting after the comments were published. McLain went on broadcaster Ernie Harwell's pregame show, trying to take back the criticism, saying he had been misquoted. But it didn't do much good. McLain was booed when he lost to the Baltimore Orioles in his next home start.

"Sometimes with the stuff he said," Gates Brown said, shaking his head, "you'd wonder what he was thinking. But that was Denny McLain. Too often the mouth ran ahead of the man."

If anything, though, the catcalls only seemed to energize McLain— after all, it was still attention and he was back in the spotlight—and it soon became evident something was clicking. The home loss to Baltimore would be his only losing effort in May. He won six of seven games during that month, pitching complete games in each of the wins including a ten-inning affair against the Twins. Then in June he won six of seven again. The following month he did one better, winning seven of eight decisions in July. By midsummer it was clear that on the mound, at least, he could do no wrong and the sports world was beginning to follow his every move.

Soon after the All-Star Game, Detroit was down 4–2 in the bottom of the ninth inning against the Baltimore Orioles. Once again the scene was set for late-inning heroics, as the Tigers won that game on rookie short-stop Tom Matchick's homer—a long fly that Baltimore outfielder Frank Robinson thought he had before the breeze carried the ball just into the second deck overhang at the Tiger Stadium. "If you weren't so ugly," Dick McAuliffe told Matchick afterward, "I'd kiss you."

With the city's two major newspapers—the *News* and *Free Press*—on strike for much of the season, fans instead listened to Tigers' announcer Ernie Harwell on the radio, calling the games in his sweet Georgia lilt. "In '68, there were still plenty of people who thought the city was going to burn to the ground. That it was all going to fire up again," Mickey Lolich said. "I had some friends in the police. They were in the city and had a good feel for what was going on. They told us to please keep winning—that things were smoldering, like how it is before it starts burning all over again. But if we could keep winning then things may not explode like they had the year before.

"In '67, you'd see four or five guys standing on a street corner, and they'd be looking for trouble. In '68, you'd see the same kind of guys standing on a street corner, but they'd have a transistor radio and they'd be gathered around, listening to Ernie calling the Tiger game, waiting to see if we could come back and win another ballgame."

Freehan felt having the newspapers on strike kept the Tigers focused during these difficult times. "I swear it helped the club," he wrote in his autobiography *Behind the Mask*. "We didn't have any of this ridiculous divisive gossip floating around. Sure, baseball writers want to write inside stories, and sometimes they do, but they can get as sloppy with their facts as we can ever get on the field."

The newspaper strike was close to being settled when the Tigers traveled to the East Coast for three games in Washington and then Baltimore starting July 23. Despite almost 46,000 rooting against him at Memorial Stadium, McLain pitched a shutout four days later, with his teammates hitting five home runs for him in the 9–0 victory. During the "Year of the Pitcher" some pitchers that season didn't see that kind of support in a month.

At 20–3, McLain was the quickest to reach the twenty-win plateau since Rube Marquard in 1912. Few in the visiting clubhouse were sure who old Rube was. But there was no doubt that McLain was flying high above the clouds—safe for now.

Luis Tiant holds court just inside the front doors of the ESPN Zone in downtown Washington. On this muggy July evening in the nation's capital, the crowd has walked over from the E Street Cinema, a few blocks away, where they have just watched the ESPN movie *The Lost Son of Havana*, in which Tiant stars.

"If it had been up to my father, I would have stayed in Havana," Tiant tells those gathered around him. "He said to me that there was no place in the major leagues back then for a black man. I listened to him. I understood what he was telling me. But I still came to America."

He pauses to look about the crowded room.

"If I'd listened," Tiant adds, "all of this and so much more wouldn't have happened."

Tiant first left Cuba in 1959 to play in the Mexican League, and for a short time he enjoyed the best of both worlds. He played baseball professionally and returned home to Cuba in the off-season, where he would usually play some more ball. Yet by his third year with the Mexico Blues, the political situation in Havana had changed markedly. Fidel Castro, the nation's new leader and an inspired ballplayer in his own youth, declared that Cuba would no longer accept the pro game on its own shores. In other words, those who lived on the island could play as amateurs only. Thus began a sea change that saw Cuba soon fade as the top exporter of talent to the major leagues, and such countries as the Dominican Republic and later Venezuela pick up the slack.

In the spring of 1961, all Tiant knew for sure was that he wanted to play professional ball and try to follow his father's footsteps. The old man once starred for the New York Cubans in the old Negro Leagues and was considered one of the top pitchers the island had ever produced. But as writer Rob Ruck documented in *Raceball: How the Major Leagues Colonized the Black and Latin Game,* his father had also never reconciled himself to the racial insults he faced playing in the States. "I didn't want him to come to America," the senior Tiant explained years later. "I didn't want him to be persecuted and spit on and treated like garbage, like I was."

Still, the major leagues were the showcase for the best players and, in the end, there was no holding back Tiant's son. On May 25, 1961, Luis Tiant Jr. left Cuba, not knowing when or if he would ever return. He played in the minor leagues—West Virginia, Florida, and North Carolina—before debuting with the Cleveland Indians in 1964.

Four years later, Tiant was merely considered the rotation's fourth-best pitcher as the 1968 season began. Yet by the close of the "Year of the Pitcher" he would seemingly come out of nowhere to establish himself alongside Bob Gibson, Don Drysdale, Mickey Lolich, and Denny McLain as one of the best hurlers in the game.

While the Senators' Frank Howard may bemoan the lousy start he got off to early in '68, a major reason was because he ran into Tiant. On April 28, Tiant pitched a two-hitter against the Washington Senators for a 2–0 victory. The key moment came when he struck out Howard on a hesitation pitch—a throw in which Tiant altered his delivery so radically that for a heartbeat he actually turned completely away from the home plate. All the batter could see was his back before Tiant finally came around with the ball.

"I still have nightmares about that pitch of his," Howard said. "To me, standing there in the batter's box, it seemed like he threw everything at me but the ball."

Tiant maintained that he didn't go to the hesitation pitch "for show. But to get batters out."

On that particular day, Tiant told the *Cleveland Press* that he'd given Howard his "shoulder, back, foot and the ball last."

During his next start on May 3, Tiant recorded another shutout, this time a three-hitter against the visiting Minnesota Twins. Before a crowd of just 5,106, he threw 122 pitches, picking up the 4–0 victory in two hours, twelve minutes. Even though the Cuban was relatively unheralded, he had already proved his durability by averaging nearly nine complete games a season during his first four years in Cleveland. In '68, he would more than double that total.

Such numbers often seem astounding today with many pitchers hoping to average six innings and pitch counts typically limited to around one hundred. While relief pitchers were certainly utilized in 1968—that year the Chicago White Sox had Wilbur Wood and Hoyt Wilhelm, a pair of knuckleballers—and had been for years by that point, starting pitchers were expected to go the distance, at least strive for nine innings. "You were expected to finish what you started," Nolan Ryan said. "There was a level of responsibility involved with pitching."

As the price to sign quality arms escalated, however, ballclubs became more cautious, some would say too conservative, about how long to extend their top-line pitchers. Eventually one hundred pitches became the game limit for most promising arms. "It's the amount of money they have tied up in these players," said Dick Bosman. Minor league pitching coordinator for the Tampa Bay Rays, Bosman toed the rubber for the Washington Senators in 1968. "Everybody plays it safe with that much on the line now."

On May 7, 1968, Tiant shut down the New York Yankees, defeating them in another complete-game shutout. In addition to throwing another

129 pitches, he also cracked a two-run single. Five days later, he went into the Indians' record book with his fourth consecutive shutout, a 2–0 victory over the Orioles in Baltimore. After the game, the Robinsons, Frank and Brooks, complained about the hesitation pitch.

Now Tiant stood within one shutout of the American League record, set by Chicago's old Doc White. But in a rematch with the Orioles, this time in Cleveland, Boog Powell cracked a three-run home run off him in a 6–2 Baltimore victory. Although the scoreless streak was history, Tiant was far from finished with his remarkable season.

Six weeks later, on July 3, Tiant went on a strikeout tear against the visiting Twins. Scoreless heading into the tenth inning, Minnesota put runners on first and third with none out. That's when Tiant struck out John Roseboro, Rich Rollins, and pitcher Jim Merritt, putting him at nineteen strikeouts, which broke Bob Feller's team record for a single game. "I've never seen a fastball thrown so hard for so many innings," Roseboro told *Baseball Digest*. That was high praise. Once a mainstay with the Dodgers, Roseboro had caught Don Drysdale and Sandy Koufax.

"I can't say enough about that performance," said home plate umpire Ed Runge. "He's a great pitcher. Every time I've seen him this year he's been great. Whenever he got into trouble tonight he just reared back and fired. He challenged them all night long."

In the victory, Tiant equaled Koufax's record of forty-one strikeouts in three consecutive games, set in 1959. After upping his record to 14–5 a few days later, Tiant was named the American League's starting pitcher for the All-Star Game in Houston's Astrodome.

Meanwhile, in Detroit, the Tigers' Denny McLain wasn't much interested in attending the Midsummer Classic if he wasn't the starting pitcher. Frankly, he had better things to do. Such grumbling prompted American League president Joe Cronin to warn the Tigers' ace, as well as Detroit manager Mayo Smith, that he expected the right-hander to be in Houston. McLain finally agreed to go but not before deciding to swing by Las Vegas first.

In his last start before the All-Star break, McLain won his sixteenth game as the Tigers rallied yet again in the late innings. This time it was Willie Horton lining a home run over the left-field fence off Oakland's Ed Sprague. The 5–4 victory marked the sixteenth time Detroit came from behind to win so far in 1968. A phenomenon Detroit sportswriter Jerry Green dubbed as another "Last Licks Victory."

McLain's victory came in the first game of a doubleheader and afterward the Detroit ace went up to the press box at Tiger Stadium to shoot the breeze with the press. In between innings, he gave the team organist a break and serenaded an unknowing crowd with a version of "Satin Doll." On the field below, the Tigers demonstrated why they were running away from the rest of the American League. Mickey Lolich, who had struggled in the first half of the season, with a 5–4 record through June, came out of the bullpen to strike out Reggie Jackson as the Tigers held on for the 7–6 victory to sweep the doubleheader. "If we can play .500 the second half, we should be OK," said Smith, acknowledging that no league leader had been better off at the All-Star break in decades than the Tigers' nine-and-a-half-game lead.

Held at Houston's Astrodome, the 1968 All-Star Game was the first one ever played indoors. The change of venue didn't help the hitters much as they continued to struggle. The year before, in Anaheim, the two squads had battled for fifteen innings before the National League won, 2–1. Many blamed the twilight conditions (an early start for East Coast television) for the lack of scoring. In Houston, some felt the sightlines were almost too perfect. The Tigers' Bill Freehan claimed that conditions inside the Astrodome "ruins your depth perception or something."

Teammate Willie Horton agreed. "[Juan] Marichal threw me a slider and I saw it so good I said to myself, 'I'm going to murder this.' And I swung and that ball hasn't got to me yet. . . . It's nothing I can put my finger on. It is odd."

For the record, the National League won, 1–0, as Willie Mays scored on a double play in the bottom of the first inning. He reached second base on Tiant's throwing error and then headed to third when the pitcher and Freehan, the American League's starting catcher, got their signals crossed. From there the American League couldn't score against Drysdale, Marichal, Steve Carlton, Tom Seaver, Ron Reed, and finally Jerry Koosman. For being the only one to cross the plate, Mays was named the game's Most Valuable Player, while Tiant ended up as the losing pitcher despite not allowing an earned run.

Afterward many complained that baseball's problem had little to do with playing baseball indoors for the first time. Rather, pitching was at fault. This facet of the game had become too good, too dominant. The 1968 All-Star Game was exhibit A—it was the first in history to end with only one run scored.

"No better example of the universal impotence that has gripped baseball in the last two seasons could have been arranged for a television audience throughout the Western Hemisphere estimated to number sixty million, and 48,321 who paid $383,733, a record gross, to attend the game," wrote Leonard Koppett in the *New York Times*.

"Pitchers Turn All-Star Classic Into a Farce," read the headline in the next morning's *Los Angeles Times*.

A few days after the game, Tiant's mother, Isabel, was able to call from Havana. She had seen the contest. A friend of the family had managed to pick up the signal from Miami and during the innings her only child pitched, Senora Tiant gazed at the flickering screen, tears in her eyes. She didn't care about the score or that her only son had lost the game.

"I watched you on television," Isabel later told Tiant in the phone call, "and all the while I watched I cried because I wanted to reach out and touch you and I couldn't."

If you believed the odds-makers in Las Vegas, the 1968 regular season was over at the All-Star break. In the National League the St. Louis Cardinals were staked to a ten-game lead. Bob Gibson finished the first half with a 3–0 shutout in San Francisco improving his record to 11–5. His ERA stood at a miniscule 1.06.

At 55–28, the Tigers were two games better than St. Louis and enjoyed a nine-and-a-half game lead in the American League over the Cleveland Indians, with the Baltimore Orioles another game back. Vegas soon made the Cardinals 7–5 favorites to win the World Series, and commissioner William Eckert announced that 1968 would be the last season that the winner of the National League pennant and the winner of the American League pennant would go directly to the Fall Classic. Starting the following year the major leagues would be split into divisional play with more teams included in the postseason hunt.

Yet not everyone was ready to concede the '68 season to the front-runners. In Baltimore, the third-place Orioles fired manager Hank Bauer, who had been at the helm two years before when Baltimore swept the Dodgers in the World Series. Bauer's dismissal didn't surprise anyone, himself included, but the naming of his successor did. Many expected Orioles' coach Billy Hunter to be promoted to skipper. Instead the job went to thirty-seven-year-old Earl Weaver, who had never played in the majors and only joined the big-league team as a coach in the off-season.

"The Orioles are not winning because they're not hitting, so I guess I'm to blame," Bauer said. "But if I could still hit, I'd be playing."

When it came to Weaver, Bauer grumbled, "I would have named Hunter. He knows the players better."

That said, Weaver certainly knew the younger players better than anybody else in the organization. Of the eleven Orioles' farm teams he had managed, all finished in the upper division. Within the Orioles' front office, he was famous for grading players, trying to get inside their heads. At his insistence, the entire minor-league ballclub in Elmira, New York, had its IQ tested one season. He did it in an effort to better understand one player, fastball phenom Steve Dalkowski. Considered one of the fastest but also most unpredictable pitchers of all time, Dalkowski later became the basis for the character Nuke LaLoosh in the movie *Bull*

Durham. Always looking for new methods to analyze and better understand performance, Weaver was one of the first proponents of the radar gun, and he also urged such stars as Brooks and Frank Robinson to study film of themselves at the plate. But most importantly to the immediate future—and to the front office—the new manager believed the Orioles could still make a run at Detroit.

"I still feel we are a pennant contender," Weaver said. "I don't think first place is unrealistic even though we are ten and a half games out."

Few paid much attention to Weaver's proclamation. With the pennant races considered by many to be a foregone conclusion, attention instead remained upon individual records and pursuits. And there were plenty. In Cleveland, Tiant continued his dominance, stringing together seven consecutive regular-season victories, and winning eleven out of twelve decisions. Meanwhile, in Atlanta, all eyes were on Hank Aaron, who was about to join what used to an be elite club. Like most sluggers, "Hammerin' Hank" struggled in the first half of the season, hitting just .247 at the break. His choices for the National League All-Star outfield were the Reds' Pete Rose, the Giants' Willie Mays, and the Cardinals' Curt Flood. Surprised to even make the team, Aaron ended up hitting cleanup in the Astrodome. In a way, being a part of the All-Star Game became excellent preparation for Aaron's next star turn.

On July 14, 1968, Aaron hit his five hundredth career home run, a three-run clout that powered the Braves past the visiting San Francisco Giants. With that dinger, Aaron joined Willie Mays, Eddie Mathews, Mel Ott, Ted Williams, Mickey Mantle, Jimmie Foxx, and Babe Ruth as the only sluggers to reach the five-hundred plateau. In recent years this select club has tripled in size (from eight to twenty-five). In 1968, though, five hundred career homers still meant something.

"In Atlanta, they're convinced he's a combination of Mary Poppins and Clark Kent, that when he takes his uniform off, there's a huge block 'S' on the front of his sweatshirt and cape on the back," wrote *Los Angeles Times* columnist Jim Murray. "Ruth and Aaron were born the same week of the year (Aaron Feb 5, 1934; Ruth, Feb 6, 1895). Ruth had 470 home runs on his 34th birthday. Aaron had 481. Ruth, of course, hit 234 home runs in the last six years of his career. Henry only has to hit 223 to tie what is generally considered the most unreachable record in the books."

Aaron would indeed pass Ruth six years later, on April 8, 1974.

But even on Aaron's big day in 1968, pitching still managed to also find its way into the headlines. Out of Cincinnati came news that Don Wilson, a right-hander with the Houston Astros, had struck out eighteen in a 6–1 victory. In doing so, Wilson tied two major league records: one for the most strikeouts for a nine-inning game (at the time), and another for striking out eight straight batters.

For all its dominance, the fact remained that pitching didn't score runs, not even in 1968. To win a game at least some measure of hitting was in order, and to that end, a lot of pitchers would have loved to have Denny McLain's good fortune in 1968. Everywhere pitchers excelled but few had any runs to work with. In Chicago, White Sox knuckleballer Hoyt Wilhelm appeared in his nine hundred and seventh game as a pitcher, breaking Cy Young's all-time record. Unfortunately for the old knuckleballer, it was in a losing effort, a 1–0 defeat to the Oakland Athletics.

"I've been a knuckleball pitcher, even in high school," Wilhelm said in an effort to explain his durability. "It's a pitch I don't think just anybody can master. I'm not sure I've mastered it yet."

A few weeks after the All-Star Game, Luis Tiant had built an impressive 17–6 record but the Indians' attack, like much of the offense at the major league level, was being worn down by exceptional opposing pitching. On July 30, the Indians were reminded that in this season for the ages defense wasn't too shabby, either, as Washington Senators shortstop Ron Hansen completed an unassisted triple play against them. It was only the eighth in major league history and the first since 1927.

In mid-August, the Tigers visited Cleveland Stadium, where Tiant awaited them. The Indians' ace went seven innings, striking out nine and walking none. That would have made him the winner most days. But Tiant lost the marquee matchup to Lolich and the Tigers 3–0.

"Luis and I would each be fighting for thirty wins if he had our kind of hitting to go with his kind of pitching," McLain said. "I've been getting more than five runs a game to work with. If I just stay close to the other team, I have a 99 percent chance of winning. If he stays close, he's got a fifty-fifty chance."

Tigers' catcher Bill Freehan added, "If Luis played for us, he'd be shooting for forty wins."

"Maybe they're right," Tiant replied. "I don't know. All I know is that I'm not a Tiger. I'm an Indian. So all I want is twenty wins. That's what I'm shooting for."

In seven of Tiant's losses to that point in the season, the Indians had scored fewer than three runs. In a dozen of his games, his teammates hadn't scored a run until the sixth inning or later. "I never have an easy inning," Tiant said. "I must throw hard all the time, and this puts strain on my elbow."

Others wondered if such arm fatigue was due to his herky-jerky motion, and perhaps even his famed hesitation pitch. After that game in Cleveland, Al Kaline said that Tiant has "got to hurt his arm throwing that way. He won't have a long career."

Of course, a lot of things are said after any game, when the players and media can dissect it all with great abandon. Yet for some reason Kaline's comments seemed to stick with Indians' manager Alvin Dark. He was the same manager who drove Orlando Cepeda, Juan Marichal, and the Alou brothers to distraction when he managed them in San Francisco from 1961 to 1964.

"Alvin Dark to me was one day the best man in the world," Marichal wrote in his autobiography, "and the next day, he was the worst. I love the guy, but I saw Alvin Dark do things that hurt me deeply."

A few weeks later, when Tiant pulled himself from a game due to a sore elbow, Dark picked up on Kaline's comment and revealed just how much it had resonated with him. He told the press that Tiant's "extreme motions had put a strain somewhere. I don't think he needs all those motions. All he has to do is throw hard. He'll just take years off his career if he keeps throwing this way."

Tiant couldn't believe his own manager didn't have his back. His delivery, his trademark motion and the hesitation pitch, wasn't to blame he said. It was the lack of run support. The pitcher pointed out that in his last twenty-three innings, the Indians had given him a grand total of two runs to work with. The reason he was sore was because he was throwing so hard, trying every trick in the book, because in 1968 he had no margin for error.

If the clubhouses in Detroit and St. Louis could be held up as model examples for building team chemistry, the situation in Cleveland became a classic example of what *not* to do. Alvin Dark wasn't the best point man when it came to race relations. In 1964, not long after the U.S. Senate passed the Civil Rights Act (after a fifty-seven-day filibuster), he told *Newsday* that the Giants sometimes struggled because "we have so many Negro and Spanish-speaking players on this team. They are just not able to perform up to the white ballplayers when it comes to mental alertness. You can't make most Negro and Spanish players have pride in their team that you get from white players."

While Dark claimed he was misquoted, his tenure in San Francisco soon ended. After two seasons managing in Kansas City, he was in Cleveland for the '68 season, where he was about to face another showdown with a prominent Latino star.

By the dog days of August, any talk of a full-fledged Olympic boycott had died down to grumbles and whispers. The stars from San Jose State's "Speed City"—Tommie Smith, John Carlos, and Lee Evans—may have been won over by Harry Edwards's rhetoric, but they were still heading to Mexico City to run for their country.

But there was a key factor that ABC-TV executive Roone Arledge and the Olympic powers still didn't fully understand at this point—competing at altitude. While scientists expressed concern about the Summer Games being held 7,400 feet above sea level, few in the running community were really that worried. After all, in 1955, Mexico City had hosted the Pan American Games and race times appeared to balance each other out. In retrospect, though, that was wishful thinking, especially by those calling the shots on the U.S. Olympic team.

"I don't think there was an American middle or long-distance runner who was as ready as he should have or could have been for his race in Mexico," Dr. Jack Daniels later wrote in a paper entitled "Science and the Altitude Factor." "For a non-acclimatized miler to race a mile at altitude would be similar, from a competitive standpoint, to having him race a sea-level two mile for the first time. It's a different race."

U.S. Track and Field named Daniels as its official altitude consultant the summer before the '68 Games. Unfortunately, the organization didn't give him much funding, nor did they bother to really listen to what he had to say. In the months leading up to the Summer Olympics, Daniels joined forces with Dr. Bruno Balke, a German medical doctor and physiologist specializing in altitude training. Balke had been brought to the United States by the Air Force to help develop the space program. At one point, Balke told the U.S. Olympic Committee, "I should not be coming to you asking for funds to do altitude research. You should be coming to me offering it." Together, he and Daniels determined that two types of acclimatization—physiological and competitive—needed to take place for even elite athletes to excel at the kind of high altitude they were going to be competing at in Mexico City.

"We should have been having major competitions at altitude for several years prior to the '68 Olympics," Daniels said.

Yet neither Daniels nor Balke could convince U.S. officials to hold a significant number of races at altitude. Instead, it fell to the athletes themselves to help foot the bill for such research and try their best to prepare. Jim Ryun, the face of the U.S. track team, went to work at a supermarket in Alamosa, Colorado, at $1.50 an hour, to help defray training costs. For many, it was inconceivable that the world-record holder in the mile would end up in such a situation. One morning, Ryun and Daniels were having breakfast at local diner in Colorado. A teenage girl and her little brother approached the runner.

"My brother thinks you look like Jim Ryun," the girl said.

"I am," Ryun replied.

Shaking her head, she said, "No, you're not."

"Yes, I am," Ryun said.

"No, you're not."

With that she led her little brother away by the hand.

In August, Curt Flood graced the cover of *Sports Illustrated*, making a leaping catch against the emerald ivy and four-hundred-foot sign at Wrigley Field. The cover line read, "Baseball's Best Centerfielder." Left unsaid, but certainly understood by many, was that Flood also played for the best team in baseball. After losing eleven of thirteen games early in the season and falling to fourth place, the Cardinals had responded in dominant fashion, putting together a 54–20 record from Memorial Day into the dog days of August. A ballclub built on pitching and defense with a touch of the unconventional (manager Red Schoendienst won one game by pinch-hitting for MVP Orlando Cepeda), the Cardinals held a fourteen-game lead in the National League as the regular season began to wind down.

Even though St. Louis and Detroit were markedly different ballclubs with varying clubhouse dynamics, they had a common trait. Both could be brutally honest with each other.

"Chemistry means you get in my butt if I'm not doing the job," the Tigers' Willie Horton explained years later. "Sure we'll have good times. But you also know we can criticize each other if one of us isn't doing the job.

"It's like having brothers at home. You'll have fights, but they don't mean anything. You probably talk more honestly to each other, especially when things are against you, than you would to others. Winning teams have fights in the clubhouse. Because they're that close. In '68, we had a lot of scrapping in the clubhouse. But that doesn't mean tomorrow we're mad at each other."

If hanging around the Cardinals sometimes resembled a fashion shoot for GQ magazine, for the Tigers, on the other hand, it could be like stepping onto the set of *Animal House*. The joke was that if anybody ever wanted a team picture just find the nearest bar. Most of the Detroit roster would be found there. When Hall of Fame slugger Eddie Mathews first joined the ballclub in 1967, he initially thought they were a bunch of drunks. Over time, though, he realized that Tigers were a well-knit group that looked out for each other, even Denny McLain, and the off-the-field shenanigans played a key role in team chemistry. Perhaps no prank better demonstrated this than the famed "Plane in the Pool" stunt. On a road trip to Anaheim, the ballplayers became enthralled with a full-sized wooden replica of an antique aircraft in the hotel lobby. It had been erected for a convention of aviation hobbyists, who were sharing the same hotel with the team. Some genius got the bright idea to steal the plane, relocate it next to the hotel's outdoor swimming pool, and just like that the game was afoot.

Several obstacles, however, lay in the Tigers' path. First, measurements were taken and it was determined that the plane was too big to go through the door leading out to the pool deck. Somehow, in short order, sufficient tools were found to take it apart. But then there was the matter of getting it out of the lobby without being caught.

The wooden plane was located just around the corner from the front desk. While the night clerk couldn't see it from his post, any noise would certainly draw his attention. As a solution, reliever John "Ratso" Hiller was sent down to the front desk to chat up the clerk, making sure to talk loud enough so that the rest of the team could get to work. While Hiller's conversation echoed throughout the lobby, the Tigers quietly took the plane apart and lugged the pieces outside. There they reassembled the plane next to the pool. For most teams that would have been enough. Yet once the Tigers got the plane rebuilt on the pool deck, they couldn't resist sliding it entirely into water, even though most got wet feet in the process. Despite the fact that the massive model was made of wood, it eventually sank. Afterward, the team reconvened in a room overlooking their hand-iwork—a pool with a full-sized replica of an antique plane resting beau-tifully in its deep end. That was certainly one way to have a team-building experience. For many of them, like Mickey Lolich, it "was one of the tran-scendental moments" of the '68 season. Deep down, Tigers management must have agreed because Detroit general manager Jim Campbell paid the hotel for damages.

While the Cardinals didn't go in for such heavy lifting, they could be just as hard on each other when it came to mental miscues. In the club-house, they often played a game called "baseball quiz." Win or lose, they would start shouting questions like, "Who couldn't advance the runner in the first?" or "Who forgot to slide into second base?"

As in their El Birdos' cheer, names from Ty Cobb to Babe Ruth to Max Patkin were tossed out until the guilty party, somebody wearing a Cardi-nals uniform, was identified. If anybody was scoring the ballclub's baseball quiz during the 1968 season, they would have noticed that Curt Flood's name was rarely brought up for such derision.

Flood had arrived in St. Louis in a minor trade with the Cincinnati Reds after the 1957 season. He made an immediate impact, allowing the ballclub to move then outfielder Ken Boyer to third base. When Lou Brock came from the Cubs to the Cardinals and became our leadoff hitter, Flood was the perfect guy to bat behind him in the second spot, Tim Mc-Carver said.

"[Flood] was patient at the plate," McCarver explained, "which gave Brock the opportunity to use his great speed and steal all those bases. Curt could go deep in the count, hit behind the runner, and steal a base, and he was consistently in the .290 to .300 range. Don Drysdale called him the toughest out in the National League."

Among the Cardinals, Flood became the most involved in the national civil rights movement. His hero was Jackie Robinson, and at Robinson's invitation Flood attended the NAACP's (National Association for the Advancement of Colored People) regional conference in Jackson, Mississippi, in 1962. There he had been joined by boxing champions Floyd Patterson and Archie Moore. In his biography of Flood, *A Well-Paid Slave*, author Brad Snyder noted how Flood did his best to stay involved with the movement despite his baseball schedule. When Martin Luther King gave his "I Have a Dream" speech in Washington, D.C., Flood was taking the field with the Cardinals in San Francisco. "I should be there instead of here," Flood later said.

When King was assassinated in Memphis, Flood joined with a St. Louis calendar company to paint a commemorative portrait of King. How much help Flood received in the project remains up for debate, but the portrait went from a small project to being reproduced as eight-by-ten color productions that were handed out at an Atlanta benefit concert in King's honor.

"I'm a child of the Sixties, a man of the Sixties," Flood told Ken Burns decades later for the documentary *Baseball*. "During that period of time, this country was coming apart at the seams. We were in Southeast Asia. Men, good men, were dying for America and for the Constitution.

"In the southern part of the United States, we were marching for civil rights, and Dr. King had been assassinated and we lost the Kennedys. And to think that merely because I was a professional baseball player I could ignore what was going on outside the walls of Busch Stadium is truly hypocrisy."

Despite being on the cover of *Sports Illustrated*, winning two World Series championships with the Cardinals and five Gold Gloves, Flood was unsatisfied. He wanted to be the game's next Jackie Robinson, to make an impact not only on the field, but on the game itself. He felt he should be doing something more.

Meanwhile, in Green Bay, Wisconsin, new Packers' coach Phil Bengtson was not only hoping to follow in the footsteps of another sports legend, but also finding the task especially difficult with that legend still hovering in the background. Of course, the big shoes Bengtson was attempting to fill belonged to Vince Lombardi, as big a name as there was in pro football at the time. As the Packers opened training camp that August, launching their campaign for a third consecutive Super Bowl championship, many would have been at a loss to name a tougher act to follow. In addition, Lombardi had remained with Green Bay as the team's general manager, and the promotion of Bengtson seemed to have as much to do with loyalty and maintaining the party line as it did with ability.

A native of Rousseau, Minnesota, Bengtson had played tackle for Bernie Bierman's teams at the University of Minnesota, earning All-American honors. The quarterback on that team was Bud Wilkinson, who would become another coaching legend at the University of Oklahoma. After his playing days were over, Bengtson coached at Stanford for twelve seasons before moving up to the professional ranks with the San Francisco 49ers. He was fired after the 1958 season and joined Lombardi's staff beginning in 1959.

As defensive coordinator, he was the only coach to stay the entire nine years of Lombardi's tenure in Green Bay. The Packers' defense, with Ray Nitschke, Willie Wood, and Herb Adderley, was a force and a key reason that Green Bay won five NFL championships and the first two Super Bowls.

At first blush, Bengtson appeared a logical choice to be the next Packers' coach. Certainly he was somebody who worked hand in glove with Lombardi and knew the organization, top to bottom. Yet beginning in training camp, the players and press noticed a huge difference in approach. While Lombardi had been volatile, willing to get in anybody's grill, Bengtson was low key. Perhaps too much so.

"The players at first expressed relief about the new regime," wrote David Maraniss in *When Pride Still Mattered*. "Bengtson was tall, calm, gentle, laconic, the opposite of Lombardi. Hawg Hanner, his defensive assistant, had advised him to run the players to the point of exhaustion during the first week, reminding them that the Lombardi tradition still lived, but Bengtson politely declined, saying he had to establish his own style. Where Lombardi conducted his practices with metronomic discipline, Bengtson was easily distracted and might pass the whole day dragging on his Camels and discussing the intricacies of a zone defense."

Players grumbled that Bengtson spoke only in a monotone and seemed more interested in how they lined up for the national anthem before a game than what happened once the ball was snapped. It didn't help the new coach that Lombardi remained such a dominating presence and iconic figure. On August 7, 1968, the city of Green Bay staged "A Salute to Vince Lombardi." Highland Avenue outside the Packers' stadium was renamed for the Hall of Fame coach. "I just want you to know that I'm not dead," Lombardi said in the dedication.

Of course, Lombardi's stepping down also resulted in implications stretching far beyond Green Bay. With Lombardi out of the coaching ranks, many believed a door had been opened for the rival American Football League. The upstarts had been crushed in the first two Super Bowls by Lombardi's Packers. Heading into the new season the consensus was they once again would be a decided underdog, but nonetheless an opportunity for recognition, perhaps even for victory, was now there.

The question was, who would take the AFL to the next level? Who could topple the established NFL in the Super Bowl?

Heading into the summer of '68, the Democratic Convention, set to be held in Chicago, still needed a home. The city's McCormick Place had burned down the year before, but Mayor Richard Daley was adamant that the show would go on. So he moved to have the event held at the Amphitheater, down near the old Union Stockyards, a lousy place for an occasion that was already ripe with disappointment and anger.

Still, if Daley and the old guard were determined to have the party in Chicago, then Tom Hayden, Rennie Davis, Abbie Hoffman, and the other leaders of the New Left were just as determined to crash it. Kennedy and McCarthy supporters soon realized that the Chicago convention would be a continuation, even an affirmation of the Johnson presidency. Lyndon Johnson wasn't on the ballot, but his number two, Hubert Humphrey, had been the front-runner for the nomination since Robert Kennedy's assassination at the Los Angeles Ambassador Hotel in June.

Inside the convention hall and back at the delegates' hotels, former Green Bay Packers coach Vince Lombardi was rumored to be possible VP choice. "If Hollywood movie stars can sit in the California statehouse and the United States Senate, what bar exists to the election of a good football coach?" the *Milwaukee Sentinel*'s editorial page asked.

The paper went on to say that Lombardi's speeches, which he was now giving across the country, were "a cut above some pronouncements made in the halls of government."

In his biography about the Packers' coach, David Maraniss detailed how Richard Nixon first considered Lombardi as his running mate. That infatuation lasted until the Republican candidate learned that Lombardi had been a strong supporter of Bobby Kennedy. In fact, when Lombardi stepped down as coach in Green Bay, Kennedy had sent him a cable reading, "Vince, now would you come and be my coach?"

In Chicago, where the Democrats gathered, talk about Lombardi continued. Miles McMillin of the *Capital Times* in Madison, Wisconsin, just down the road from Green Bay, maintained that Lombardi's name came up in discussions of vice presidential short lists. In the end, though, nothing came of such speculation, and soon enough it was overshadowed by much larger issues.

Although Jesse Jackson and other civil rights leaders had told their followers to stay away from Chicago, enough advocates from all sides made the trek to the shores of Lake Michigan to set off a cultural explosion. All summer long, a strong undercurrent of anger had been steadily building, igniting in the aftermath of King's assassination and again following Kennedy's, all the while gathering greater and greater force. Such emotion could be seen in the baseball ballparks, notably Tiger Stadium in Detroit. There fans were allowed to bring their own booze to the game as long as they concealed it in brown bags. Empty bottles and firecrackers were often deployed to protest umpires' calls or poor play by the home squad.

In a mid-June contest at Tiger Stadium, Boston outfielder Ken Harrelson was nearly hit in the back by a cherry bomb. A plea over the public address system for "good sportsmanship" only led to additional objects being thrown, including another explosive that went off over Harrelson's head. With that the outfielder threw down his glove and began walking in from right field. He'd had enough.

"I'd hit a couple home runs and the second one had put us ahead, so when I go to take up my position again in right field, I hear this strange sound going on around me. It was like, 'Zip, Zip,' and I saw that they were throwing ball bearings, about the size of a quarter at me," Harrelson recalled. "Then a cherry bomb goes off over my head. It wasn't that close, maybe ten to fifteen feet away, but I'm getting unnerved about all of this.

"I came in and start to discuss the situation with the umpires. Our manager, Dick Williams, came out and there's talk about forfeiting the game. But then somebody tells me, 'If it's a forfeit, you lose those two home runs and five RBI you have.' That's when I went and got a helmet and decided to ride it out."

With the Tigers trailing, 8–5, in the bottom of the ninth Harrelson hung around, but just barely. He positioned himself twenty feet or so behind Boston second baseman Mike Andrews—as far away as he could from the mob in right field.

"No wonder they have trouble in this town," Harrelson said after the game. "It's people like that, just a few jerks, who give a city a bad name."

Years later, Harrelson said of that night: "Now I wasn't privy to what happened later, but I do know that Mr. Yawkey, our owner, and Mr. Fetzer, the Tigers' owner, talked on the phone. And the next night I went out there, the upper deck in right field had been cleared out. They had done that to keep me and the other guys safe."

Unfortunately, the Harrelson incident was far from the exception that season.

"Has the whole world gone crazy?" asked Bill Rohr, a relief pitcher for the Cleveland Indians, after so much debris rained down from the second deck in Detroit that he was unable to warm up. "In the stands there were a couple of guys standing together, slugging . . . really hitting each other. There were a couple of people beating up an old man. It is nuts."

Mickey Lolich added, "A guy doesn't need (military) basic training. Just play the outfield in Detroit."

Such flashpoints were possible omens—precursors to what was to happen later that summer in Chicago, where the Democratic National Convention was scheduled to begin. City officials there, in an effort to discourage demonstrations, refused to issue permits for any marches or overnight stays in the parks. No matter that the Boy Scouts routinely camped in Lincoln Park, an impressive swath of urban openness that hugged the west shore of Lake Michigan. The hippies and Abbie Hoffman's Yippies and anybody else in town to protest the political powers were required to vacate the park by 11 p.m. Chicago's finest were charged with enforcing the curfew, and for consecutive nights they aggressively did so, while television cameras rolled in the background. During the day the youthful protesters and city police could actually be seen playing catch, but inevitably each night by 11 p.m.—in time to be featured on the late evening news—the violence escalated to fever pitch yet again. Police clubbed many of those in their way. Cars with Eugene McCarthy bumper stickers had their tires slashed. Across the country the public was transfixed as more than 16 million tuned in on television.

The Tigers were supposed to be in Chicago, too. But all the rooms in the city were booked due to the convention, so the first game of their series with the White Sox was switched to Milwaukee. In hindsight, it would be a fortunate substitution. Other ballclubs weren't as lucky.

By August 28, demonstrations made their way closer to downtown Chicago. Plans were made to march on the Amphitheatre, where Hubert Humphrey was about to accept the nomination and the party was expected to take a position of supporting the ongoing war in Vietnam. The protesters gathered in Grant Park, a smaller venue opposite the Conrad Hilton Hotel, where many delegates were staying. Protesters listened to the convention's proceedings on transistor radios, and when the prowar plank passed many decided to march.

"After everything that had happened this year," Mark Kurlansky wrote in *1968: The Year That Rocked the World*, "after Tet, Johnson's resignation, McCarthy's campaign, Martin Luther King's death, Bobby Kennedy's campaign and death, and four months of futile Paris peace talks—after all that, both parties were to have pro-war stances."

That's when Chicago law enforcement, which now numbered more than twenty-five thousand, moved in, again with billy clubs swinging.

Most of the time sport exists in a different orbit from the real news of the day. Even sports writers like to kid that they work in the "toy department"—fortunate to be caught up in less serious matters. But in '68, time after time, those lines became blurred.

That evening in Chicago, Larry Dierker, a young pitcher with the Houston Astros, checked into the Conrad Hilton with the ballclub. He was pitching well in 1968, with one of his victories coming against Bob Gibson, a triumph he would always treasure. In September, he would turn twenty-two, and after spending the winter pitching in the Dominican Republic, Dierker was thrilled to be part of a big-league rotation. He was holding his own, feeling good about himself. Despite his age it was actually his fourth full year in the major leagues, but nothing he had experienced up to that point had prepared him for what was about to unfold before him.

"We flew into Chicago while those riots were going on," he recalled decades later. "When the team bus came to the Conrad Hilton, we couldn't pull up in front of the hotel. Instead we had to enter through the back entrance—through the kitchen to get into the lobby.

"When we got into the lobby, you could smell the smoke and tear gas. It wasn't like our eyes were watering or anything, but you could tell it was an unusual scene. You could hear the sirens and you could hear the bullhorns. Once we got up to our room, our room was facing the park. That was back when you could still open windows in a hotel. We ordered up some beer and sandwiches and opened the windows. We sat out there and watched what was going on down below."

From eight stories above the fray, Dierker and his roommate, Jim Ray, witnessed the police and National Guardsmen wade into the crowd. Their wrath on that night knew no bounds. As Kurlansky notes, the authorities beat "children and elderly people and those who watched behind police lines. . . . They dragged women through the streets. A crowd was pressed so hard against the windows of a hotel restaurant—middle-aged women and children, according to *The New York Times*—that the windows caved in and the crowd escaped inside. The police pursued them through the windows, clubbing anyone they could find, even in the hotel lobby."

Although the police seemingly went out of their way to smash cameras, perhaps to keep images off the network feed, additional television cameras had been mounted above the hotel entrance, offering roughly the same angle Dierker and his teammates had. The mayhem went on for seventeen minutes—a bloodbath that can now be viewed on YouTube. Many who witnessed it firsthand were changed forever.

"Jim and I were just amazed by what was going on down below," Dierker said. "I was in the same age group as the people who were upset about the war. Certainly protesting not only what was going on in Vietnam and Chicago, but what was going on in a cultural way with the music and fashion.

"I knew I was a part of that generation that was boiling up down below. At the time, I was more selfishly concerned with my own life and career. I didn't feel a great kinship with the ones protesting. But once you see something like that, you don't forget it so easily. Looking back on it, that night changed me . . .

"I wasn't worried that they would call up my Guard unit and send me to Vietnam. I was somewhat insulated from the potential dangers that a lot of guys my age felt that they were in. I don't consider myself unpatriotic, but if I had a chance to say whether I'd like to go to Vietnam and fight for my country or I'd like to stay home and have someone else do it, my choice was not to go, to play major league ball, and let someone else do it. That night I wasn't proud of that."

The Tigers' Dick McAuliffe averaged .247 during his sixteen-year career. He never hit above .274 in a season and his high-water marks in home runs and runs batted in were twenty-four and sixty-six respectively, both in the 1964 season. To the average fan, he wasn't anything special, just a guy who could play second base and shortstop. But his teammates knew better.

Today they still use words like aggressive, determined, and fiery to describe a player they nicknamed "Mad Dog." Several remember a four-hit game when he singled each time and ended up on second due to his derring-do on the base paths. "He was the guy who made us go in '68," Gates Brown said. "Dick McAuliffe was the kind of player you could always count on and you know will cover your back. It's hard to picture that '68 team without him."

In late August, as things were about to erupt in Chicago, the Tigers and their fans were about to be reminded how valuable McAuliffe was. Born into an Irish-Italian family in Hartford, McAuliffe learned early on never to back down from anybody. In high school, he had batted against the legendary fireballer Steve Dalkowski. When he and McAuliffe confronted each other, Dalkowski was as fast and wild as ever. His fastball hit McAuliffe square in the back.

"That was as hard as I've ever been hit by a ball," McAuliffe said. "I didn't think I was going to breathe again."

Despite being hunched over at the waist, McAuliffe made his way to first base that day. His teammates decided he must have really been hurting because he wasn't able to shout out anything in Dalkowski's direction.

That wasn't the case on August 22, 1968. The White Sox were in town to play the Tigers, and there was no love lost between the two ballclubs.

Over the past two seasons, former White Sox manager Eddie Stanky (who had been fired in July after a disappointing first half) had questioned Detroit's makeup. He agreed that the Tigers certainly had the talent, but wondered aloud if they have the fortitude to win it all? McAuliffe was among those who remembered such slights.

Early on the storyline that day appeared to be Mickey Lolich's return to the rotation. After weeks in bullpen purgatory, winning four games in the process, the enigmatic left-hander was back in the rotation and pitching well. He had made a half-dozen appearances out of the bullpen and recalled struggling not only with his control but also in regaining the quality sinking action on his pitches. "They just sat there," Lolich said, "and people hit them. Simple as that." Certainly McAuliffe was doing his best to make him a winner in his return. With his distinctive batting style— bat held high, kicking his front leg toward the mound as the pitch arrived—McAuliffe led off the first inning with a single and scored the Tigers' first run of the game.

In the third inning, McAuliffe was back at the plate, again facing White Sox starter Tommy John. The second pitch was a little chin music and McAuliffe turned to talk with home plate umpire Al Salerno. "If he hits me in the head, I'm dead," McAuliffe said.

When the count ran to three and two, John came inside again, spilling McAuliffe face-first to the ground. As he started toward first base, he and John began to jaw at each other. About thirty feet up the line, McAuliffe suddenly made a beeline for the mound, where John waited for him. As McAuliffe charged, John dropped down, ready to throw a shoulder block. The two of them cracked together, with McAuliffe sprawling over the top. John's left shoulder, his pitching arm, took the major force of the impact.

As far as baseball fights go, this one was over quickly. Nothing compared to the Cardinals-Reds brawl. In fact, McLain missed the whole thing because he was back in the clubhouse eating a hot dog. McAuliffe was ejected by Salerno and order was soon restored. That's when everybody noticed John holding his left arm. Afterward, it would be determined that he had suffered torn ligaments in his pitching shoulder.

The Tigers went on to record a 4–2 victory. In his return to the rotation, Lolich was the winner, even though he failed to finish the game after beating out an infield single and later coming around to score. "He ran out of gas," manager Mayo Smith told Jerry Green. "He didn't even have a tiger in his tank."

After the game, umpire Salerno said that he was required to send a report to American League president Joe Cronin about the McAuliffe-John altercation. In it he would say that McAuliffe was the aggressor. "I doubt he'll be suspended, though," Salerno said. "I don't think John was throwing at him on a three-two pitch. But John did cuss him."

With that the incident appeared to be over. But the following day, with the Tigers in New York to play the Yankees, word came down that McAuliffe was suspended for five days. With a doubleheader thrown in, he would miss the next six of Detroit's games.

At the time, the Tigers held a relatively comfortable seven-and-a-half-game lead over second-place Baltimore, but they were about to find out the difference one player can make. McAuliffe's suspension exposed a key weakness with the Tigers' roster.

In the first game without McAuliffe, Detroit lost 2–1 to the Yankees. The second game of the doubleheader went into extra innings, tied at 3–3. Just past one in the morning, it was called due to curfew—slated to be made up as a brand-new ballgame.

The next day not even McLain could stop the bleeding. He lost to the Yankees 2–1 on Roy White's two-run homer. It was the first time all season McLain had lost two games in a row. From there things continued to snowball downhill for Detroit. At first, it looked as though the Tigers would take the first game of Sunday's doubleheader easily, staking themselves to a 5–1 lead. But when Yankees manager Ralph Houk brought in outfielder Rocky Colavito to pitch in order to avoid depleting his bullpen in a losing effort, incredibly "The Rock" shut down the Detroit bats and the Yankees rallied for a 6–5 victory, with Colavito the game's winner.

The victory couldn't have been sweeter for The Rock. He had previously played for the Tigers, an integral member of the 1961 ballclub that had given the New York Yankees a run for their money. But Colavito never felt at home in the Motor City and often seemed to resent the adoration that Al Kaline in particular received. Colavito was no stranger to the mound, having pitched for the Indians in 1958, and he loved to mess around with throwing changeups and curveballs during warm-ups. "I feel so funky," he said after his victory.

In comparison, the Tigers weren't feeling very funky at all, especially after Lolich walked seven batters and the Yankees completed the four-game sweep, winning 5–4 in the day's second game. With the losses, Detroit's lead had been shaved to five games over Baltimore, with the Orioles coming to Detroit the following week for a three-game showdown. In the cramped visitors' clubhouse at Yankee Stadium stood a blackboard. On it, someone had written, ANYBODY WHO THINKS THE WORLD ENDED TODAY DOESN'T BELONG HERE.

To this day, nobody is sure who the author was. Catcher Bill Freehan often receives credit, while others insist it had to be Eddie Mathews. Whoever the author was the Tigers were about to be tested after coasting for so long.

On September 4, 1968, bothered by a sore arm, Luis Tiant took the mound in Anaheim. Even though he lasted only five and two-thirds innings, allowing four earned runs, the Indians hitters did the job this time around and he was credited with the win. Five days later, on the road against the Twins, Tiant went the distance, giving up only one run, and at last secured his twentieth victory. But while he led the American League and ERA, the season had taken its toll and the damage was done. His next start was at home, against Baltimore. Before the contest, his arm throbbed so badly that second-year pitcher Steve Bailey was called on to take his place. After the Orioles beat the last-minute substitute, Alvin Dark questioned his top pitcher in the press. The next morning's paper quoted Dark as being "surprised" that Tiant had quit. The quote prompted a confrontation later recounted in Tiant's autobiography.

Storming into Dark's office, Tiant flung the morning paper across the desk, hitting the manager in the chest.

"I never come in here with excuses," Tiant said. "You should know that better than I do. The rest of these guys are always getting dizzy or having colds or not feeling good, but you never say anything in the papers about them. Why did you have to say this about me?"

"You're taking it the wrong way," Dark replied.

"I don't care how I'm taking it," Tiant answered. "You're not supposed to say those things about your players in the papers. I do my job for you and for this ballclub, so I should be respected. You never hear any excuses from me, but I've been pitching with a sore elbow and you know it."

Dark tried to get a word in edgewise, but Tiant cut him off.

"From now on, if I don't feel good, I don't pitch," the staff ace said. "I don't care if you get mad, or if you trade me, or whatever else happens. If I'm not one hundred percent, I don't pitch."

Moments later, Tiant walked out of his manager's office. Many of his teammates thought his impressive 1968 campaign was history.

The city of Detroit burned during the summer of 1967 in one of the deadliest riots in U.S. history. As the new baseball season began, many in the city and on the hometown team feared such protests would break out again.

The Detroit News Archives

Willie Horton, left, shown here in the Tigers' clubhouse with his good friend and Tigers teammate Gates Brown, risked his life trying to stop the '67 riots. Many on the ballclub lived year-round in the Detroit area. They knew how far a winning ballclub could go in healing a divided city.

The Detroit News Archives

Just after 6 p.m. on April 4, 1968, Dr. Martin Luther King, Jr. was shot in Memphis, Tennessee. He was standing on the balcony outside his room at the Lorraine Hotel, about to leave for dinner at his friend Billy Kyles' house. Afterward, members of his party pointed in the direction where the shots were fired.

Getty Images

Entering the '68 season, the St. Louis Cardinals were poised to win their third World Series championship in five years. Ahead of their time, the Cardinals' lineup was made up of blacks, whites, and Latinos.

National Baseball Hall of Fame Library, Cooperstown, N.Y.

Tim McCarver, like any good catcher, knew how to earn a pitcher's trust. During his twenty-one years in the majors, he called the signals for such Hall of Fame pitchers as Bob Gibson and Steve Carlton. McCarver went on to a successful second career in the broadcast booth.

National Baseball Hall of Fame Library, Cooperstown, N.Y.

Orlando Cepeda was heartbroken when he was dealt from the San Francisco Giants to the Cardinals early in the 1966 season. But the Puerto Rican star soon realized he had joined a team built to win titles.

National Baseball Hall of Fame Library, Cooperstown, N.Y.

Mike Shannon helped supply the power for a Cardinals' team built on pitching, speed and defense. He also became a popular broadcaster after retiring as a player.

National Baseball Hall of Fame Library, Cooperstown, N.Y.

No one was more eloquent than presidential candidate Robert Kennedy in the hours after Dr. Martin Luther King, Jr.'s assassination. Speaking from the heart and from few notes, he urged a crowd in Indianapolis, shown here, "to tame the savageness of man and make gentle the life of this world." When he was finished, many rushed the platform to reach out to him.

Associated Press

Robert Kennedy was assassinated eight weeks after Dr. Martin Luther King, Jr. was shot. Maury Wills, then playing for the Pittsburgh Pirates, refused to play the day after Kennedy's murder. Instead Wills stayed in the training room, reading Kennedy's book *To Seek a Newer World*.

National Baseball Hall of Fame Library, Cooperstown, N.Y.

Pirates' star Roberto Clemente was also ready to sit out the game, as well, but changed his mind after meeting with Pittsburgh manager Larry Shepard. "I preferred not to play," Clemente later said.

National Baseball Hall of Fame Library, Cooperstown, N.Y.

In Cincinnati, pitcher Milt Pappas was adamant that his team shouldn't take the field against the visiting St. Louis Cardinals. After the game, Pappas resigned as player rep. Less than seventy-two hours later, Pappas was traded to Atlanta.

National Baseball Hall of Fame Library, Cooperstown, N.Y.

Don Drysdale of the Los Angeles Dodgers set the bar high for pitching excellence in 1968 by hurling six consecutive shutouts. His fifty-eight-scoreless-inning record would stand for twenty years until another Dodger pitcher, Orel Hershiser, broke it. Drysdale is shown in his first start after Robert Kennedy's assassination. Note the black armband.

National Baseball Hall of Fame Library, Cooperstown, N.Y.

Despite pitching five no-hitters in high school, some ballclubs considered Jim "Catfish" Hunter to be damaged goods due to a hunting accident. Athletics' owner Charlie Finley was convinced that the right-hander could win at the big-league level and Hunter rewarded him with a perfect game in 1968.

National Baseball Hall of Fame Library, Cooperstown, N.Y.

Few sluggers had more success in the "Year of the Pitcher" than Frank Howard of the Washington Senators. He hit ten home runs in six games early in the season.

National Baseball Hall of Fame Library, Cooperstown, N.Y.

Nearing the end of his eighteen-year career in the major leagues, New York Yankees' star Mickey Mantle proved he could still go deep, especially if he had a little help from his friends.

National Baseball Hall of Fame Library, Cooperstown, N.Y.

While Dr. Martin Luther King, Jr.'s assassination "jolted" Bob Gibson, Robert Kennedy's death "infuriated" the Cardinals' pitching star. Admittedly, Gibson pitched better angry and he soon put together one of the best seasons by a pitcher ever to play the game.

National Baseball Hall of Fame Library, Cooperstown, N.Y.

During the regular season, Bob Gibson compiled a 1.12 ERA—the third-best mark since 1900 and the lowest in a season not played in the "deadball" era. He completed 28 of his 34 starts, with 13 of them being shutouts.

Associated Press

After a disappointing 1967, Denny McLain established himself as the winningest pitcher in baseball. He became the first pitcher since Dizzy Dean thirty-four years earlier to reach the thirty-victory plateau.

National Baseball Hall of Fame Library, Cooperstown, N.Y.

Ever the showman, Denny McLain used his 31–6 record in 1968 to make a big splash in the entertainment world. Here he shows an ailing Jerry Koosman of the New York Mets how to hit the right notes.

National Baseball Hall of Fame Library, Cooperstown, N.Y.

As the '68 season began, Tigers' left-hander Mickey Lolich was determined to win the big games and deliver a championship to Detroit.

National Baseball Hall of Fame Library, Cooperstown, N.Y.

Lolich often rode one of his several motorcycles to Tiger Stadium for his home starts. He said the wind in his face helped him relax.

National Baseball Hall of Fame Library, Cooperstown, N.Y.

A major reason for Lolich's inconsistency on the mound was the time he spent away from the ballclub due to his National Guard obligations. Despite the aggravation, Lolich often joked about the situation.

Associated Press

While Denny McLain won thirty-one games, many considered Luis Tiant of the Cleveland Indians to be as good or better in 1968. When Tiant started the All-Star Game for the American League, his mother back in Havana was able to catch a glimpse of him on television. Tiant had left his home country of Cuba six years earlier unsure of when he would see his family again.

National Baseball Hall of Fame Library, Cooperstown, N.Y.

Only twenty-one years old during the 1968 season, Larry Dierker was a starting pitcher for the Houston Astros, going against the likes of Don Drysdale and Bob Gibson. But what rocked his world was witnessing the demonstrations in Chicago surrounding the Democratic National Convention late that summer.

National Baseball Hall of Fame Library, Cooperstown, N.Y.

Nolan Ryan won only six games in eighteen starts in 1968 and nearly walked away from the game for good. He, like the Tigers' Mickey Lolich, spent time away from the game due to his National Guard commitment.

National Baseball Hall of Fame Library, Cooperstown, N.Y.

Detroit catcher Bill Freehan was a rock behind the plate. He hit a career-high twenty-five home runs in 1968 and played his entire fifteen-year career in a Tigers' uniform.

The Detroit News Archives

The Tigers were reminded how valuable second baseman Dick McAuliffe, shown here turning a double play against the Yankees, was when he was suspended for five days after an altercation with Chicago White Sox pitcher Tommy John. The Tigers went winless during that stretch, allowing the Baltimore Orioles to briefly climb back into the race in the American League.

National Baseball Hall of Fame Library, Cooperstown, N.Y.

Al Kaline won the American League batting championship in 1955 at the age of 20—one day younger than Ty Cobb, who accomplished the feat in 1907—and over the course of his career he became one of the most popular Tigers of all time. But Kaline missed significant time with a broken arm in 1968. Some argued the Tigers shouldn't upset team chemistry by trying to get him back in the everyday lineup so late in the season.

National Baseball Hall of Fame Library, Cooperstown, N.Y.

Although Willie Horton was born in Arno, Virginia, his family soon moved to Detroit and he grew up in the local Jeffries Housing Projects. Nobody was a bigger local hero in the Motor City, then and now, than Horton.

The Detroit News Archives

In 1968, *Sports Illustrated* called the Cardinals' Curt Flood "Baseball's Best Centerfielder." After he was traded to the Philadelphia Phillies following the '69 season, Flood sued Major League Baseball over its reserve clause. The case would go all the way to the Supreme Court and eventually open the door to free agency.

National Baseball Hall of Fame Library, Cooperstown, N.Y.

Brock was at his best in World Series play. In three Fall Classics, he batted .391 with 14 stolen bases.

National Baseball Hall of Fame Library, Cooperstown, N.Y.

Nobody was faster on the base paths than St. Louis outfielder Lou Brock. His career standard for stolen bases (938) would stand until Rickey Henderson came along.

National Baseball Hall of Fame Library, Cooperstown, N.Y.

After a stellar season in center field for Detroit, Mickey Stanley was shifted to shortstop against the St. Louis Cardinals. Tigers' announcer Ernie Harwell warned it could be "a bad move."

The Detroit News Archives

In one of the boldest decisions in World Series history, before Gamer One in St. Louis, Detroit manager Mayo Smith announced that Stanley would play shortstop. The gamble opened a spot in the regular lineup for outfielder Al Kaline, which soon paid off for the Tigers.

National Baseball Hall of Fame Library, Cooperstown, N.Y.

Ahead three games to one, the Cardinals had a great opportunity to capture their second consecutive World Series when Lou Brock headed for home in pivotal Game Five. The St. Louis speedster was thrown out, however, on a perfect peg to the plate from outfielder Willie Horton to Tigers' catcher Bill Freehan. Brock didn't slide, missing home plate by inches, and the Tigers later rallied on Al Kaline's bases-loaded single.

National Baseball Hall of Fame Library, Cooperstown, N.Y.

Thanks to complete-game victories by Denny McLain and Mickey Lolich, the Tigers took the final two games in St. Louis to win their first World Series title since 1945. Moments after the final out, the streets of Detroit, where there had been riots only the summer before, filled with fans celebrating their team's victory for the ages.

Getty Images

PART
V

Rewriting the Record Book

Action is character.
—F. SCOTT FITZGERALD

Despite the riots in Chicago, the Democrats moved ahead with their selection of Hubert Humphrey, Lyndon Johnson's vice president, as their presidential nominee. He would oppose Richard Nixon in the November election, and those new to the game, the ones who had supported Eugene McCarthy and Robert Kennedy, realized that when it came to the Vietnam War, the most divisive issue in the land, little was going to change in terms of public policy.

"After the convention, I was on pins and needles awaiting possible (federal) indictment," remembered Tom Hayden, one of the Chicago Seven, who was charged with conspiracy and inciting to riot in connection to the Windy City protests. "I thought Humphrey had blown it. Later on, he did break with LBJ when it came to the war and rose in the polls, but it was not enough."

Hayden grew up in southeastern Michigan, and in fact had played youth ball against several of the 1968 Tigers. Detroit catcher Bill Freehan remembered Hayden as "a little guy, always arguing with the umpires and getting thrown out of games."

Decades later, Hayden reluctantly agreed with Freehan's scouting report. "Bill has a good memory," he said. "We were kids together and we both loved playing ball. I was scrawny, he was a big man. Bill had a great arm, even back then, and he'd sometimes pitch. I managed to get a clutch hit off him once, and made a diving catch in left field on a line drive of his, while he was otherwise mowing us down. Those remain the baseball highlights of my youth."

In the late fifties and early sixties, before the riots and talk of revolution, the Motor City "played some of the best amateur baseball in America," Freehan wrote in his memoir, *Behind the Mask*. In high school, when his family moved to St. Petersburg, Florida, Freehan still returned to the Detroit area in the summers, living with his grandparents, so he could play against several of his future Tigers' teammates and such prospects as Alex Johnson and future basketball star Dave DeBusschere. Willie Horton, who graduated from Northwestern High School in Detroit, believes that's where the '68 ballclub really began, where it learned about determination and resiliency—qualities that were about to be tested again.

On August 28, 1968, second baseman Dick McAuliffe returned to the Tigers' lineup, having served his five-day suspension. Still, the losing streak the team suffered while he was out had taken its toll, and a sense of foreboding had settled in Detroit. The California Angels were coming to town, followed by the hard-charging Baltimore Orioles. It had been the Angels the year before who had eliminated the Tigers on the final day of the season, in that wild dog pile with four teams in contention down the stretch. Now with the '68 pennant race on the line, they relished the chance to play spoilers once more.

"Wouldn't it be funny if we did it again?" asked Angels manager Bill Rigney before the start of the two-game set.

In the first game, ace Denny McLain was on the mound for the Tigers, looking to break his two-game losing streak—his longest of the season. Facing off against him was Tom Burgmeier, pitching for the Angels.

From the start, the contest was a heated one, with McAuliffe's first at-bat returning from suspension nearly echoing the one that sent him there. It appeared Rigney had taken a page from the White Sox's playbook— Burgmeier came in high and tight, moving the Tigers' lead-off hitter off the plate. For a moment, McAuliffe glared out at Burgmeier, ready to charge the mound. "It took a lot for me to stop there," McAuliffe said decades later. "But I knew I couldn't risk another suspension. Not with the way we were struggling."

With McAuliffe still in the game, igniting the attack, the Tigers scored three times in the second inning with Freehan cracking a two-run homer. In the eighth inning, Freehan was hit by a pitch for the twenty-second time that season. He stared out at California reliever Bobby Locke as he made his way to first. Later he came around to score on Jim Northrup's home run.

With the victory, McLain became the first American League pitcher to win twenty-six games since Bob Feller and Hal Newhouser in 1946. Afterward he was asked how he could pitch and somehow win with such a sore shoulder. "Because we were only four games ahead of Baltimore," he replied.

Back in Baltimore, Frank Howard made the Tigers' victory especially sweet as his home run propelled the Washington Senators past the Orioles, 3–2. Detroit's lead was back up to five games.

The next afternoon, Mickey Lolich made his third start since being released from the bullpen. He allowed three Angel hits in the first two frames but then settled down, retiring twenty consecutive batters. Willie Horton supplied the firepower, walloping his thirty-first homer of the year. The blast landed in the center-field stands, the same area where he once delivered a homer at the tender age of sixteen in the Detroit Public School League championships. The Tigers won 2–0, and back in Baltimore the lowly Senators somehow did it again, this time tripping up the Orioles 5–4 in eleven innings.

Always eager to play the prophet, Rigney told the media if Detroit took just one from Baltimore in the upcoming series "it will just about be over."

The big home stand against Baltimore opened on Friday, August 30, and 53,575 packed Tiger Stadium, the largest crowd since 1961. A highway sign on the Lodge Expressway leading to the ballpark read, Go GET 'EM TIGERS!!! Detroit right-hander Earl Wilson didn't disappoint, pitching a four-hitter and driving in four runs with a single and home run.

The Orioles won the next day, 5–1, behind Dave McNally's pitching gem and Paul Blair's three-run home run. Afterward Weaver said, "If we beat them tomorrow, the pressure's back on them."

Rain delayed the start of the rubber game of the three-game series for forty-five minutes, complicating pregame preparation for McLain, who still nursed a sore shoulder. Unable to get loose, he fell behind 2–0 when the first two Orioles he faced singled and homered.

With that Smith hustled out to the mound and asked McLain if he wanted out. Was the shoulder too painful to continue?

"It's the first goddamn inning," McLain replied. "There's 42,000 people here—it'll get better."

Smith looked to Freehan, who had joined the discussion on the mound.

"How's he throwing, Billy?" Smith asked.

"How would I know?" the catcher said. "I haven't caught anything yet."

That broke the tension and McLain remained in the game.

Northrup tied it with a two-run shot in the bottom of the first inning. But then yet another rain delay exasperated McLain. As the rain fell, he took a hot shower in the home clubhouse, trying to loosen up his aching shoulder. When the clouds lifted, McLain was back on the mound and the Tigers soon pegged him to a 4–2 lead. But the Orioles answered and after a walk, a single, and an RBI by Frank Robinson, trimmed the margin to a single run.

With men on first and second base, with none out, up stepped the Orioles' Boog Powell, the last guy McLain wanted to face in that situation. "I could never get that son of a bitch out," McLain recalled. "I hated hitters who hung out over the plate, and Powell was one of those. I'd already tried everything with him. I used to yell to him, 'Fastball's coming—I might as well tell you so we can speed up the game.' And I'd throw him a fastball. Other times, I'd lie and see if that would help, but it never did."

This time McLain wanted to come inside, but instead the pitch caught too much of the plate. Powell smashed the offering right back at the pitcher. In self-defense, McLain stabbed at it and somehow caught the screaming line drive for the first out.

With that he turned and fired to shortstop Tom Matchick at second base for the second out, and Matchick threw on to first baseman Norm Cash to double off Robinson for the third out. Bing-Bang-Boom. Triple play.

"As was discovered long ago, Denny McLain had this flair for showmanship, this knack of doing things a little differently," Jerry Green wrote. "What other ballplayer had met his future wife when his bat flew into the grandstands at a kids' game and struck her? Who else in the big leagues played the organ?"

And who else but Denny McLain could escape trouble by starting a triple play?

"The ball was heading right at my head," he said. "If I hadn't caught it, it would've killed me."

No matter that the ball was actually headed for his midsection. Why let the truth get in the way of a good story, right? From there, McLain cruised, striking out nine and raising his record to 27–5. Afterward, the winning pitcher announced with confidence, "I think the pennant race is getting near over."

Can a guy stuff too much good fortune into a single season? Can somebody's good luck be so bright and beguiling before one starts to wonder when the proverbial piper will need to be paid? While McLain's teammates were beginning to wonder, meanwhile the winningest pitcher since Dizzy Dean thirty-four years before continued racing full-bore toward the horizon.

After the Orioles series, the Tigers traveled to the West Coast, where their ace ushered Ed Sullivan and singer Glen Campbell around the Detroit clubhouse, introducing them to his teammates. While his fellow Tigers were shy or even envious, McLain reveled in the attention. It was all good, he told anybody who would listen, as if he were convincing himself. Even a piece in *Life* magazine hinting that he might be too distracted in flying and his music for his own good didn't upset McLain that much. The talkative right-hander remained eager to embrace the moment.

Soon afterward McLain was scheduled to go for his thirtieth victory on a Saturday—September 14, 1968—against the Oakland Athletics. The night before the game Sandy Koufax and Dizzy Dean visited the ballpark. Koufax was a member of the NBC television crew in town to nationally broadcast Saturday's game. Dean, meanwhile, had traveled from his home in Wiggins, Mississippi, to bear witness to the thirty-victory torch being passed. "I'm getting more publicity now with Denny winning thirty than I did when I won thirty," Dean said.

Years later, McLain remembered Koufax as a class act, while Dean "was just a good ole boy who wanted to talk about the football season and point spreads."

Unable to resist a dig at his larger-than-life teammate, Lolich put up a sign on the pillar in the middle of the home clubhouse. "Attention Sportswriters," it read, "Denny McLain's Locker This Way," with big arrow pointing stage right. In perhaps the most intriguing interview conducted that season, he spoke with the *Detroit News* as the media hordes swirled about McLain.

"How could I be a thirty-game winner?" Lolich asked. "How could I ride my motorcycle on the *Ed Sullivan Show*?"

Lolich explained that he was getting into music, too, learning to play the drums. But in a stream-of-consciousness ramble, Lolich honestly summed up what it was like to live in McLain's large shadow that season. "If I have a good year next year and win twenty, they'll say, 'So what?'"

Looking back over at McLain and all of the attention that enveloped him, Lolich added, "He's sort of ruined things for everybody around here."

After such a buildup, McLain's thirtieth could have been anticlimatic. Instead it was again the kind of thriller that had become so indicative of the Tigers' remarkable season.

By this point in the season, the game really didn't have any pennant implications as the Tigers were only days away from clinching. The Orioles were history, reconciled with positioning themselves to win it all the following season. Yet on that sunny afternoon in Detroit, 33,688 fans still jammed into the old ballpark at the corner of Michigan and Trumbull. McLain's opposing number was Oakland's Chuck Dobson and before the game Jim Pagliaroni, the Athletics' backup catcher—the one who had caught Catfish Hunter's perfect game—did up a sign of his own that read "Dobson goes for #12 today."

Usually pitchers don't talk to the press before a start. Yet when McLain saw the crowd around his locker, no one was very surprised when he found he had plenty to say. "I never understood how a writer could have anything to do with my performance," he later explained. "What a special day it was and what an absolutely marvelous time to be alive. I loved it all. I was a circus leader and these were my animals following me around. I told the writers that I'd been on the phone until midnight. Logically, one of them asked me what I'd dreamt. I said, 'I dreamt about losing my contact lenses, and I spend more on contact lenses than most guys make.'"

McLain held Oakland scoreless the first time through the order. Yet in the fourth inning, Reggie Jackson clubbed a curveball into the lower deck in right field. Danny Carter had been aboard, giving the A's a 2–0 lead.

Detroit fought back to take a one-run advantage on Norm Cash's three-run homer, only to see Oakland tie it in the fifth inning. An inning later, Jackson homered again to give the A's a 4–3 lead. That's the way it stayed until the bottom of the ninth.

McLain left the game for a pinch hitter (Al Kaline) but remained the pitcher of record. Kaline walked to start the ninth inning and went around to third base on Mickey Stanley's single with one out. The Tigers' Jim Northrup then bounced a grounder to Cater at first base. Even though Cater led American League first basemen in fielding, Kaline took off for home plate. Unbelievably, Cater's throw sailed high, but Kaline fell trying to avoid running into Oakland catcher Dave Duncan. After the ball flew over Duncan's head, Kaline scrambled on all fours back to touch home, and the game was tied, 4–4.

With Stanley now at third base, the A's had no choice but to bring the infield in. As McLain paced in the home dugout, Horton drove a 2–2 pitch over the left fielder's head and Stanley, clapping his hands together, came home with the lead run.

When Horton connected, McLain jumped so high he hit his head against the underside of the Tigers' dugout. Still woozy, he was half-carried out to join the celebration by Kaline. The image made the cover of the following week's *Sports Illustrated*.

Still seeing stars, McLain answered questions from the media who had rushed onto the field, too. The mob included Koufax and Dean. As McLain turned to acknowledge the cheering hometown crowd, many of whom had probably booed him back in May after he called Tigers fans the worst in the world, he saw a woman behind the dugout throw her panties at him. Soon afterward McLain was ushered back into the Detroit clubhouse. But ten minutes later, he returned as the fans refused to leave without a curtain call from him.

With the Motown crowd still chanting, "We want Denny. We want Denny," the Tigers' ace walked back down the tunnel from the clubhouse and stood atop the dugout steps to wave at the crowd, which included several thousand Detroit school safety-patrol boys, who had been given free passes for the day's game. The kids screamed their lungs out, making the scene reminiscent of a Children's Crusade to *Detroit Free Press* reporter George Cantor.

"Isn't this incredible. Isn't this incredible," repeated Sandy Koufax, who was still at McLain's side. The veteran of four World Series was as amazed as everybody else by what was going down that day in Detroit.

McLain responded by blowing kisses to the crowd. For one of the few times in his career, the pitcher who lived the high life like none other was at a loss for words. "Right now," he said, "I'm numb."

A day later, the St. Louis Cardinals clinched the National League pennant at the Astrodome. In the 7–4 victory, Roger Maris hit his 275th and final home run in the major leagues, while Curt Flood collected five hits.

About the only thing left to determine in the regular season was whether Bob Gibson could continue his amazing run. Since Robert Kennedy's assassination, he had willed himself into becoming the best pitcher in baseball. Entering August, he held an astonishing 0.96 ERA. It hovered around 1.00 into early September and crept up to only 1.16 heading into his final start of the regular season. Even with a mediocre outing, Gibson was almost assured of breaking what many considered to be the National League record of 1.22 set by Grover Cleveland Alexander in 1915. But the all-time record—1.14 held by Walter Johnson—was there for the taking.

That day, Gibson took no prisoners. He pitched a complete-game shutout, his thirteenth of the year, and struck out eleven Astros. When he returned to the Cardinals' clubhouse, he found a stuffed Tiger hanging by a rope in his locker. Yes, everyone was gearing up for the pending World Series.

Gibson finished the regular season with a 22–9 record; something that appears almost pedestrian when linked with his record 1.12 ERA. Bill Deane from the Hall of Fame in Cooperstown, New York, later pointed out that Gibson was victimized again and again by poor offense in '68. Nine times during the season, Gibson had allowed three earned runs or less, only to lose every time. Granted, he was often matched against the top pitchers around the league (Don Drysdale, Ferguson Jenkins, Gaylord Perry). Still, St. Louis's offense rarely did him any favors.

In that nine-game stretch, all losses, Gibson's ERA was 2.14. As Deane detailed, if the Cardinals had scored 3.43 runs a game, the league average in the "Year of the Pitcher," Gibson would have finished with a 30–4 record, which would put him in the same conversation with the Tigers' Denny McLain when it came to victories. Even if the Cardinals had averaged only one run a game for their ace in 1968, Gibson still would have had a winning record, 13–10. Suffice it to say that Gibson was the best in the National League, perhaps in all of baseball. Five times during the season, he had a streak of twenty-plus scoreless innings. Perhaps more incredibly, he had a 1.83 ERA in games in which he did not pitch a shutout.

"In the summer of 1968, I mastered my craft," Gibson later wrote. "This is not to say that I was a perfect pitcher, because I made mistakes (although not as many as other years) and a perfect pitcher is an impossible concept, anyway, as long as major-league hitters remain capable, as many are (damn them), of hitting perfect pitches. But in 1968, we of the pitching profession came as close to perfect as we've ever come in modern history and probably ever will."

Denny McLain and Mickey Mantle were both fun-loving guys, willing to skirt the rules when possible, so it didn't come as any surprise when one of the most curious moments of the '68 season occurred when the two of them got together. Only a few weeks remained in the regular season, and with the pennants already decided McLain came to the conclusion he needed to have some more fun.

"Denny McLain always gave you a ball to hit," Reggie Jackson said. "I think he liked home runs almost as much as hitters did."

Despite past heroics (Triple Crown winner in 1956, twelve World Series appearances), in 1968 Mickey Mantle did about as well as any other power hitter not named Frank Howard. In other words, he was scuffling. But unlike other sluggers, Mantle, who was in his eighteenth major league season, had more at stake as the regular season came to an end. With 534 career home runs, he stood tied with Jimmie Foxx for third place on the all-time list. Even though "the Mick" didn't realize it at the time, McLain had grown up a huge fan of his. As a kid, McLain had worn the number seven, tried to hit from both sides of the plate, and even played center field until better success on the pitching mound took him in that direction.

Facing off against his childhood hero on September 19, 1968, staked to a 6–1 lead in the sixth inning, his thirty-first victory well in hand, McLain found himself in a giving mood. That's when he motioned for Jim Price, who was catching that day in place of Bill Freehan, to come out to the mound. There McLain told Price, "I want Mantle to hit one."

At first Price didn't know what McLain was talking about. So McLain spelled it out for him. "I'm going to throw a pitch and I want him to hit a home run. He needs one more to move up on the all-time home-run list."

Dumbfounded, Price stared back at McLain, then slowly realized what was about to happen. They were about to groove a pitch to one of the top sluggers of all time.

"All you gotta say is, 'Be ready, Mick,'" McLain told Price.

With that, the catcher nodded and walked back behind the plate. But somehow, the message didn't make it to Mantle. McLain saw Price say something, but the only one really paying attention was home-plate umpire Russ Goetz. Sure enough the Tigers' ace served up the first pitch on a platter. It arrived at barely sixty miles per hour, splitting the heart of the plate. Everything went according to plan, only Mantle didn't swing.

Instead he turned around to ask Price, "What the hell was that?"

The catcher replied simply, "Be ready."

It was a response reminiscent of the cryptic line from W. P. Kinsella's novel, later immortalized by Kevin Costner in the movie *Field of*

Dreams—"Go the distance." Indeed, everything seemed set for the Mick to do just that as McLain lobbed the next one right in there, as well. Yet a confused Mantle once again took the pitch, this time for strike two.

"Is he gonna do it again?" Mantle asked, incredulously.

"I'm not sure," Price replied. "Let me ask him."

Unbelievably, Price took another trip out to the mound to ask McLain if the fix was still in now that everybody in uniform and a growing number of spectators had already figured out something was going on.

"Mick wants to know if you're going to do it again," Price told McLain.

"Of course I'm going to do it again," McLain answered, barely able to contain his laughter. "Tell him to be ready this time."

Price went back behind the plate and confirmed to Mantle, "Yeah, he's gonna do it again."

Not quite as memorable as "Be ready," but this time it would do the trick. McLain wasn't leaving anything to chance, however, and so he yelled in from the mound, asking Mantle where he wanted the ball. The slugger motioned for an offering almost letter-high, on the inner half of the plate. After nodding in reply, that's exactly where McLain put his next pitch and Mantle promptly jacked it out of the park. As he circled the bases, Mantle doffed his cap and yelled "Thank you" to McLain.

When the celebration was over, Joe Pepitone, the next batter up, stepped into the box and mimicked Mantle, motioning for the ball about letter-high, right out over the plate. McLain's first pitch came in just under Pepitone's chin, sending him to the ground in self-defense.

The Tigers won the game, 6–2, which made McLain 31–5 for the season. He was the first thirty-plus game winner in the majors since Lefty Grove in 1931. But, of course, what everybody wanted to talk about after the game was the incident in the eighth inning.

"I'm a big fan of Denny McLain," Mantle told reporters.

At the time, McLain refused to acknowledge that he had orchestrated the at-bat. But years later, in his second autobiography, the pitcher declared, "It was a Hall of Famer being honored in the best fashion of all, having him perform what he was most famous for. I cherish it as one of my warmest baseball memories."

When told that McLain had served up a home-run ball to Mantle in a measure of respect, Bob Gibson couldn't believe it. "My method of showing respect for a guy like Mantle," Gibson said, "would have been to reach back for something extra with which to blow his ass away."

Commissioner William Eckert announced an investigation into the Mantle incident but nothing really came of it. The Yankees returned to the Bronx to play the Red Sox and that's where Mantle hit the last home run of his eighteen-year career—a two-out shot in the third inning off Boston's Jim Lonborg, the previous season's Cy Young.

Of course, McLain wasn't the first pitcher to play favorites. In fact Milt Pappas, who took such a strong stand after Robert Kennedy's assassination, had nearly changed the course of baseball history by doing so. In 1961, the Yankees' Roger Maris was chasing Babe Ruth's single-season home-run record. Ford Frick, the commissioner at that time, decreed that if Maris didn't break the Babe's record in the same number of games (154), any new mark would have an asterisk.

"In so many words, Frick was telling Roger that his achievement wasn't worth full recognition and he, Roger Maris, wasn't as good as the great Babe Ruth," Pappas later accounted. "What a crappy thing to do to a nice guy like Roger. Frick had a lot of shortcomings as commissioner, and this was the lousiest of them all."

The Yankees played games 153, 154, 155, and 156 that season in Baltimore against the Orioles, Pappas's team at the time. And lo and behold, Pappas was scheduled to start game Number 154. The night before the contest, Pappas ran into Maris and Mantle deep in the bowels of Memorial Stadium in Baltimore. At that point, the outspoken pitcher laid it out for Maris. As a disbelieving Mantle looked on, Pappas told Maris that he was going to throw him nothing but fastballs the next day.

"I want to see you break the record," Pappas said. "So if I'm shaking my head, I'm calling off either a slider or a changeup. I'm throwing nothing but fastballs."

"Are you serious?" Maris asked.

"Damn right, Roger," Pappas replied.

The next night, Pappas's plan nearly rewrote the record book. True to his word, he grooved fastball after fastball to Maris. In his first at-bat, Maris didn't quite get under the ball enough, lining out to right field. In his second appearance at the plate, Maris drove a Pappas fastball deep for his fifty-ninth home run of the season, putting him one behind the Babe.

Yet Pappas also threw one too many fastballs to the rest of the Yankees' lineup. New York was ahead 4–0 when Maris came up next and Pappas had already been lifted for a reliever. Maris went homer-less in his next three at-bats in Baltimore.

As Pappas remembered, "That was the end of Roger's attempt to equal Ruth's record in 154 games."

Maris did finally hit his sixty-first home run, on the last day of the season, off Boston's Tracy Stallard. For his part, Frick rolled out a designation in the record book that there was a 154-game record (Ruth) and a 162-game record (Maris).

Regardless of skill or ability, there are often many intangibles that remain outside a pitcher's control. How else to explain Bob Gibson's nine losses in a season when his ERA was an as-yet-unsurpassed record 1.12? Or Milt Pappas's inability to take baseball history into his own hands? As Nolan Ryan once said, "To have any hope at succeeding as a pitcher, you can have the best stuff in the world, but can you put it where you need to with several thousand people at a given time watching? That's the real challenge."

Since reaching the big leagues in 1961, right-hander Ray Washburn had been an enigma for the Cardinals. Despite a quality fastball and outstanding slider—stuff that drew comparisons with Gibson at times—

Washburn rarely had the record to show for it. Beginning the '68 season, his major-league record stood at just 51–44. Yet, perhaps to the surprise of many, he would be the author of one of the most fitting footnotes to the regular season.

On September 17, 1968, the Giants' Gaylord Perry no-hit the visiting Cardinals at Candlestick Park. Undoubtedly Perry received a major assist from the fact the contest came days after St. Louis clinched the National League pennant in Houston. Matched against Gibson, Perry allowed walks to Mike Shannon and Phil Gagliano in no-hitting the Cardinals. Tim McCarver and Gibson himself were the only visiting hitters to even get the ball out of the infield. With the feat, Perry became the second pitcher from eastern North Carolina to no-hit a team in the majors that year. The A's Jim "Catfish" Hunter, who grew up in Hertford, North Carolina, about sixty-five miles from the Perry's family farm, twirled his perfect game on May 8, 1968.

Perry's no-no highlighted how hit and miss the Cardinals' attack had become, and how much the team depended upon such speedsters as Brock and Flood to reach and steal bases. "The tendency was to view the Cards as the same club that beat the Red Sox in the 1967 World Series," wrote the *Washington Post*'s Shirley Povich. "They are not. They have the same personnel but they are playing like imposters. Their hitting is sadly off."

The following day, many of the 4,703 fans at Candlestick must have thought they were witnessing a Yogi Berra moment of déjà vu all over again. For Washburn went out and matched Perry's accomplishment of the previous day almost batter for batter. The performance didn't surprise Cardinals' trainer Bob Bauman. Before the second game at Candlestick, he predicted a great outing for Washburn. "I told him, 'You are going to pitch a no-hitter today because you're going to get even with those guys.'" Bauman said in the *Sporting News*. "It was as simple as that. I wanted Ray to make up for that no-hitter Gaylord Perry threw at us the night before."

Back in Williamston, North Carolina, Perry's mother usually stayed up late, listening to her son's starts on the radio. Yet she somehow missed the no-hitter, thinking Gaylord's start wasn't until the following day, September 18. No matter. She tuned in the next day, an unlikely witness to baseball history.

In Washburn's start, there were again only two batters who managed to hit the ball out of the infield. This time it was the Giants' Hal Lanier in the sixth inning and Willie McCovey, who popped out to Flood for the final out. Washburn escaped a two-men-on, two-out jam in the seventh inning by striking out Dick Dietz, who had done his utmost to break up Don Drysdale's scoreless streak earlier in the summer.

Sixteen hours after Perry's feat, Washburn had pitched the second consecutive no-hitter in the same ballpark. It marked the first time in major-league history that back-to-back no-hitters were pitched by the same two teams on consecutive days in the same place. "In Gaylord's no-hitter, only two balls were hit out of the infield," Washburn said. "The same thing happened with me."

"They talk about '68 being the 'Year of the Pitcher,'" Perry later said. "Those forty-eight hours at Candlestick kind of summed that up, didn't they?"

The no-hitters were the fourth and fifth in baseball that season. Perry threw 101 pitches in "the biggest thrill of my career," while Washburn delivered his in 138 pitches.

"It was a fine day to pitch," Washburn said. "The wind wasn't strong. I felt real good going into the ninth. I had control of my breaking pitches when I was behind the batters. My slow curve was working. If you have good motion and can keep it away from hitters, it's a very effective pitch."

That Candlestick Park would host back-to-back no-hitters was especially improbable. Anybody who remembers the old ballyard can recall that games at the 'Stick were part punishment, part comedy, and part wonder for players and fans alike.

As part of the enticement to move his team west along with the Brooklyn Dodgers following the 1957 season, New York Giants' owner Horace Stoneham had been promised 40,000 seats and 12,000 parking spaces.

Such real estate was difficult to come by in San Francisco even back then. As a solution, the city scrambled to build a new ballpark on a jagged stretch of land well south of downtown that extended out into the bay. In 1960, then-vice president Richard Nixon threw out the first ball at the stadium's opener, declaring, "San Francisco can say this is the finest ballpark in America." It wouldn't be the last time Nixon stretched the truth. During the summer, thanks to the prevailing weather pattern, fog and strong winds funneled through the hills to the west and down through the Golden Gate, causing cold temperatures and plenty of mayhem. It soon became known as one of the game's most notorious and unpredictable homes. It was where reliever Stu Miller was once blown off the mound by a gust of wind. (A balk was called.) In the late 1980s, the Giants handed out "Croix de Candlestick" pins to those who stuck it out to the end of extra-inning games. Players had it written into their contracts that they couldn't be traded to San Francisco.

Unlike the Dodgers' idyllic home at Chavez Ravine, the elements were nearly always in play at the Giants' venue. Some nights the flags beyond the center-field fence didn't blow in or out but rather straight up. The gale-force conditions blew many a foul ball fair over the years. Center fielder Brett Butler was once asked how he managed to persevere under such conditions, with wind currents that could take a ball in any direction as if it were on a string.

"Prayer," he answered.

By 1968, the American Football League was steadily gaining a following thanks to its explosive offenses and a growing legion of quality quarterbacks. Within the game, though, the upstart league was also turning heads in another significant way. While the more established National Football League had such African American stars as running back Jim Brown and Super Bowl hero Herb Adderley, as the 1968 season unfolded, black stars in the AFL were making serious inroads playing in notable positions that had long been held by white players. Marlin Briscoe started as quarterback for the Denver Broncos. Willie Lanier took over as the starting middle linebacker for the Kansas City Chiefs, calling the shots on defense. These were the developments that Dr. Martin Luther King and his inner cadre had kept abreast of; watching sports, as Rev. Billy Kyles said, with "an historical eye."

"Not just in style of play, but also in its social fabric, the culture of the new league was distinct from that of the NFL, particularly in race relations," wrote Michael MacCambridge in *America's Game: The Epic Story of How Pro Football Captured a Nation*. "The AFL was hardly an idealistic utopia of racial equality, but the topic was more contemplated, more easily confronted, and better understood than in the NFL."

Ironically, nobody better understood or seemed more comfortable with this transformation than a white quarterback who wore distinctive white cleats and played in New York, the largest media market. Football and the sporting world in general may not have been ready for Joseph William Namath. But, frankly, he didn't give a damn.

Raised in western Pennsylvania, a football-crazed region that would later produce such legendary quarterbacks as Dan Marino and Jim Kelly, Namath went south to play his college ball. At Alabama, he headlined Bear Bryant's Crimson Tide. Somewhere along the way, Namath became comfortable with blurring the lines of segregation that extended throughout sports in this watershed season. As a handsome bachelor, he certainly transcended the game, but what really turned heads within the game was how he could, in an almost off-hand way, bring blacks and whites together in a fashion that perhaps only the St. Louis Cardinals and Detroit Tigers could really duplicate at the time.

As an example, MacCambridge cites the observations of acclaimed sportswriter Paul Zimmerman. In 1968, Zimmerman covered Namath's team, the New York Jets, for the *New York Post*. "Most teams, no matter how close they are, break down into some loose kind of black-white arrangement at meal times," Zimmerman wrote. "To a casual observer, it would give the appearance of a segregated dining room. But I have seen Namath plunk his tray down at one of those all-black tables, and then a few white players join him, and soon it becomes a mixed table. I've seen this happen too many times to assume it's accidental. The same thing on buses. I've seen Namath integrate a little knot of black players by his presence."

As the 1968 season got rolling in football, Namath's Jets were by no means considered the best team in the sport. They had plenty of competition within the supposedly inferior AFL, from the Oakland Raiders, Kansas City Chiefs, even Briscoe's Denver Broncos, whom they lost to early in the 1968 regular season. Few could foresee them toppling the power structure of professional football, let alone that of sports in America. Yet that's exactly what they were about to do.

"Baseball is a game that was designed to be played on a Sunday afternoon at Wrigley Field in the 1920s," Roone Arledge told *Sports Illustrated*, "not on a 21-inch screen. It is a game of sporadic action interspersed with long lulls. Last year we tried re-running plays in slow motion. It was redundant."

If anything, the sixties was a decade of change, with the lines often drawn between those who embraced change and those who resisted it. And time after time, it was those who embraced it who prevailed. Even though few saw it coming, football was about to supplant baseball as the top sport in the country, and it would be none other than the quarterback with the Fu Manchu mustache and the signature white shoes who would soon deliver the unlikely but decisive blow.

The stretch drive in '68 held plenty of heartbreak and disappointment for Luis Tiant. The right-hander was struggling, and he was doing so alone. In addition to being apart from his wife and children, who were in Mexico City where they made their year-round home, after the heated argument with Alvin Dark, Tiant didn't trust his manager anymore. Instead the right-hander tried to carry on as best he could on his own—now insisting that he was healthy enough to take the ball even though his elbow was still killing him.

During that stretch, he allowed seven earned runs, while his ballclub scored only five runs for him. At one point, Tiant sprayed the team bat rack with ladies perfume in the hope of attracting more hits from the baseball gods. It may have worked. His nineteenth victory came in one of his worst outings of the season, a 9–5 victory in Anaheim. Five days later, Tiant won his twentieth against Minnesota, striking out sixteen. In today's era, that would have been it. Tiant would have been shut down for the season, told to rest up for next year. But Tiant had other ideas.

"I'm a pitcher," he said, "and what I'm meant to do is pitch."

So on September 25, 1968, Tiant made his last start of the season against the Yankees in the Bronx. His teammates weren't surprised to see him on the mound for what many considered a meaningless game. While McLain was the hands-down favorite to win the American League Cy Young Award, in the Indians' clubhouse they still talked about what a competitor Tiant was. How his nostrils "flared like a bull" when he pitched. Even the Cleveland radio broadcasters began to call him "the little bull" during the '68 season. So perhaps what happened at Yankee Stadium as the regular season drew to a close shouldn't have surprised anyone.

In the first inning, the Yankees' Mickey Mantle singled through the infield. From there, Tiant didn't allow another hit for the rest of the game, shutting down New York, 3–0. He struck out eleven in the process, raising his season total to 264, what would be the highest number in his nineteen-year career. More importantly, his ERA of 1.60 was the lowest in the American League since Walter Johnson's 1.49 in 1919. One could argue he was the best pitcher in the game after Bob Gibson, regardless of what McLain and Drysdale had accomplished.

"Yeah, Denny won thirty-one, but if anybody had asked me which one was the better player, I'd have taken Luis one hundred times in a row," said Stan Williams, Tiant's teammate that season. "We have a little saying, it's called 'bowing the neck.' It means getting a little tougher when the situation is tougher. Some pitchers can do it and some can't. Luis could."

With the regular season over, Tiant prepared to move his family to Venezuela for winterball action. He had played there the previous off-seasons and believed the extra work had played a major role in helping him transform into one of the game's best pitchers. He maintained that the winter games made his arm stronger, more durable. The Indians had other ideas, however.

The organization determined Tiant needed a break and ordered him not to pitch until next spring. No winterball allowed. The pitcher replied that if he didn't pitch, his arm would stiffen and the muscles could even shorten. The front office dismissed his protests. Even though Tiant would be named the team's "Man of the Year" by the Cleveland press, Dark's criticism of Tiant, that the pitcher supposedly abused his arm with that funky delivery of his, had struck a chord with the front office. Instead of heading to Venezuela to pitch in the off-season, Tiant was advised to rejoin his family in Mexico City and instructed not pick up a ball until training camp opened in the spring. The right-hander predicted that without following his regular training regimen, he wouldn't fare well next season. Nobody cared to listen.

"Instead they told me to stay home," Tiant said, "and watch TV."

While the rest of the league finished out their regular season games, the Tigers and Cardinals prepared for the upcoming World Series. With no wild-card teams or divisional rounds, by clinching the pennants, Detroit and St. Louis were headed directly to the Fall Classic. "It was the end of an era for baseball," historian William Mead said. "But like so many things of consequence, nobody really realized it at the time. So much in sports was about to change forever."

For hitters, their season-long struggles and futility in the face of the "Year of the Pitcher" was written on the wall. Boston's Carl Yastrzemski went 0-for-5 on the final day of the regular season, dropping his average to .3005, which was good enough to take the batting crown in the American League. Washington's Frank Howard finished with forty-four home runs to lead baseball, while the Red Sox's Ken Harrelson had a league-best 109 RBI. The National League offered a bit more offense, especially in Cincinnati. There Pete Rose and Alex Johnson hit better than .300.

"I never said I would lead the National League in hitting in 1968, but I would not trade places with anyone," said Rose, who was twenty-seven years old at the time and playing his third position since joining Cincinnati five years before. (He went from second base to left field and now right in '68.) Looking ahead Rose said he didn't care where he played, but he shared the same financial goal as Detroit's Denny McLain—he also thought $100,000 annually sounded like a beautiful figure.

The Tigers and Cardinals had plenty of time to get their World Series rotations in order, with Roger Maris warning his St. Louis teammates that Mickey Lolich, rather than Denny McLain, was the guy to be concerned about. Certainly Detroit manager Mayo Smith had confidence in the left-hander as well. He decided Lolich would pitch the second game of the World Series—an impressive ascension, especially considering he had spent part of the '68 season in the bullpen.

The headlines, however, were all about McLain versus Bob Gibson. Both pitchers would win the Cy Young and Most Valuable Player awards in their respective leagues. Already the World Series was being billed as the greatest pitching matchup of all time.

Behind the scenes, Tigers' manager Mayo Smith worried about his team's everyday lineup and decided to make a major gamble. Up to that point, Detroit had won many of its games without the help of "Mr. Tiger" himself, Al Kaline, who had missed significant time with a broken arm. Now he was healthy and Smith desperately wanted to get Kaline's bat back in the offense for the Series. Understandably, part of his motivation had to do with Kaline's standing in the organization. In 1955, he had won the American League batting championship at the age of twenty—one day younger than Ty Cobb, who accomplished the feat in 1907—and over

the course of his career he had become one of the most popular and recognized Tigers of all-time. Still, Kaline was an aging star, with his best
power days pretty much behind him. By 1968 some wondered if the ballclub still needed him on a full-time basis. The Tigers' outfield of Willie
Horton, Jim Northrup, and Mickey Stanley combined to hit sixty-eight
home runs and played solid defense without him. Would wedging Kaline
into the outfield mix disrupt team chemistry? But Kaline was still Kaline
and Smith couldn't resist trying to get him on the field full time.

On September 17, Kaline pinch-hit for Norm Cash and ended up scoring the winning run as the Tigers clinched the pennant. After the game,
Kaline told Smith that he didn't deserve to be a regular in the World Series. The kids had done the job and they were the ones who should play.
Yet Smith wasn't buying it. In the World Series, on the biggest stage in
the game, the Tigers' manager wanted his best-known player out there.
The rub was how to do it.

With the adoption of the designated hitter rule five years away, Smith
was seemingly left with little choice: either break up his outfield and
bench one of its starters or face Bob Gibson and the rest of the St. Louis
pitching staff without Kaline's bat. But as the regular season wound to a
close, Smith proved to be resourceful and full of surprises. He tweaked
and experimented with his players' lineup and positions, searching for
other viable options. What turned heads was when the Tigers' manager
moved Stanley in from center field to play shortstop for several games.
He even let Horton manage the team for a game. Days before the World
Series opened in St. Louis, Smith announced that Stanley would be in the
infield, with Northrup moving from right to center field, opening up a
place for Kaline in right. It was anything but a popular tactic. Ernie Harwell, the Tigers' broadcaster, openly complained that "it was a bad move,"
and went as far as to ask twenty-five so-called experts what they thought
about Stanley at short. They all agreed it was a misuse of personnel.

Several Tigers didn't agree with the move, either. On a team with
plenty of jokesters and free spirits, Stanley was one of the few straight ar-
rows, a self-proclaimed workaholic. Horton and Bill Freehan, who had

known Stanley since youth ball, wondered if the added pressure of playing a position he wasn't used to would be too much for their friend. After all, Stanley had been credited with a perfect fielding percentage playing the outfield in 1968 and would win his first Gold Glove. During one game earlier in the season he had raced some sixty yards to make a diving grab against the White Sox. Afterward Smith had told Jerry Green that it had been the best catch he'd ever seen. Although Stanley often took infield practice and occasionally spelled Norm Cash at first base, shifting positions for the Fall Classic was another matter. Could he hold up under all the scrutiny? The manager countered that Stanley had accrued some experience at shortstop and second base during McAuliffe's suspension. Of course that hadn't resulted in any Tigers' victories. Was Smith putting the team's World Series in jeopardy?

One of the great American beliefs is that everything and everybody deserves representation in the nation's capital. To that end, it should come as no surprise that on the first Wednesday of every month, at the Hawk 'n' Dove, a few blocks east of the Capitol Dome on Pennsylvania Avenue in Washington, D.C., the Mayo Smith Society convenes its monthly meeting. Hunkered down at one of the tables in the restaurant's lower level, ideally near a large-screen television to watch the night's action, the group adeptly protects its turf against the onslaught of interns and lobbyists that populate the Hill like pigs to the trough.

Founded in 1983, the society's roster goes hundreds deep worldwide. Annual outings include catching the visiting Tigers at Camden Yards in Baltimore and making an annual pilgrimage to Detroit for a weekend series. But such events are gravy, really. The real fun is simply catching up every month, sharing a drink or two, recalling the great games of the Tigers' past, and reaffirming the genius of one Mayo Smith.

"As a baseball man, Smith was really ahead of his time," said Dave Raglin, creator of the society's Facebook page. "Certainly he was low-key, sometimes overlooked, but he was an innovator throughout his career, and he was exactly what the Tigers needed in '68."

Smith had managed the Philadelphia Phillies and Cincinnati Reds before taking the Detroit job in October 1966. The Tigers were reeling after previous managers Charlie Dressen and Bob Swift both died during the '66 season. In Philadelphia, Smith had bought the team's first pitching machine and in Cincinnati he had moved Frank Robinson to first base. Along the way, he targeted Lou Brock for stardom in a *Sport* magazine piece, two years before his trade to St. Louis. Soon after taking over the Tigers, Smith moved Dick McAuliffe from shortstop to second base. And although shifting Mickey Stanley to the infield before the '68 Series seemed to come out of the blue, members of the Mayo Smith Society pointed out that the signs were there all along. The year before, Dick Young wrote about the possible ploy in the *Sporting News* (an insight that likely came from Smith himself), and during the 1968 season the Tigers' manager hinted that such a move could work nicely with the Detroit lineup.

"Even his own players joked that Smith sometimes seemed asleep at the switch," Raglin said. "But the man was always thinking and often he was a step ahead of everybody."

Certainly managers have been playing hunches since the game's origins. In Game One of the 1929 World Series, the Philadelphia Athletics' Connie Mack went with Howard Ehmke (7–2) over pitching legend Lefty Grove (20–6) or George Earnshaw (24–8). (Ehmke went the distance, striking out a record thirteen.) In 1950, the Phillies gave closer Jim Konstanty his first start of the season in the opening game of the Fall Classic. Although Konstanty allowed only a single run over eight innings, this time around such a gambit failed to pay off as he lost the contest to the Yankees' Vic Raschi, who pitched a complete-game shutout. We've also seen such strategic innovations as the Boudreau Shift—an infield alignment first devised by the Cleveland Indians against Boston's Ted Williams and redeployed in the 1946 World Series by the Cardinals—and on the offensive side of things, in recent years St. Louis manager Tony La Russa has batted the pitcher eighth instead of at the end of the batting order. All interesting twists, but they seem to take a backseat to Smith's bold decision to move his best outfielder to shortstop for the biggest games of the 1968 season.

Since the All-Star break, Tigers scouts had been charting St. Louis games. Nobody read those reports more closely than Mickey Stanley. A major component to the Cardinals' offense was outfielder Lou Brock. After coming over from the Chicago Cubs in 1964, his speed energized the St. Louis attack. Brock stole sixty-two bases during the '68 regular season and was in the midst of a run that would see him lead the National League in thefts eight times in nine seasons. His success on the base paths intimidated ballclubs to the point that many gave up trying to make the basic plays.

The Tigers' scouts, for example, noticed that if Brock was on second base he rarely drew a throw to the plate on a single to the outfield. The mindset of opposing outfielders appeared to be why bother? Brock had the wheels and he would score, throw or no throw. As a result, some in the Detroit clubhouse believed that Brock wasn't running full out all the time. He rarely slid into home plate, often going in standing up. Perhaps a strong, accurate throw could catch him. Stanley pointed this out to his teammates, especially Horton.

Even though he had plenty of work to put in at his new position at shortstop, with the World Series days away, Stanley once again played the role of teacher. Brock could be thrown out, Stanley told his teammates. But every aspect, from fielding the ball to throwing home to the catcher being ready to snare the catch, had to be automatic and perfect.

"That's what we started to practice," Horton said. "From the scouting reports, we knew that Brock sometimes drifted around second base. Same way when going home from second.

"He'd slow a bit going around third base. Of course, he'd brought base-stealing back into [the game], so for a lot of outfielders it was why throw in those situations? He's going to score anyway.

"As a result, he'd picked up bad habits. The third-base coach picked up bad habits. Even the guy in the on-deck circle picked up bad habits. He wasn't up there to help Brock by signaling him to slide or pick it up. But we all agreed: The chance would be there, and we'd have maybe one crack at it. Could we throw out the great Lou Brock?"

The Tigers and the sports world would soon find out.

PART VI

The Great Confrontation

There is no loser in the World Series, just two winners,
one bigger than the other.

—BOB GIBSON

The regular-season numbers didn't lie. By the end of the 1968 season, the collective ERA for all twenty major-league teams was just 2.98. Five no-hitters were pitched (by Tom Phoebus, Catfish Hunter, George Culver, Gaylord Perry, and Ray Washburn) and folks were still complaining about the 1–0 final in the All-Star Game, with the only run scoring on a double-play ball. It seemed only appropriate, then, that Game One of the World Series would be a showdown between arguably the two best pitchers in the sport—Bob Gibson and Denny McLain. For their part, both pitchers stayed in character.

Gibson, the St. Louis staff ace, maintained that he found satisfaction in winning the big games because that simply meant more money. But even his own teammates weren't buying that. "It's not this easy to always win the big game," Cardinals' shortstop Dal Maxvill told *Newsday*'s Steve Jacobson before Game One. "He says it's money, money, money."

With that Maxvill pointed at the left side of his chest. "There's a big heart in there. Right now there's so much pride in it that it would fill up that room. He says money. It's the World Series ring."

Soon after Detroit and St. Louis clinched the pennant in their respective leagues, McLain put his foot in his mouth, claiming that he didn't want to just beat the Cardinals. "I want to humiliate them," he said. Several Cardinals didn't appreciate the comment, especially Gibson. A newspaper story with the quote was tacked to the bulletin board in the St. Louis clubhouse. "I said it, but I didn't mean it," McLain tried to explain. "I was under the influence of champagne and happiness." Any further brash talk dissipated like tiny bubbles when McLain and Gibson met the afternoon before Game One, a gathering that the press dubbed "The Great Confrontation."

"It's not a match between two pitchers," Gibson said, "but a game between two teams."

McLain concurred: "The thing between Gibson and me has been blown all out of proportion."

With that McLain couldn't resist a nod to his burgeoning music career, adding that he expected to be more nervous in a few weeks for his opening night in Vegas—which had just been scheduled—than pitching on the road in the World Series. Perhaps with that in mind, the night before Game One McLain strolled into the Gas House Lounge in the Sheraton-Jefferson, the Tigers' official hotel in St. Louis. The crowd soon recognized him and without much coaxing McLain played the organ for nearly ninety minutes. At one point, teammate Jim Northrup joined him on stage.

"How many Tiger fans are in here" Northrup asked and most of the room applauded.

"How many Cardinals fans?"

One person yelled out.

"Get him out of here," McLain joked.

With that Northrup broke into a tune nobody really recognized, closing with the impromptu line, "We didn't come to St. Looey to sing the blues."

Northrup went by several nicknames on the ballclub. He was called "The Gray Fox" for his premature silver hair and "Sweet Lips" for his gift of gab. "Lay some sweet words on me, Sweet Lips," his teammates would often say.

After his attempt to sing along with McLain, Northrup introduced many of his fellow Tigers in the audience—Gates Brown, Willie Horton, Ray Oyler, Joe Sparma, Norm Cash, Mickey Lolich, and Bill Freehan. When the all-star catcher and his wife were singled out, receiving a warm round of applause, Freehan decided to call it a night. Yet most of the Tigers, along with their family and friends, stuck around as McLain serenaded them with such tunes as "One of These Days," "Restless Wind," and "Money Is the Game." A newspaper photographer took McLain's picture and the hubbub the next morning was how many of the Tigers had broken Mayo Smith's much-maligned curfew. Not that any curfew was held in high esteem within the Tigers' ranks. If the Cardinals were the defending champions the fall of '68, the game's proud professionals, the Tigers, were still eager to be perceived as equal parts frat brothers and misfits.

October 2, 1968

Game One, Busch Stadium, St. Louis, Missouri

NBC held the television and radio rights to the 1968 World Series, and the network rolled out an impressive team of announcers for their coverage of the Fall Classic. Curt Gowdy held things down as the TV voice, with Harry Caray as his partner for games in St. Louis and George Kell joining him in the booth for games back in Detroit. Jim Simpson and Sandy Koufax headed the pregame show. (On the way to Busch Stadium, Koufax told a St. Louis cabbie that whoever won Game One would take the Series.) On the radio, Joe Garagiola led things off with Pee Wee Reese up in the booth, with help from Jack Buck and later Ernie Harwell. Tony Kubek would be on the field for all games.

Before Game One, Smith watched McLain warm up in the Tigers' bullpen and didn't like what he saw. Almost everything his ace threw was high in the zone. Unbeknownst to either of them, the Cardinals planned to take pitches against McLain. After throwing a league-high 336 innings, word had it that he was running on empty. In the '68 season, McLain started forty-one games and went the distance an impressive twenty-eight times. His relentless drive for celebrity, to constantly be in the spotlight, had helped fuel that fire, along with Pepsi, cortisone, Xylocaine, Contac, and amphetamines. But now it was all visibly taking a toll. In addition, thanks to the fact that any such fatigue had yet to impact the running of his mouth, McLain now also had a lineup of angry Cardinals batters to contend with. Even though he tried to distance himself from his comments about humiliating them nobody in St. Louis had forgotten.

"Our guys were charged up," Gibson later wrote in a column he penned during the '68 Series for the *St. Louis Post-Dispatch*. "The reason might have been McLain's statement about wanting to humiliate us, if he really made that statement.

"McLain is a good pitcher," he conceded, before adding, "Whether he'd win thirty-one games in our league, I really couldn't say."

If the Cardinals were charged up, so was the sellout crowd at Busch Memorial Stadium. In the afternoon sunshine, Dixieland bands played and *Sports Illustrated* decided half the crowd was wearing straw hats with either cotton tigers or cardinals stapled to them.

As Game One unfolded, Mickey Stanley was the only Tiger batter to have any early success against Gibson. Although he singled in the first inning, nothing came of it. In the field, Stanley quickly settled into his new post at shortstop, throwing out the Cardinals' Lou Brock for the first out in the bottom of the first inning. Not bad for a guy who was starting his ninth game at shortstop in the big leagues.

"I hope I can just be adequate," Stanley said the day before the Series began. "That's all Mayo wants from me. I know I'll be tight, but then I'd feel that way in center field for my first Series game."

With Stanley in the infield, Detroit's outfield consisted of Kaline in right, former catcher Willie Horton in left, and Jim Northrup in center field. None of them was Stanley's equal, defensively.

Game One remained scoreless through the first three innings, with Gibson clearly the more impressive pitcher. As Gibson dispatched one Tiger hitter after another (often taking ten seconds or less between pitches), McLain struggled both on and off the mound. In the top of the third inning, he bunted a third strike foul, failing to move Don Wert over. In the bottom of the fourth inning, the Tigers' starter walked a pair of Cardinals, and Mike Shannon and Julian Javier then singled to bring them around, staking St. Louis to a 3–0 lead.

"We'd never seen McLain," St. Louis manager Red Schoendienst later said, "but we knew if we'd lay off his high stuff—pitches above the shoulder, up around the neck and eye level—and make him throw strikes, we'd have him."

Meanwhile, the Tigers' scouting report on Gibson didn't do much good. Detroit hitters had been told to be ready for the right-hander's high heat, but advised that Gibson didn't have much in his arsenal after his epic fastball. But the St. Louis starter and his batterymate, Tim McCarver, soon realized that the Tigers were too eager to swing at anything that appeared to be a strike. As a result, they began going with breaking stuff. "They were swinging at my curve like it was a fastball," Gibson said.

In the top of the sixth inning, down 3–0, Detroit pinch-hit for McLain and with that, for this day at least, the "Great Confrontation" was over. The way Gibson was pitching, a three-run lead may as well have been a thirty-run advantage.

McLain later grumbled about his early exit. "Surprised? I was very surprised," he said. "You don't pitch 336 innings and get yanked out of a ballgame. . . . I think this could be the worst I pitched this year—no, I can't say that. I was making good pitches, but they weren't going where they were supposed to go."

When asked about Gibson's dominating performance, McLain replied, "I know he's got that 1.12 ERA and he doesn't give up three runs often, but I don't give up many runs, either. This is the World Series and it's different. I won thirty-some games and he won twenty-some, but that's all wiped out. It doesn't matter. Not in the World Series."

McLain bristled when asked about the previous night's concert at the Gas House Lounge. "It wouldn't have mattered if we'd been in bed by eight the night before because Gibson was unhittable. Al Kaline and Norm Cash struck out three times and all of us looked like we were in shock."

By the final frames of Game One, the lone constant remained Gibson. He had fanned every Tiger at least once. The only time Detroit really threatened came in the sixth inning, with two outs, when Dick McAuliffe singled and went to third base on Kaline's two-out double. Then, after a quick meeting on the mound, the Cardinals' starter proceeded to strike out Cash with a sizzling fastball, ending the threat and closing the inning.

Unfortunately for Cash, he would be on the losing end of another memorable out in the top of the ninth inning, as well. Stanley singled to open the inning, giving Detroit one last measure of hope. Then Gibson struck out Kaline to tie Sandy Koufax's single-game World Series record of fifteen, which had been set in 1963. With that McCarver hurried to the mound with the ball in his mitt, trying to tell the right-hander what he had done. An exasperated Gibson waved him away, ordering his catcher to get back behind the plate.

"Give me the ball," Gibson yelled as McCarver pointed at the scoreboard.

McCarver stood his ground, trying to get a word in edgewise.

"Give me the damn ball," Gibson shouted, getting really agitated now.

Finally, McCarver got a chance to explain why the hometown crowd, which included Frank Sinatra and Julie Nixon, daughter of presidential candidate Richard Nixon, was on its feet and raising such a ruckus. Gibson had tied Koufax's World Series record, and now he had a chance to surpass it. At last, the Cardinals' ace understood.

"All right, now give me the ball," Gibson told McCarver.

With that he promptly established a new mark by once again fanning Cash.

Cash didn't need such reminding that he was the record strikeout. "I read it on the board," he said, "but I've made a lot of history in my life."

"Who follows Cash?" Gibson then asked.

"What difference does it make?" McCarver shouted back.

Of course, it was poor Willie Horton, who admired Gibson perhaps more than anybody else on the Tigers' ballclub. Proving that sports has little time for sentimentality, the Detroit left fielder became the seventeenth strikeout victim on a wicked slider. The pitch broke so sharply and Horton swung at it so hard that McCarver later claimed he heard the Tigers' slugger grunt in resignation.

Bob Gibson's Game One performance would become one of the most iconic of that period in sports. Images of him in action that afternoon can be placed alongside the famous photographs of Muhammad Ali yelling for Sonny Liston to get off the canvas in 1965, or the moment when sprinters Tommie Smith and John Carlos raised their gloved fists into the air (which would take place in Mexico City just days after the '68 World Series concluded). For there is something in the way that Gibson pitched that perhaps wasn't simply directed at the hitters he faced, but rather at the world in general. It is something that, decades later, still manages to reach out to us through still photographs of him frozen in action—a countenance of determination and perhaps even scorn that crackles with energy and purpose. Gibson unleashed his pitches as if he were a man on fire. He delivered his offerings with such power and conviction that he fell violently off to the first-base side in his followthrough, as if he had difficulty controlling what he conjured up. Seeing images of him captured in this act can be striking, even startling. His frame held motionless at an impossible angle, everything about the action that flung it there screaming in defiance against convention, expectation, what was accepted. Looking at such photos of Gibson, it is at once easy to imagine him springing to life before your eyes and yet nearly impossible to anticipate exactly what will happen next. Which is likely similar to what the Tigers' lineup must have been feeling that October afternoon in St. Louis.

"That day Bob Gibson was the toughest pitcher I ever faced in any particular game," Horton said years later. "That last pitch, the one he struck me out with to end the game, tied me up but good.

"But in looking back on that day, what I still cannot believe is Tim Mc-Carver trying to tell him that he'd tied that all-time strikeout record, running out to tell him and Gibson wanting no part of any kind of interruption. He just kept yelling to McCarver, 'Give me the damn ball.' I never saw a guy so focused. That day nobody in the world could beat him."

Almost to a man, the Tigers agreed that Gibson's performance was among the best they had ever witnessed. "I've never seen anybody pitch like that before," Kaline said. "If he continues to pitch like that, we can't beat him."

"It was impossible to detect what he was throwing," Detroit pitching coach Johnny Sain added. "He is a wonderful pitcher—a machine."

"I would say that with the possible exception of Luis Tiant at his best, this man throws harder than anyone we have in our league," Jim Northrup said, "and he is certainly the best we have seen in some time."

Yet Detroit hitters also wondered if they had unwittingly played into Gibson's hands. Busch Stadium's larger confines, at least compared with those of cozy Tiger Stadium, had them swinging from the heels, looking too much for Gibson's famous fastball, and believing they had to hit the ball that much harder to do any damage.

"I'd rather pitch to guys who swing for home runs," said Gibson, who threw 144 pitches in the victory.

After his dominating performance, the Cardinals pitcher received a phone call in the St. Louis clubhouse. Vice president and Democratic nominee Hubert Humphrey was on the line. "I'm with you all the way," he told Gibson.

In the losing clubhouse, some wondered whether manager Mayo Smith would avoid another "Great Confrontation" by moving McLain up to start Game Three back in Detroit. Instead, he confirmed that the rematch would take place. "I'll put them head to head again," he said. "I know [Gibson] can't be any better."

That evening McLain was back playing at the Gas House Lounge, entertaining the crowd. "Mr. Gibson was super today," he told his audience. "I don't even feel bad about getting beat. He pitched one helluva ballgame."

FINAL SCORE: CARDINALS 4, TIGERS 0

St. Louis leads Series, 1–0

Detroit	0	0	0	0	0	0	0	0	0		0	5	3
St. Louis	0	0	0	3	0	0	1	0	x		4	6	0

October 3, 1968

Game Two, Busch Stadium, St. Louis, Missouri

After Bob Gibson's record-setting performance, Tigers manager Mayo Smith made it official: Mickey Lolich would start Game Two instead of Earl Wilson. His stated rationale? Wilson swung a better bat and Tiger Stadium—where Games Three, Four, and Five were scheduled—was considered a better hitting ballpark. Of course, this was long before the designated hitter rule and its alternating use, depending on whether the game was in an American League or National League venue. Back in '68, pitchers had to hit, or at least give it a try. "[Wilson] gives us another bat," said Smith, "and we need it."

Before anybody took the mound in Game Two, however, Eugene McCarthy had free rein of the field. *Life* magazine had commissioned the former Democratic presidential candidate to write a series of stories about the Fall Classic, and now a flock of photographers followed him, recording his every move. As a college student, McCarthy had played first base at St. John's College in Minnesota, and on the Watkins semipro team in the Sioux League. "My grandfather and my uncle played," McCarthy explained, "so I did. . . . I wasn't a bad hitter, but I didn't like certain pitches. You could say I ran for Congress so that I could outlaw the inside curve."

When Tigers' coach Tony Cuccinello asked about his ability, McCarthy said there were times he "could have been mistaken for Gil Hodges. I hit a lot of long fouls."

With all the great players assembled in St. Louis that afternoon, McCarthy curiously targeted Cardinals' reliever Joe Hoerner for an interview. Besides saving seventeen games in 1968, Hoerner was known for wielding a mean fungo bat. His towering blasts during pregame infield practice had once glanced off the underside of Houston's famed Astrodome. McCarthy wanted a firsthand demonstration and Hoerner indulged him by lofting several high fly balls toward the outfield.

In bypassing seven future Hall of Famers who were participating in the 1968 World Series (Al Kaline, Bob Gibson, Eddie Mathews, Lou Brock, Orlando Cepeda, Tim McCarver, and Steve Carlton) for a relief pitcher swinging a fungo bat, McCarthy perhaps underscored, in some way, why he had lost the nomination to Hubert Humphrey

"That was the problem and the attraction of McCarthy," Tom Hayden said. "He was . . . odd.

"Imagine this was September, just before the election in perhaps the worst of all years since 1865 or 1918. Hundreds of thousands of young people gave up a year of their lives for him. Then he got interested in fungo bats? Sounds like a common reaction to the traumas of the year, but he was supposed to lead."

After summerlike conditions for Game One, a cold front moved through St. Louis, dropping temperatures into the fifties by the first pitch. Overnight, Lolich had developed a groin infection and required medication in order to make his surprise start. "I never did get nervous before the game," he later explained. "I was a little groggy because (team physician Dr. Clarence Livengood) gave me a couple of capsules and I just never tightened up."

If anything, Lolich appeared a little too groggy for his own good early on. The Cardinals' Julian Javier singled and Curt Flood walked in the first inning. That left it up to Kaline, back in right field, to single-handedly keep the game scoreless. First the Tiger known simply as "Six" (for his jersey number) made a running grab of Orlando Cepeda's foul fly ball, and moments later he tracked down Mike Shannon's liner to right-center field. No report as to whether McCarthy was impressed.

St. Louis starter Nellie Briles, meanwhile, set down the first four Tigers he faced before Willie Horton turned on a fastball, launching it deep into the left-center field bleachers. With the home run the Tigers held their first lead of the Series.

The following inning the sports gods once again demonstrated their penchant for irony. Even though Smith had started Lolich ahead of Wilson in order to have a better bat in the lineup for Game Three back in Detroit, it was actually Lolich who helped supply the long ball there in St. Louis. In the top of the third inning, he pulled a ball deep down the left-field line. To everyone's amazement, the ball stayed fair, falling softly into the left-field seats for a home run. The dinger would in fact be the very first and very last of Lolich's sixteen-year professional career.

As he began his home-run trot, Lolich missed first base, prompting coach Wally Moses to call him back to make sure he touched them all. "I'm not used to this sort of thing," Lolich told him.

"I still won't believe he hit a home run," McLain later said, "until I see a replay."

From then on, the Tigers were in control. Norm Cash, who had been Gibson's record-setting strikeout victim the day before, clubbed a solo home run. Briles departed after two batters in the sixth, and prompting a string of Cardinals' relievers that included twenty-three-year-old Steve Carlton.

"It wasn't my day," Briles said. "And often when it isn't the pitcher's day, it often isn't the team's day, either."

Carlton replaced Briles with a man on before Jim Northrup's single and Don Wert's walk loaded the bases. Dick McAuliffe then hit a sinking line drive to center field that glanced off Curt Flood's glove. Two runs came around on the rare miscue by the game's best center fielder, and with that Detroit had a 5–0 lead. McAuliffe's liner was certainly a difficult play, but one that Flood had often made throughout the '68 season.

A day after being baffled by Bob Gibson's dazzling repertoire, the Tigers were beginning to resemble their old selves. Soon they were once again playing with swagger and plenty of trash talk in the dugout.

"Oh, we had some fun," Gates Brown recalled. "I mean we had fun most of the time anyway. The guys on that ballclub recognized that you were much more prone to win when you were loose and happy with yourself."

In the seventh inning, with Detroit comfortably ahead 6–1, manager Mayo Smith moved Stanley back to center field. Northrup shifted to left and Ray Oyler came in to play shortstop. The odd man out was Horton, who stewed in the Tigers' dugout after leaving the field. "I want my three best arms out there when we're ahead," Smith had told the press. The Tigers' manager didn't fully communicate his game plan to Horton, however.

"I sure wasn't happy," Horton later said. "I had played out there the whole year, with Al Kaline hurt. I wasn't that bad an outfielder. I'd worked hard on my game. I felt the least Mayo could have done was tell me before he started pulling people out."

Regardless, the way Lolich was pitching that afternoon, he could have had the Three Stooges in the outfield and won. The only concern remained Lou Brock, who stole another two bases after having stolen one in the first game. In fact, the only time Lolich lost his composure occurred when Brock stole second base despite Detroit holding a 6–1 lead in the eighth inning.

"It was definitely for his own self-glory," Lolich said, a comment he later claimed was taken out of context. "He wants to set a record for stolen bases or something, There can't be any other reason. . . . Sure, I could disregard him. But when he takes a big lead like that, it's almost an insult."

Out in the Detroit bullpen, rookie Jon Warden, Pat Dobson, and John Hiller kept a keen eye on Lolich. Due to the medication he was on nobody really expected the left-hander to go the distance. Yet in a methodical, al-most understated way, that's exactly what he did, securing the victory after allowing just six hits. While his nine strikeouts paled in comparison to Gibson's seventeen the day before, Lolich had been in control throughout. "None of the Cardinals' six hits off Lolich was stroked with much author-ity," the *Sporting News* reported.

Through it all, Gates Brown, who would have pinch-hit for Lolich if the pitcher had come out of the game, took a more relaxed approach to it all. "I enjoy days like this," he said, "just sitting back and watching my guys run around the bases."

With the Series heading to Detroit for the first time in twenty-three years, the Tigers' hitters had regained their mojo. "We're in good shape now," Smith declared, "all even and going back to our own park for three games."

But what the Detroit manager left unsaid was that the Tigers would have to face Bob Gibson twice more if the Series went seven games.

FINAL SCORE: TIGERS 8, CARDINALS 1
Series tied at one game apiece

Detroit	0	1	1	0	0	3	1	0	2		8	13	1
St. Louis	0	0	0	0	0	1	0	0	0		1	6	1

During the off-day, before Game Three in Detroit, Tigers' manager Mayo Smith called outfielder Willie Horton into his office for a private meeting. There Smith told Horton that he would continue his defensive strategy: If the Tigers held a lead late in a game, Mickey Stanley would shift back to center field, with Al Kaline staying in right and Jim Northrup taking over for Horton in left. The Tigers had several good-field, no-hit infielders in Ray Oyler and Dick Tracewski. One of them would man shortstop.

As Smith explained to Horton, the manager knew he could cover as much ground as Northrup, but he didn't think he could throw as well. "I wasn't really that mad to hear it," Horton later said. "He's the manager and I understand he has to make decisions."

Still, the strategy annoyed Horton. After coming up as a catcher, he had significantly improved his throwing mechanics. During spring training and routinely before regular-season games, Stanley had taught him how to deliver a ball with more pace and distance from the far reaches of the outfield.

"Personally, I owe a lot to Mickey Stanley," Horton said. "Playing catcher as a kid—that's a different throwing motion. Mickey spent a lot of time with me, teaching me how to play the outfield. One of the main things he did was redo my throwing mechanics. He told me to pretend that I was on a bus and pulling down the rope to get off. That motion from top to bottom—a good throwing motion. That was so important to me because until that point I had thrown more like a catcher—everything compact and from the chest. Years later, I had to learn something that basic while at the major league level, and Mickey Stanley was the guy who took the time to teach me."

Of course, such discussions didn't make headlines back in 1968. Instead the front page of the *St. Louis Post-Dispatch* ran another photo of Bob Gibson from Game One. Along on the front page was a story about George Wallace, who was also running for president, naming retired Air Force general Curtis LeMay as his vice-presidential choice. The architect of the systematic bombing of Japan in World War II, LeMay advocated that more military pressure be brought to bear upon North Vietnam, perhaps even the use of nuclear weapons. "When you get in it, get in it with both feet," LeMay said, "and get it over with as soon as you can."

Other top headlines included student demonstrators clashing with government troops in the Tlateloco section of Mexico City—this just ten days before the Summer Olympics were scheduled to begin. Mexican authorities blamed extremists and Communist agitators within the students' ranks for initiating the violence. But decades later, in documents released by the National Security Archive, it was revealed that the Mexican Army fired indiscriminately at the demonstrators. After the bloodbath, surviving protesters were dragged away and many were never heard from again. Ironically, the dove of peace was the symbol for Games of the XIX Olympiad, with billboards in Mexico City already proclaiming, "Everything Is Possible with Peace."

"We have conferred with Mexican authorities and we have been assured that nothing will interfere with the peaceful entrance of the Olympic flame into the stadium on October 12, nor with the competition which follows," Avery Brundage, president of the International Olympic Committee, said in a statement. "As guests of Mexico, we have full confidence that the Mexican people, universally known for their sportsmanship and great hospitality, will join the participants and spectators in celebrating the Games, a veritable oasis in a troubled world."

October 5, 1968

Game Three, Tiger Stadium, Detroit, Michigan

In the Motor City, the riots of a year ago were forgotten for now. In the days before Game Three, Detroit city street workers stenciled orange and black Tiger faces on the downtown streets, and Washington Boulevard was renamed Tiger Drive with orange stripes running down the center of it. By game time, the old ballpark at Michigan and Trumbull was packed with 53,634 boisterous fans, and even though it wasn't his day to pitch, Denny McLain couldn't help stealing some of the limelight. "Whoever wins today will win the World Series," he told the press.

Early on in Game Three, Al Kaline proved himself worthy of inclusion in the Tigers' lineup yet again when he laced Ray Washburn's pitch into the left-field seats, staking Detroit to an early 2–0 lead. Much to their fans' delight the hometown team appeared to be in good shape as starter Earl Wilson proceeded to shut out the Cardinals through the first four innings.

Throughout the regular season, however, Wilson's luck had often gone south at the most inopportune times. Repeatedly, he had gotten hurt when it mattered most. So it happened again in Game Three.

In the fifth inning, Lou Brock singled and once again swiped second base. To put his base-stealing in proper perspective, during the regular season Brock had stolen sixty-two bases, while the entire Detroit team recorded just twenty-six. The Tigers had no answer for him, and as a result the stage was set for the Series to run away from them.

"Speed, running on the base paths, starts rallies," Brock explained years later. "When a team runs, it forces the other team into mistakes. When a runner takes off from first, the shortstop and the second baseman move to cover him—and that opens a hole in the infield that shouldn't be there.

"That gives the batter a break, because most batters like nothing better than fastballs—especially when they are anticipating fastballs." In other words, an infusion of speed can hotwire any offense.

A year after dominating the Red Sox in the '67 World Series—in which he hit .414 and stole seven bases—Brock was back at it against another American League foe. He wasn't satisfied with merely getting on base, however. He wanted to excel at all facets of the game.

"Look at Ty Cobb," Brock said. "He stole 892 bases but people say, 'Hey, Ty Cobb got 4,000 hits; he must've been a great hitter, too.'

"But what do people say about Maury Wills now? They say, 'That guy, Maury Wills, stole 104 bases one season. He must've been fast, good on the bases.' When I leave the game, I want to be remembered as a complete ballplayer—not only as a good base-stealer. . . . If you leave the stats in the record book, they speak for themselves."

Speed can unnerve the best of opponents. With Brock on second and Curt Flood up, Wilson hurried his delivery, slipping as he followed through to the plate. Tigers' catcher Bill Freehan called time and spoke with Wilson on the mound. While the Detroit starter admitted that he may have pulled a muscle in his leg, he was determined to get out of the inning. Yet when Flood doubled, bringing around Brock, and Roger Maris then walked, Smith had no choice but take Wilson out of the game.

The manager's reasoning behind flipping Wilson and Mickey Lolich in the postseason rotation had been to have Wilson's bat in the lineup at the smaller Tiger Stadium. But with Wilson now sidelined, the better-hitting pitcher had gone just 0 for 1 in Game Three, while Lolich had hit his improbable home run in Game Two at Busch Stadium.

"Is there any way to stop Brock from stealing," Smith was later asked.

"Sure," the Tigers manager replied. "All we have to do is play without bases."

Right-hander Pat Dobson relieved Wilson, and after he got Orlando Cepeda to pop up he served up a three-run home run to Tim McCarver. In the span of five hitters, the Cardinals had taken a 4–2 lead. "That's how quickly the Cardinals of that era could strike," baseball historian William Mead said. "They always had speed with Brock and Flood. The pitching with Gibson and the others was there. The defense was excellent, too. So when the power came around for them, it was a very potent combination and pretty much unbeatable."

Less than a month after pitching a no-hitter against San Francisco, Ray Washburn went just one inning longer than Wilson. Yet that was good enough to secure the victory on this blustery afternoon in downtown Detroit. "It was cold out there," Washburn said of the temperatures in the mid-fifties, "but it wasn't that bad. My control of the curve just wasn't good. It's the worst my control has been in some time."

In the bottom of the fifth inning Dick McAuliffe launched a solo homer off Washburn that pulled the Tigers within a run, at 4–3. When Washburn walked Horton and Norm Cash with one out in the sixth, it looked as though Detroit was on the verge of another signature comeback. But St. Louis manager Red Schoendienst lifted Washburn and called on reliever Joe Hoerner of fungo bat fame. Hoerner snuffed out the rally, along with the Tigers' hopes of winning Game Three, retiring Jim Northrup and Freehan.

In the top of the next inning, the Cardinals' Cepeda blasted a three-run shot off Detroit reliever Don McMahon. The home run was Cepeda's first in sixty World Series at-bats. With some derring-do on the base paths, coupled with a pair of home runs, St. Louis had jumped out to a commanding

7–3 lead. "Even now I can close my eyes and still see innings like that in my head," Cepeda said. "It was beautiful what we could do sometimes. When it all came together for us."

On the other side, everything came unhinged for the Tigers' bullpen, a cruel reminder of the final days of the '67 season, when another championship had been within their grasp only to slip away. After Wilson allowed three earned runs in four and one-third innings, Dobson quickly gave up another earned run in two-thirds of an inning. McMahon was rocked for three runs in an inning and John Hiller serving up four hits in his two innings of action.

Through it all, Detroit rookie pitcher Jon Warden stayed loose, ready to pitch. But he never got into the ballgame.

After the Cardinals' 7–3 victory, McLain couldn't help thinking that the Tigers "were cooked."

Just like that, whatever momentum Detroit had gained by winning Game Two appeared to be lost.

FINAL SCORE, CARDINALS 7, TIGERS 3

St. Louis leads Series, two games to one

St. Louis	0	0	0	0	4	0	3	0	0	7	13	0
Detroit	0	0	2	0	1	0	0	0	0	3	4	0

October 6, 1968

Game Four, Tiger Stadium, Detroit, Michigan

The rain came down in buckets, reminding Gates Brown of that Beatles song they played on the radio. The one with the chorus that stretched out the word itself, "Raaaaiiiaaaiiiaaaiiinnnn, I don't mind."

Baseball commissioner William D. Eckert likely didn't have such lyrics running through his head on this gloomy Sunday afternoon in Motown. Before the game, he walked the field and stared up at the heavens, as if asking for divine intervention. Clearly none was forthcoming as the rain continued to fall.

Across the country, everybody was talking baseball, eager to tune in for round two of the "Great Confrontation" between Bob Gibson and Denny McLain. On the presidential campaign trail, Richard Nixon, much more of a football fan, couldn't resist a baseball allusion or two. In a stop in Hempstead, New York, he noted that Bob Gibson stuck out seventeen batters in Game One, adding, "This administration has struck out for America. It struck out on peace aboard; it struck out on peace at home; it struck out on stopping the rise in crime and it struck out in stopping rising prices."

In comparison, Democratic nominee Hubert Humphrey took the afternoon off to attend the game, now ready to cheer for the hometown Tigers. In both clubhouses, the players expected the game to be played at some point, no matter how hard it rained down on Tiger Stadium. "Too many people watching on TV, too much money to be had," Gates Brown recalled. "No way the big bosses would pass that up."

After a thirty-seven-minute rain delay, the pivotal Game Four began in the darkness and mist. On its biggest stage, with so many tuning in, baseball was about to give itself another black eye. Once again many in sports would blame Eckert, pointing out it was the second major decision of the season he had whiffed mightily on. Usually the umpires have the final say on weather—if a game will be played or not, or when it would be stopped. But for World Series play, the commissioner decided he would make the final call.

"For 162 games a year we're permitted to decide rain or shine whether a game is going to be played," umpire Jim Honochick told pool reporters Milt Richman of United Press International and Murray Chass of the Associated Press. "Then suddenly along comes the World Series games and they take it away from us."

Before the rain came, Al Kaline had been concerned about facing Bob Gibson at Tiger Stadium. He couldn't help worrying about how the shadows usually fell down over the field late in the day, and how Gibson's blazing fastball would be coming right out of that darkness. Of course, with the rain and overcast conditions shadows weren't the issue on this day. Still, Gibson promised to be a formidable foe. He didn't mind pitching in the rain. On May 22, he battled the elements for eight innings while narrowly dropping a 2–0 decision to the Dodgers' Don Drysdale (the third consecutive shutout in Drysdale's record-setting streak).

In comparison, the Game Four rain delay and slippery conditions created havoc with McLain's pregame preparations. The Tigers' right-hander used the extra time to take a hot shower, trying to loosen up his sore right shoulder. Yet by the time the game actually started, it was no good. "I'm not a mudder, and Game Four was as bad as it gets," McLain said. "When I walked out for the first inning, it was drizzling, and when I threw the first pitch, it was coming down in buckets. Actually, the first pitch went OK. It was the second pitch that (Lou) Brock hit into the center-field stands four hundred and thirty feet away."

The Cardinals tacked on another run when McLain stumbled trying to cover first base on Roger Maris's dribbler and then Mickey Stanley couldn't come up with Mike Shannon's grounder deep in the hole. At the end of the first inning, the Cardinals held a 2–0 lead, and the skies showed little chance of clearing. For McLain, the fun-loving days of summer seemed long ago.

In the third inning, the Cardinals doubled their total against McLain. Curt Flood singled and came around on Tim McCarver's triple. McCarver then scored on Mike Shannon's double. After Julian Javier walked, the rain began to come down even harder and home plate umpire Bill Kinnamon suspended play. While commissioner Eckert would be the final arbitrator if the game was called or not, Humphrey had already cast his vote. After joining Eckert in the commissioner's box for early innings, the presidential candidate ducked and ran for cover.

By the time Bob Gibson appeared in his second consecutive World Series in 1968, opposing players had learned never to get the Cardinal's ace hot under the collar. One would have thought fans would have gotten the message, too.

The year before, on the eve of Game Seven against the Red Sox in Boston, Gibson had tried to share breakfast with teammates Tim Mc-Carver and Dal Maxvill and the players' families at the Sheraton Motor Inn in Quincy, Massachusetts. Everyone else's order promptly arrived, except for Gibson's. After forty-five minutes, and several complaints, the waitress brought out burnt toast for the Cardinals' ace.

"This toast is burnt," Gibson told the waitress. "Please take it away."

"We'll take you away," the waitress replied.

Gibson got by with a ham-and-egg sandwich, purchased by the *St. Louis Post-Dispatch*'s Bob Broeg at a diner near Fenway Park. Gibson won Game Seven over the Red Sox's ace Jim Lonborg. "It was evident by that time, and to my good fortune, that Boston didn't understand me," Gibson wrote in his autobiography. "Anger was a part of my preparation. The people at the hotel, despite their best efforts to the contrary, were getting me extremely ready for the ballgame."

A year later, in their own sweet way, Detroit fans did their part to assist Gibson in his game preparation, as well. The night before Game Four, after taping *The Bob Hope Show* with McLain of all people, Gibson returned to the team hotel in Detroit around midnight. At two in the morning, somebody hammered on his door yelling, "Telegram." When Gibson opened the door, nobody was there. An hour later, the telephone rang. When he picked it up, the person on the other end of the line asked, "Is Denny McLain there?" and promptly hung up.

After a fitful night, Gibson awoke to find the hallway outside his hotel room decorated with flowers. Within baseball circles, flowers are considered bad luck, especially before a big game.

Gibson took such abuse in stride, however. While McLain was busy soaking his aching shoulder in a hot shower during the rain delay, Gibson ate an ice cream cone and worked on a crossword puzzle in Tiger Stadium's visiting clubhouse.

———————

After a second rain delay, this one lasting an hour and fourteen minutes, Game Four continued. But Denny McLain was no longer involved as Detroit manager Mayo Smith lifted him for right-hander Joe Sparma. The Tigers' starter had lasted only two and two-thirds innings, giving up four runs, three of which were earned.

Of all the characters on the Tigers' pitching staff, Sparma was the one nobody could really figure out. He possessed perhaps the best fastball on the ballclub, coupled with a hard-breaking overhand curveball. A well-rounded athlete, he played quarterback for Woody Hayes at Ohio State, keying the Buckeyes' 50–20 victory over rival Michigan in 1961. Yet despite all the tools, Sparma was inconsistent at best on the mound. Perhaps it seemed only fitting then that he would be called on to throw in a ballgame that would soon turn into a fiasco.

"Rain, rain, rain," the Tigers' fans chanted, eager for the game to be called due to the weather. Their ranks on this blustery afternoon included actor George C. Scott and his wife, actress Colleen Dewhurst. Despite the outcry, commissioner Eckert ordered the infield tarp rolled up and the game continued. As the sporting world watched, baseball once again made a mockery of itself.

Soon after action resumed, Gibson reminded everyone that he was an exceptional athlete, homering off Sparma to lead off the fourth inning. With the contest becoming a rout, the teams struggled in the wet conditions, often at cross-purposes. Detroit started to stall, holding out hope for a postponement. Catcher Bill Freehan repeatedly went to the mound to talk with a long line of relievers—Sparma, Daryl Patterson, Fred Lasher, John Hiller, and Pat Dobson. Meanwhile, the Cardinals tried to hurry things along so the game would become official once five innings were in the book. Hence St. Louis's Julian Javier trying to steal with Patterson still holding the ball on the mound. At one point the umpires called out both managers and told them to stop such gamesmanship.

"Sure I was trying to stall," Tigers' first baseman Norm Cash said, "when I went over to talk to Daryl Patterson in the fourth inning I didn't have anything to say to him. I wanted to get in an argument with the umpire, which I did."

Gibson knew as well as anybody what was at stake and, as was his wont, he decided to do something about it. Not only did he homer in the fourth inning, becoming the first pitcher in World Series history to hit two home runs, but he made sure that the game became official—rain or no rain. While the Tigers showed signs of life in the bottom of the fourth, with Jim Northrup homering into the right-field stands, Gibson did his utmost to end things once and for all. After striking the two previous batters he got Mickey Stanley to fly out to end the fifth.

"In rain or shine," catcher Tim McCarver said afterward in the winning clubhouse, "that Gibson is fine."

Through it all, commissioner Eckert sat stoically in the rain, alongside Hall of Famer Jackie Robinson. Humphrey never did return. "The Tigers attempted to stall, and the Cardinals attempted to hasten the lopsided game. The World Series had become a farce," Jerry Green wrote. "The players sloshed around and deliberately attempted to make outs and the rain fell and the nation watched the incredible spectacle in its living rooms."

Of course, baseball has suffered its share of mediocre commissioners. Ford Frick and Bowie Kuhn come to mind. Yet few reached the level of Eckert's incompetence. As the rain fell in Detroit, his critics remembered how the commissioner had also failed to cancel all the scheduled games after Robert Kennedy's assassination. Once again, the national pastime didn't do right by its fans or its players. In another twist, Eckert could be blamed for at least opening the door to steroid abuse in baseball. Despite being tone-deaf about the demonstrations in Mexico City and complaints from the "Speed City" athletes on the U.S. team, one thing the International Olympic Committee did manage to accomplish was banning the use of steroids on the eve of the Summer Games. While baseball had a similar opportunity to address the use of performance-enhancing drugs in 1968, Eckert opted to pass.

The Cardinals' Lou Brock rarely let any opportunity slip by. So, in the eighth inning, after his double staked St. Louis to a 10–1 lead, he took off for third base, sliding in safely. The stolen base was Brock's seventh of the '68 Series, which tied his record from the previous year, and his fourteenth in postseason play, which tied Eddie Collins's all-time record. "I didn't know about the record until someone on the bench told me," he later told the *Sporting News*. "Then I figured I owed it to myself to try it. You don't get to play in too many World Series in your career."

As the rain came down, Tigers' rookie Jon Warden watched the action like any relief pitcher would: wondering if the score would become so lopsided that he might get in the game.

Back in April, when the season began, Warden had been the Tigers' hottest pitcher. Not only had he won the team's first victory of the campaign, but his 3–1 record early on had been the best in the American League. Yet as the season progressed, Warden became the forgotten man in the Detroit bullpen. The Tigers' staff often threw complete games, tossing a dozen in a row at one point during the regular season. Despite Warden's early success and his impressive fastball, others were soon being called on and eating up any available innings.

On August 25 Warden had thrown three shutout innings at Yankee Stadium and then pitched only one more time in the regular season. Yet as the World Series' Game Four unfolded, Warden thought he might get another chance. Joe Sparma gave up two runs in one-third of an inning. John Hiller couldn't record an out as the Cardinals battered him for three earned runs.

"I almost got in," Warden said. "I was up several times, kind of champing at the bit. I mean it was a perfect situation. Bring in the kid and let him mop up and we look ahead to another day.

"I hate to say it but sometimes Mayo Smith wasn't the sharpest manager around. But in a way he was exactly the right kind of guy to manage
that team. What I mean by that is he'd let things play out sometimes. Now
I don't know if that's what he wanted or if he'd just kind of tuned out at
times, just went to sleep. But he wasn't micro-managing everything so
you always had a right-hander pitching to a right-handed batter, playing
every angle like that. He'd kind of forget. He'd let the players take it over.

"But on that day, Game Four, that kind of managing sure didn't work
in my favor. He let Hiller stay out there and get pounded when I would
have loved a chance to have that experience. I mean let me have a chance
to get pounded, too. Unlike Denny, I could throw in the rain."

After the game, Humphrey appeared in the Tigers' clubhouse. No matter that the hometown team had suffered the most lopsided defeat since
the New York Yankees defeated the Pittsburgh Pirates 12–0 in 1960, the
candidate was ready to press the flesh.

"Willie, you've had a great year," he told Horton, shaking the slugger's
hand.

"Who's that cat?" Mickey Stanley asked as Humphrey headed for the
door.

FINAL: CARDINALS 10, TIGERS 1
St. Louis leads the series, 3–1

St. Louis	2	0	2	2	0	0	0	4	0	10	13	0
Detroit	0	0	0	1	0	0	0	0	0	1	5	4

October 7, 1968

Game Five, Tiger Stadium, Detroit, Michigan

Before the 1968 season, only two teams had rallied from a 3–1 deficit in
games to win the World Series (the 1925 Pittsburgh Pirates and the 1958

New York Yankees). After being humiliated in the rain, dominated twice by Bob Gibson and driven to distraction by Lou Brock's base-running, the Detroit Tigers didn't appear to have much of a chance. If anything, they just wanted to put together one last good game for their fans at home, something more reminiscent of the regular-season heroics, regardless of how the Series played out.

"A lot of people watching us must think we're a lousy club," Al Kaline told the *Detroit News*. "And we aren't."

Indeed, lousy clubs often overreach and try to do too much when their backs are against the wall. Good teams, however, ones that believe in themselves, emphasize the everyday routine, the little things that got them to the championship in the first place. That's why heading into Game Five Willie Horton and Mickey Stanley continued to discuss outfield defensive strategy. No matter that manager Mayo Smith planned to lift Horton if the Tigers ever got the lead in the late innings again. No matter that Stanley remained the starting shortstop rather than the Gold Glove center fielder. The two of them, bringing Kaline, Bill Freehan, and Jim Northrup into the conversation, maintained that Brock could be thrown out. Even though the St. Louis speedster had already tied his World Series record of seven stolen bases set the year before—and in addition had added a triple and home run—he wasn't perfect. It only seemed that way.

"Some would say we were grasping at straws," Horton said. "But we still talked about those scouting reports. How (Brock) would drift and slow down a bit going around third base. How he didn't slide.

"In the Series, we were still practicing our relays, making good throws because that's the only chance we knew we'd have against him. Everything may have been against us, but we had to find something to believe in."

While the Cardinals were the consummate pros, a rainbow coalition of understanding and discussion, the Tigers, even with their backs against the wall, remained a gang of misfits, an irreverent band of brothers. In the hometown clubhouse, catcher Bill Freehan squinted through the gun sight of a new Winchester rifle that he stowed in his locker. "That is how we're going to stop Lou Brock," shouted Mickey Lolich from across the room.

If anything, the Tigers realized that they had already endured their trial by fire the season before. In losing the pennant on the final day, in playing on in a city literally going up flames, they had learned that they could rely upon their teammates. "We looked out for each other," said Lolich, Detroit's starting pitcher for Game Five. "Always have, always did. Sometimes that's the only thing you can do, the only thing you have left in the world. The guy on either side of you."

Tigers play-by-play announcer Ernie Harwell invited Jose Feliciano, whose cover of The Doors' "Light My Fire" was high on the pop charts, to sing the national anthem before Game Five. The rendition soon ignited the kind of public-relations firestorm that could seemingly only take place in 1968.

"It was a long version of the song and at that point in time, singers weren't supposed to give their own interpretations," McLain recalled. "This was the height of the Vietnam War and the protest movement. The National Guard was all over the field in a patriotic display, and here's this blind Latino supposedly 'butchering' the anthem. It was viewed as sacrilegious rather than an impressive artistic interpretation."

As Feliciano finished his soulful version, angry fans were already calling NBC affiliates and local newspapers nationwide. More importantly, in terms of the game at hand, the artistic interpretation derailed Lolich's pregame routine. Usually the Tigers' left-hander took about twelve minutes to warm up. That tired his arm a touch, allowing his deliveries to sink, just like pitching coach Gerry Staley back in Portland had taught him. Yet before Game Five, "[They] played it early," Lolich said. "It took the guy three minutes to sing. Then the umps came out and started the game. I decided to rear back and throw as hard as I could. When I do that the ball comes in straight."

The Cardinals wasted no time in capitalizing on Lolich's mistakes. For the second game in a row, lead-off hitter Lou Brock smoked the second pitch he saw, this time doubling to left field. He came around on Curt Flood's single. Flood then stole second base and he, too, scored when Orlando Cepeda hit a home run into the left-field stands. In roughly the amount of time it took Feliciano to finish his much-maligned anthem, the Cardinals had struck what many believed would be the closing notes of the World Series.

"I thought we would wrap it up, the whole Series, when I hit that homer," Cepeda said. "I definitely thought so. But Lolich got tough after that."

St. Louis manager Red Schoendienst considered starting left-hander Steve Carlton for Game Five. In '68, however, Carlton was still years away from the Hall of Fame numbers he would put up for the Philadelphia Phillies, when he would lead the National League in victories four times. This was only Carlton's second full season in the majors, during which he posted a respectable but unremarkable 13–11 record and 2.99 ERA. In the end, Schoendienst decided the pitcher nicknamed "Lefty" better served the team out of the bullpen, and instead he gave Nellie Briles, who had gone 19–11 during the regular season, the opportunity to redeem his losing Game Two performance and close out the Series. Early on, after St. Louis raced out to that 3–0 lead, it appeared Schoendienst had made the right decision. Briles was in charge and shutting the Tigers down.

"There are stretches as a pitcher when you feel you can do no wrong," Briles later said. "The first [few] innings of that game, I was in control. I thought I was going to be the one to bring the championship back to St. Louis."

Briles nearly benefited from another run in the third, but Tigers' catcher Bill Freehan somehow threw out Brock trying to steal second base. After that things began to swing in the Tigers' favor.

In the fourth inning, Detroit's Mickey Stanley tripled down the right-field line off Briles. At first base, Cepeda claimed that Stanley hadn't touched the bag but the umpires didn't buy it. For a moment, it appeared that Briles would escape the inning unscathed as he induced a grounder from Al Kaline, holding Stanley at third base. Yet Stanley scored on a Norm Cash sacrifice fly, Horton then tripled and came in to score on Jim Northrup's single. That sliced St. Louis's lead to 3–2 through four innings, but the Cardinals were still just five innings away from capturing the World Series for the second consecutive season and for the third time in the last five years.

In the top of the fifth inning, Brock was back at it, doubling off Lolich with one out. Just like that the Tigers' pitcher was back in hot water. "We'd just made it a ballgame, with the two runs in the bottom of the fourth, and here I was about to give 'em more in the next inning," Lolich remembered. "Let's just say it wasn't the game plan."

Out in left field, Horton told himself to be ready. Julian Javier was at the plate for St. Louis and Horton knew that Brock would try to score on any hit to the outfield. As if on cue, Javier singled sharply to Horton in left field. In a play that the Tigers' players and their fans would still picture clearly in their minds decades later, Horton fielded the ball about waist high. Without any hesitation he threw a bullet to home plate—just like his teammate Mickey Stanley had taught him.

In previous games, the Cardinals had noticed that Horton's arm was better than advertised. In fact, some were amused when Detroit Tigers manager Mayo Smith took him out for a late-inning replacement.

"He's not Carl Yastrzemski or Reggie Jackson," Tigers' coach Tony Cuccinello later said in Doug Feldman's *El Birdos: The 1967 and 1968 St. Louis Cardinals*, "but he's a little better than average. He fools a lot of people."

On that afternoon, Horton's throw to the plate was right on target, with plenty on it. At home plate, Freehan straddled the plate and didn't say a word. That was the signal to third baseman Don Wert to let the throw go through rather than cutting off Horton's effort. The Tigers would try for a play at the plate.

In a decision that Lou Brock would try to live down for years to come, the St. Louis speedster decided not to slide just as the ball arrived, on one hop, into Freehan's glove. Instead he stretched his left leg toward the plate, attempting to angle his foot between Freehan's legs. The Detroit catcher stood his ground, blocking the dish.

Several of the Cardinals were shocked that their top base runner didn't slide. In fact, years later, at banquets and public appearances Bob Gibson would sometimes introduce his good friend as the guy who forgot to slide in the biggest play of the 1968 World Series. Yet Horton, who had made the throw, maintained Brock had no choice but to go in standing up. "It's a good thing that he didn't slide," Horton said. "[Brock] would have broken his leg with Bill Freehan standing in there like he did. The only one I ever saw cover the plate like Bill, from back in our day, was Phil Roof from Kansas City."

"I was safe," Brock later insisted. "If I slide, he could come down on my knee and I wouldn't reach the plate. I tried to run through him."

Yet even Brock's own manager didn't buy that reasoning. "I don't know why Brock didn't slide," Schoendienst said.

In a bang-bang play, home-plate umpire Doug Harvey called Brock out. As the Cardinals' dugout roared in protest, Harvey gestured to Brock's spike marks in the dirt, seemingly inches in front of home plate.

"The umpire said Brock didn't touch the plate," Freehan said. "There is no way I could see whether he did or not, it all happened so fast. . . . [Harvey] said he probably would have been safe if he had slid."

On television, NBC replayed the collision at the plate. While largely inconclusive, the replays began debates in living rooms across the country. The score remained St. Louis 3, Detroit 2. Yet just like that the World Series became the main topic of conversation again in the sports world.

"I give the umpire credit," St. Louis sportswriter Bob Broeg said. "He didn't prejudge it. He didn't automatically assume (Brock) was safe."

In fact, Broeg would become so intrigued with the play that he made a special trip to the National Baseball Hall of Fame in Cooperstown, New

York, and watched tape of the play over and over again. "The film at Cooperstown bears it out," Broeg said. "It was the right call."

The play at the plate had been studied from as many angles as NBC's cameras allowed by the time Lolich stepped up to the plate in the bottom of the seventh inning. Even though the Tigers still trailed by a run, 3–2, Mayo Smith allowed his pitcher to swing away, perhaps thinking back to Lolich's unlikely homer back in Game Two. In any event, Lolich responded with a looping single to right field. "The writers have done such a good job of managing my ballclub, I decided to go against the consensus," Smith said afterward. "I should have called the press box and found out whether you boys thought I should have used a pinch hitter."

With Lolich aboard, the Cardinals brought in Joe Hoerner, their top reliever, to face Dick McAuliffe. The Tigers' gritty second baseman hung in against the tough left-hander, smacking a ground ball through the right side of the infield for a single. Mickey Stanley then followed with a walk to load the bases. As they had done all year, the Tigers began to mount a comeback in the late innings. The only difference was this time the entire season was on the line.

Fittingly, Al Kaline, who had waited sixteen seasons to appear in his first World Series, was next up. His single to right field drove in Lolich and McAuliffe, putting the Tigers ahead, 4–3. The next batter, Norm Cash, also singled to score Stanley, padding Detroit's lead to two runs.

Despite Willie Horton's epic throw to the plate back in the fifth inning, Smith still lifted him for a defensive replacement after the Tigers took the lead. "Some superstitions die hard, I guess," Horton said. "Mayo had won some games that way and maybe he got to believing it was the only way it could happen."

Once again Ray Oyler entered the game to play short, with Stanley returning to the outfield. Even though the Cardinals threatened in the eighth and ninth innings, Lolich hung in, going the distance with eight scoreless innings following the three-run first, striking out eight along the way.

After the game, Feliciano's rendition of the national anthem garnered almost as much attention as Brock's play at the plate.

"I picked him because he's one of the outstanding singers in America today," Ernie Harwell told the *Detroit Free Press*. "I had heard from people in music whose opinion I respect that he had an interesting version of the national anthem. I feel a fellow has a right to sing any way he can sing it."

For his part, Feliciano tried to explain his soulful, sometimes meandering performance. "I wanted to contribute something to this country, to express my gratification for what it has done for me," said Feliciano, who had flown in from Las Vegas. "I love this country. When anyone knocks it, I'm the first to defend it."

Amid the uproar, the Tigers focused on what they had accomplished during the game, itself. They had done what they set out to do, winning in front of their hometown fans and avoiding elimination. The Series was headed back to St. Louis for Game Six.

FINAL SCORE: TIGERS 5, CARDINALS 3
St. Louis leads the Series, 3–2

	1	2	3	4	5	6	7	8	9	R	H	E
St. Louis	3	0	0	0	0	0	0	0	0	3	9	0
Detroit	0	0	0	2	0	0	3	0	x	5	9	1

A few weeks before the World Series opened, *Hawaii Five-0* debuted on CBS, where it would become the longest-running crime show in television history until it was eventually surpassed by *Law & Order*. Veteran newsman Walter Cronkite had advocated for a longer news show and that same week CBS rolled out the initial broadcast of *60 Minutes*. It would air twice monthly before soon settling in as a weekly show that remains on the air today.

In the years ahead, such programming and advancements in technology (cable, satellite, large-screen TVs) would have a profound effect on how fans followed their teams and sports in general. But of course much had also changed over the course of the previous twenty-three years—since Detroit last won a World Series title—as well.

"What had made this wait so acute for Detroit's fans was that they had never watched their team win on TV," George Cantor wrote. "The revolution in communications since 1945 had skipped right over the Tigers. Watching the team you root for play on network TV, seen by the entire nation, seemed to validate your experience as a fan. Television brought an immediacy to sports unlike anything that had gone before. . . . The wait of twenty-three years seemed longer than it actually was because in that span every one of the other original teams, except the Cubs and A's, had taken their turn on the tube."

Perhaps that's what Al Kaline was trying to address when he said he wanted his Tigers to at least put on a good show. After all, so many more people were watching now. Still, the experts expected the Cardinals to ultimately win it all. After all, they had two cracks at it, with Bob Gibson ready to go again.

October 9, 1968

Game Six, Busch Stadium, St. Louis, Missouri

Denny McLain's shoulder felt markedly better on the eve of Game Six. Perhaps it was the day of rest, as the teams traveled back to St. Louis for the remainder of the Series. More than likely it was the assortment of painkillers he had taken. In Detroit, McLain had received another cortisone shot. The Tigers' doctors had convinced him to submit to it in hopes that Detroit could prolong the Series with Mickey Lolich on the mound. Lolich did his job and McLain now literally took another one for the team.

"What Denny has is an inflamed shoulder," said Dr. Harry Wright, the team's physician. "Up to now we've been manipulating the muscle, attempting to work the soreness out. But it wasn't enough anymore."

At the time, McLain told the press that the cortisone shot was his first of the season. Years later, though, he confirmed to historian William Mead that "late 1965 was the first time I had a cortisone shot, and it just multiplied from there. In 1968, I probably got a dozen."

In his memoir, McLain added that by the time he was playing in the World Series that season, "I had guys coming at me with needles from all directions.... By '68, there was never a time I pitched without some pain."

An hour before Game Six, McLain received another shot, this one of Xylocaine, in his aching shoulder. While the drug can prolong the cortisone's pain-killing power, one of Xylocaine's side effects is that it will temporarily deaden the immediate area where the injection is made. On past occasions with Xylocaine, McLain said his shoulder felt "like a dead weight the first thirty minutes before it springs back to life." This time, though, the shot hit "the right spot." As he prepared for Game Six he felt no lag time or much pain at all.

"I think I had a letdown myself after I won thirty and we won the pennant," McLain told reporters beforehand. "To tell you the truth, I don't think I've gotten up for the Series yet.... I think the only thing that has been damaged has been my pride. I think I have enough pride to overcome that."

Manager Mayo Smith again watched McLain warm up in the bullpen. This time around, the ball was down in the strike zone, with plenty of zip, and the manager confirmed what everybody expected: McLain would start on two days' rest over Earl Wilson, Pat Dobson, and Joe Sparma.

Following a more conventional national anthem presentation, sung by Miss Lydia Hunter of the Washington University music department, the Tigers' right-hander began to show the Cardinals' crowd why he was the American League's counterpart to St Louis's Bob Gibson. Why he was the game's first thirty-game winner since the Cardinals' Dizzy Dean in 1934. A pitcher who knew no bounds in 1968.

"The rules for Denny just don't seem to be the same as for the rest of us," catcher Bill Freehan wrote in his memoir. "Most of us have to be at the park at least two and a half hours before game time. Denny sometimes shows up five or ten minutes before a game. People used to say, before night games, that the best thing about baseball was that you couldn't beat the hours. In Denny's case, anyway, that's still true."

Gates Brown said he and teammates learned to steer clear of the various get-rich schemes McLain masterminded over the years. "Denny was one of those guys who could look you in the face and lie and lie some more," Brown said. "But he was such an outgoing, funny guy that you didn't mind the money flying out of your pocket ... Plus, the SOB knew how to win ballgames."

Through it all in 1968, the Tigers put runs on the scoreboard for McLain, and he usually responded with scoreless innings. Thus far in the Series things had been different, but in Game Six it was back to old times. In the second inning, Detroit scored two runs off Cardinals' starter Ray Washburn, who looked nothing like the pitcher who won Game Three or pitched the second of two no-hitters at Candlestick Park back in September. Despite averaging just two walks per nine innings during the '68 regular season Washburn walked Norm Cash in the second inning and Willie Horton got the Tigers off and running, stroking a double to the left-centerfield wall scoring him. Bill Freehan soon followed by breaking out of a five-game hitless string, his single bringing in Horton. After two innings Detroit held a 2–0 lead, with plenty more to come.

When Bob Gibson pitched, catcher Tim McCarver said the Cardinals had a tendency "to fall into a stupor." For his part, McCarver reminded himself not to "just become a fan.... [The] only thing that saved me was that he worked so fast and was so difficult to catch, he never gave me a chance to fall into an enraptured state."

In Game Six, of course, Gibson wasn't on the mound for St. Louis. Round Three of the Great Confrontation wasn't to be. Since the Tigers were on the ropes, they were starting McLain on short rest as their best hope of staying alive. Yet Gibson's presence hovered over proceedings like the Cheshire Cat. For the Cardinals knew that even if they lost, their ace, the man who had so thoroughly dominated the Tigers in Game One and Game Four, would once again be on the mound for them in Game Seven. McCarver told the press that the Tigers were a better ballclub than New York Yankees and Boston Red Sox—the teams the Cardinals had vanquished in 1964 and 1967. So why was St. Louis on the verge of its third championship in five years? "There are two good reasons," McCarver said, nodding at Brock and Gibson.

Years later, McCarver decided the safety net and assurance that Gibson provided perhaps didn't help the ballclub as much as everybody thought at the time. In his autobiography, Gibson wrote, "McCarver recently commented that, after thinking about the 1968 Series for twenty-five years, he has come to believe that the Cardinals may have been overconfident in the knowledge that no matter what happened in Games Five and Six, I would be on the mound for Game Seven. It's a dangerous thing to let another team gain momentum."

That's exactly what the Cardinals did in Game Six in St. Louis. But when does a manager play his ace? Per conventional thinking, Gibson was scheduled for Games One, Four, and Seven, if necessary. Nevertheless, hadn't Red Schoendienst been tempted to go to the hammer earlier, with the Cardinals back in St. Louis with a three games to two lead, needing just one more win to close the Series out? Certainly the manager's decision would have been criticized if Gibson lost an earlier-than-scheduled start that left the team facing a Game Seven without him. Looking back at it, some wondered if Gibson was better off with the usual rest. Perhaps the "rain game" had taken more out of him than it appeared to most, especially the Tigers' hitters. But as Smith's decision to pitch McLain on two-days' rest proved, the option was there. Schoendienst may very well have been just as confident that Washburn could close out the Series after his strong performance in Game Three, but still, one wonders—like McCarver—whether the assurance Gibson provided also resulted in a lack of urgency.

Conversely, there are examples of skippers who have gone all in at such times in the World Series. In 2003, Florida Marlins' Jack McKeon repeatedly said during the postseason that he was managing to win at all costs, and he lived up to his word. With the Marlins ahead three games to two over the favored New York Yankees, McKeon made the call to send his staff ace to the mound for Game Six, going with Josh Beckett on short rest. McKeon maintained a Game Seven offered too many intangibles. "You have an error, somebody gets hurt," he said. "We had the momentum at the time, why not go for it?"

In going all-in, McKeon certainly raised the stakes. Beckett, the twenty-three-year-old right-hander, had pitched seven and one-third innings in his previous World Series outing. He had gone only 9–8, with 3.04 ERA, during the regular season. Some warned that McKeon was jeopardizing the young star's future.

In the end, though, Beckett shut out the Yankees, 2–0, and became the youngest Series MVP since Livan Hernandez in 1997. More impressively, Beckett became the youngest pitcher since Bret Saberhagen in 1985 to win the deciding game. For his part, the young pitcher didn't see what the big deal was. "I think you condition yourself well enough to throw on [short] rest," Beckett said.

McKeon added, "Who are all the experts who say you can't pitch on three days' rest? You're not an expert until you're in my shoes. We had confidence in the game."

Thirty-five years earlier, the Cardinals certainly had confidence in their staff ace. Yet they held him in reserve, awaiting a possible Game Seven. For the Tigers, meanwhile, it meant for at least one more game they had a chance.

Before Game Six, Denny McLain told Jim Northrup that he needed eight runs to assure the elimination-game victory. That would have been a joke between most teammates, but if anybody could make good on such requests it was Northrup. In '68, the left-handed hitting outfielder remained an integral member of the Tigers' Michigan gang. He, Bill Freehan,

Mickey Stanley, and Willie Horton had been playing with and against each other since high school.

"We didn't have a lot of mystery guys on that '68 team," Horton said. "Most of us had known each other for ages. During that time frame, 75 percent of the guys had come up through spring training in Tiger Town, being in the minor leagues together. Guys in the dorms used to have pillow fights or sneaked out after curfew. That was just like college to us."

"Cheeseburger, fries, vanilla shake," Lolich added. "That's what Gates Brown always ordered. I know that because when we were together in the minor leagues, in the South, he wasn't allowed to go into the restaurants. We'd always stop after a road game, when we were on the bus, and I'd order for him."

Years later, many of the Tigers players still gathered for lunch in the Detroit area and Lolich would often order for Brown. "Cheeseburger, fries, vanilla shake," the pitcher said. "I can repeat that order in my sleep."

While Northrup's lunch order wasn't as predictable, his teammates soon learned that they could count on him for the timely long ball. With such teammates as Horton, Mickey Stanley, and Al Kaline, Northrup was sometimes overlooked on that '68 ballclub. Yet he led that squad in hits (153) and RBI (90). Amazingly, he picked up sixteen of those runs batted in with just four at-bats.

Back in late June, Northrup hit two grand slams in consecutive at-bats as Detroit defeated the Cleveland Indians, 14–3. Five days later, he blasted another bases-loaded homer, which paced McLain to his fourteenth victory of the season. The grand slam was Northrup's fourth in three weeks.

An avid fisherman, Northrup couldn't help thinking about the ones that had gotten away, though. In the first inning of the Cleveland game, he had taken a called third strike with the bases loaded. In the Chicago game, he swung at a ball in the dirt, again with the bases full. "So I had the opportunity to hit five grand slams in a week," Northrup said, "and I didn't do too well on a couple of 'em."

A notorious streak hitter, Northrup hadn't done much at the plate heading into Game Six of the World Series. Smith's radical shift of Stanley to shortstop not only put Kaline in the everyday lineup, it also allowed him to keep Horton and Northrup in the starting outfield. Through five games of the Fall Classic, however, it seemed to be much ado about nothing. While Kaline had done his part at bat and in the field, Northrup had struggled. He entered Game Six having gone only three of nineteen, with a two RBI. Striking out in his first at-bat in the second inning, it looked unlikely he was going to turn things around.

With Detroit holding an early 2–0 lead, the Tigers' Dick McAuliffe drew a walk off Washburn to open the top of the third. Stanley followed with a single and Kaline brought McAuliffe around with another single. That marked a disappointing early end to Washburn's day as he was replaced by Larry Jaster. The left-hander had posted a 9–13 record in 1968, with a respectable 3.51 ERA. Still, Jaster was a journeyman—somebody to bolster the back end of a bullpen. He would retire in 1972 with a 35–33 career record. Certainly it was early in the game, but with St. Louis down only 3–0 at the time, Cardinals' manager Red Schoendienst had other choices. They included Steve Carlton, rookie Wayne Granger (4–2 in '68) and Dick Hughes, who had won sixteen games the year before and made two starts in the 1967 World Series. They would all pitch in Game Six, but not before the contest got out of hand.

Cash greeted Jaster by driving in the Tigers' second run of the inning. Then Horton worked a walk to load the bases. That brought up Northrup. Even though Jaster hadn't gotten a batter out to this point, the Cardinals decided to leave him in the game to play the percentages. Jaster was a left-handed pitcher and Northrup a left-handed batter. In such situations, the pitcher is considered to have the advantage. Of course, what that doesn't take into account is a batter's propensity for hitting grand slams.

"He was the emotional backbone of our team that year," McLain said decades later of Northrup. "He'd get mad at you if he even saw you exchanging pleasantries with guys from the other team. Jimmy was a big reason why we were just a grind-it-out team."

The Tigers' slugger drove Jaster's low fastball deep to right field, where it touched down well back in the grandstand. Just like that Northrup had given McLain the eight runs the pitcher had requested. "Home run was going through my mind while waiting in the on-deck circle," Northrup admitted.

With the clout, the Tigers had scored six times in the inning with none out. Ron Willis relieved Jaster, but he only managed to throw gas on the fire, walking Freehan and hitting Don Wert, who was playing third base that day. McLain moved both runners up ninety feet with a sacrifice bunt. Next was McAuliffe, making his second appearance at the plate that inning. With only one out, Detroit had already batted around.

The Tigers' lead-off hitter was intentionally walked, once again loading the bases. Stanley's grounder forced Freehan at the plate for the second out of the inning. At last, St. Louis could see the light at the end of the tunnel. Yet it quickly proved to be a runaway train as Kaline's single, his second hit of the inning, brought in two more runs.

With that Dick Hughes came on as the Cardinals' third pitcher of the inning. Cash and Horton both greeted him with hits, scoring two more. Finally, Northrup, of all people, made the final out when Lou Brock ran down his long fly at the wall.

In total, fifteen Tigers came to the plate in the third inning—an exhibition that left Schoendienst wondering if it would ever end. The ten runs they produced matched the single-inning scoring record set by the Philadelphia Athletics in Game Four of the 1929 World Series against the Chicago Cubs.

"[McLain] proved to be a much better pitcher with a lead to work with," Gibson remembered, "especially one the size that the Tigers built for him."

With the Tigers on cruise control, Mickey Lolich began to lobby Smith in the Detroit dugout. If McLain could start, and more importantly win, on short rest, then Lolich felt he could do the same. Once again, Lolich was determined to keep up with his teammate and frequent nemesis. On paper, McLain and Lolich remain a baseball combination for the ages—an awesome one-two pitching punch. But off the field, in the Tigers' clubhouse, their relationship was based more on envy and competitive jealousy than any friendship or team loyalty.

"I didn't hate [Denny], no," Lolich told George Cantor years later. "It didn't bother me that he had become the number-one pitcher. I never admitted to myself that I was number two. But I didn't like how he made his own rules and got away with it. I came up with the Detroit organization, and you were taught that there was a certain way that you conducted yourself. It was fairly well regimented. I didn't mind that, and neither did the other guys—just as long as the rules applied to everyone.

"Denny never wanted to go along with the program. He always seemed to be challenging management, flaunting it, seeing what he could get away with.

"I think Mayo took out a lot of his frustration on me in 1968. He didn't dare touch Denny, not with the kind of season he was having. So I became the whipping boy."

McLain doesn't buy that characterization.

"Lolich was so miserable in the middle of the '68 season because I was going so well and he was pitching so badly," the Tigers' ace later wrote. "There's nothing worse than somebody wallowing in his own misery, and Mickey was a miserable guy."

Early on, McLain recognized that the rules, especially in sports, are rarely applied equally. In Boston, Celtics' coach Red Auerbach drove a journeyman player like Larry Siegfried harder than his captain Bill Russell. Heading to Mexico City, the U.S. Olympic team made allowances to assure that star miler Jim Ryun was on the roster. Arguably, corners had even been cut for Lolich back in 1962, when the Tigers allowed him to play the year in his hometown of Portland. Still, when does one player's celebrity become too much for a team to bear? One could argue that the Tigers were fast approaching that point. When the 1968 World Series concluded, Lolich positioned himself to become a nightclub performer, too, while McLain had already booked fifty gigs across the country, including a two-week engagement at the Riviera in Las Vegas. Matters would finally boil over between the two pitchers at the next year's All-Star Game in Washington. McLain invited Lolich to fly with him in his private plane, but neglected to tell him it would be a one-way ticket. He left his teammate there in D.C. to find his own way back to Detroit.

"There wasn't a lot of love lost between Denny and Mickey," rookie Jon Warden said. "Anybody on the ballclub could see that. Keeping up with Denny really drove Mickey. As for Denny? He could have cared less what Mickey Lolich or what anybody thought of him. That's just the way the two of them were."

During the regular season, in the run-up to McLain's thirty victories, *Life* magazine sent a writer to travel with the Tigers. When McLain lost the 2–1 heartbreaker to New York, *Life* quoted an unnamed teammate saying, "It's good he lost. He was starting to act like he already won 30."

McLain was incensed when he found out "the overwhelmingly jealous Mickey Lolich" had been the source of those quotes.

"I was the last guy he wanted to see win thirty games," McLain recalled, "and Lolich's toughest time was in '68."

On this afternoon in St. Louis, however, McLain's redemptive performance set the stage for Game Seven. He rolled along, en route to striking out seven and walking none, and as it became more and more obvious that the Series was headed to a one-game showdown, Lolich couldn't help thinking that at long last he was going to have his chance in the spotlight, on baseball's biggest stage. Perhaps the only thing that could have bothered him was that he had Denny McLain to thank for it.

With two out in the ninth inning, McLain gave up his first and only run of this game. In didn't matter as Detroit won 13–1, forcing a Game Seven in the World Series.

"We battled back—this has been the trademark of our team," Al Kaline said afterward. "The big thing is we won the way we'd been winning before. Games you can't lose. Now we've won these games and the Cards have a game they can't lose."

A few locker stalls over from Kaline, McLain insisted his performance had nothing to do with saving face or redemption. As always he had an eye on what was on the horizon. "I didn't have to prove a goddamn thing today," he told Jerry Green. "I want to thank the players. I wish I could take each of them into salary negotiations with me. Like Northrup. He's hit five grand slams this year, and four of them were while I was pitching."

When asked about being booed by the St. Louis crowd, fans known for their courtesy and civility, McLain smiled and proved that redemption was perhaps on his mind, after all, "I've been booed before and I've been booed by better fans than these. I've been booed by the best fans in the world in Detroit."

In his post-game press conference, Tigers' manager Mayo Smith said, "We were down three to one and we're happy to be going against Mr. Gibson."

Then he officially announced what everyone expected: Mickey Lolich would start Game Seven for Detroit. The left-hander, like McLain, would be pitching on short rest. Little brother was going have his chance to be the hero. All he had to do was figure out a way to do what McLain and the rest of the Tigers couldn't—find a way to beat Bob Gibson.

FINAL SCORE: TIGERS 13, CARDINALS 1

Series is tied at three games apiece.

	1	2	3	4	5	6	7	8	9	R	H	E
Detroit	0	2	(10)	0	1	0	0	0	0	13	12	1
St. Louis	0	0	0	0	0	0	0	0	1	1	9	1

October 10, 1968

Game Seven, Busch Stadium, St. Louis, Missouri

Before Game Seven, several of the Tigers players hung a SOCK IT TO 'EM sign in the visiting clubhouse. The saying was a popular refrain from

Rowan & Martin's Laugh-In, one of the most popular shows on television, along with *Gomer Pyle, Bonanza,* and *Mayberry R.F.D.* Part rallying cry, part inside joke, SOCK IT TO 'EM summed up the Tigers' dilemma in going against Bob Gibson again—this time in a winner-take-all.

As scribes eyed the sign, McLain told them that he would join Pat Dobson, John Hiller, Joe Sparma, and Jon Warden in the Detroit bullpen, where he would be "trying to put together a comedy act."

Manager Mayo Smith explained that he was "not a good psychologist, so he wasn't sure if his pregame conferences with Norm Cash, Bill Freehan, Dick McAuliffe, and Willie Horton did much good." As for Gibson, Mayo added that the Cardinals' ace "is not Superman. He's beatable." But his heart didn't appear to be in such an assessment as he soon added, "But even if we don't win, we've had a hell of a year."

The capacity crowd in St. Louis gave Gibson a standing ovation after he finished warming up. As was his habit, the Cardinals' ace stared straight ahead, barely acknowledging the overwhelming show of support. "It was down to me and Lolich in Game Seven," Gibson wrote in his memoir. "I thrived on this sort of situation—to me, it was the whole reason for being an athlete—and there was no sense of panic on the club even after the disasters of Game Five and Six."

Over in the Tigers' bullpen, as Lolich prepared to take the mound, things were far less certain, even bordering upon the chaotic.

"Nobody was sure how far Mickey would go in the game—two, three innings? Nobody really knew," Jon Warden said. "So everybody was up, doing a little bit to get loose. It was all hands on deck and nobody was sure when they could be going in."

But as teammates stole glimpses at Lolich, they saw that he was throwing loose and easy. More importantly, his ball exhibited great pace and movement. "I felt fine," Lolich said. "I wasn't issuing any guarantees on how many innings I could go. Nothing like that. I was just going to pitch until I wasn't effective. No more, no less. That kind of freed me up in a way."

While McLain's arm had received a shot before his recent victory, Lolich benefited from deep massage. Earlier, back at the team hotel, Dr. Russell Wright rigged up a shock-wave machine for Lolich's tired left arm. "It was one of those crazy looking machines that look like something out of a *Frankenstein* movie," the pitcher explained. "It increased the circulation in my arm and left me relaxed."

With that and a few sleeping tablets, Lolich got a nap and woke ready to pitch. It was time for him to face his own Great Confrontation.

As expected, Bob Gibson came out strong and once again dominated, breaking Sandy Koufax's single-series World Series record for strikeouts in the second inning. Through six innings, Gibson had sat down twenty of the twenty-one Detroit hitters he had faced. "I firmly believed that if I could hold the Tigers in check awhile, we would get to Lolich by the sixth or seven (inning)," he recalled. "Things were going pretty much as planned, but it was high time to do something about Lolich."

Though not quite as impressive, Lolich somehow matched the Cardinals' ace, zero for zero, on the scoreboard. Through five innings, he had allowed only two singles.

"Frankly, I don't know how I got to that point in the game," Lolich said. "I wasn't feeling that good really. Every time I got back to the dugout, I told them to make sure to have people warmed up and good and ready. I didn't know how long I'd last."

In the bottom of the sixth inning, Lou Brock singled to left field and everybody in the ballpark knew what was coming next. Brock would try to pick up his eighth steal of the Series. Tigers' catcher Bill Freehan went out to the mound to talk to Lolich, resulting in perhaps one of the most curious conversations in Fall Classic history.

"You all right?" Freehan asked his pitcher. "Anything I can do for you?"

"Yeah," Lolich replied. "Can you get me a couple of hamburgers between innings?"

"What's the matter?" Freehan said.

"Can't get myself together," Lolich explained. "I don't know what I'm doing wrong."

Usually Freehan didn't coach his pitchers, especially in the middle of a contest as intense as Game Seven. He left that up to legendary pitching coach Johnny Sain. But with no burgers on hand, and the whole world watching, Freehan decided to throw in his two cents' worth. The Tigers catcher suggested that Lolich was trying to throw too hard. He told him to keep his front shoulder in, instead of rearing back too much. "Just try to throw strikes," Freehan said, "and you'll still get good velocity from there."

Through it all, Brock remained patiently, for the moment, at first base. Often when he would take off for second base he would beat the relay throw from the first baseman. The key to stopping him was to have Brock make the first move, to briefly hold him in his tracks, which didn't allow him to reach full speed in a hurry.

With the conference over, Brock edged off first, taking a fifteen-foot lead, ready to break for second. Lolich kept an eye on him, refusing to deliver the ball to the plate. It was a showdown, reminiscent of the old-style Westerns that were so popular on television. Who would draw first? That's when Lolich suddenly snapped a throw over to Detroit first baseman Norm Cash. And Brock took off for second base. At the time, many in baseball felt he was the fastest man on the base paths. Still, there are times to run and times to stay put.

"I really don't understand why he did it," Cash said. "That was too much of a risk with the score tied in a game like this."

Cash got the ball out of his glove as fast as he could, throwing on to Mickey Stanley, who had shifted over to cover second base. In a split-second play, Stanley slapped down the tag and Brock was out, caught stealing. For one of the few times in the Series, the Tigers had stopped the Cardinals' speed game.

Yet that single putout didn't mean Lolich was out of the woods. But it helped when the Cardinals' next batter, Julian Javier, lined out to Stanley.

If Brock had safely reached second base on the play before, the infield would have been drawn in and the drive would likely have been a hit, probably scoring Brock. Thanks to the pick-off, the game remained scoreless.

Afterward, Curt Flood beat out an infield hit and the St. Louis running game was back in business. Even though he was often lost in Brock's shadow, Flood also certainly had the wheels to steal a base. Like Brock before him, Flood took a long lead, waiting for Lolich to throw home. But once again the Tiger's left-hander won the waiting game. After another beat or two, he threw over to Cash, a perfect pick-off move, and Flood was caught in no man's land. In between bases, Flood tried to race on to second, only to be tagged out. Amazingly, Lolich had gotten out of the inning by picking off the Cardinals' top two threats on the base paths.

The game remained scoreless with Gibson realizing he now "had to navigate one more time through the fat part of Detroit's lineup."

Mickey Stanley led off for Detroit in the top of the seventh inning and Gibson promptly struck him out. For a moment, it appeared it would be another easy inning for the St. Louis ace as Al Kaline then grounded out to Cardinals' Mike Shannon for the second out. Still, often the most memorable moments begin with small, almost innocent events. So it was in the seventh.

Concerned that Norm Cash could hit one out of the ballpark, breaking up the scoreless tie, Gibson kept the ball low in the strike zone, and Cash got enough of the bat on the ball to bounce one over Javier's head and into right field. Willie Horton followed him by grounding a single through the left side of the Cardinals' infield.

"Gates [Brown] had been in my ear about Gibson," recalled Horton, who was 0-for-7 against Gibson in the Series coming into the game and zero for two in this contest. "He was telling to me to get that ball in play, just put it out there and see what happens. We had to do better against Gibson than just going up there and striking out all the time."

Years later, those two pedestrian singles would grate on Mike Shannon, the Cardinals' third baseman that afternoon. Cash's hit was a bad hop past Javier, while Shannon believes he could have corralled Horton's single if he hadn't been guarding the third-base line so closely. In any event, the Tigers had two men on, two out, with Jim Northrup stepping up to the plate. He was the last guy Gibson wanted to see in this situation. Later, Gibson said that Northrup "had given me more trouble than any other Tiger."

With two men on, Gibson couldn't afford to walk a batter. He needed to get ahead in the count, move the odds in his favor. Unfortunately, for the Cardinals and their hopes for a repeat championship, Northrup was thinking the same thing.

Gibson threw a fastball, looking for strike one. Northrup was ready for it and laced a solid line drive to center field. When Gibson turned to follow the flight of the ball, his first thought was that Curt Flood, his good friend and roommate, would track this one down as he had done so many times before. But Flood initially broke in a few steps before reversing direction in an attempt to catch up with Northrup's hard liner. Later, Flood said that he initially lost sight of the ball in the background of white shirts in the stands behind home plate.

To this day, Flood's teammates defend his play on the ball.

McCarver said the wet field caused the centerfielder to slip. "On a dry field, he gobbles that ball up," he said.

Shannon added that Flood "didn't misjudge" the line drive. "His first step was in," Shannon said. "That's what you're supposed to do. When the ball's hit over your head, you've got to come in a little to push off and go back. He slipped."

The condition of the outfield certainly didn't help Flood at this pivotal moment. Four afternoons before, the hometown football Cardinals had hosted the Dallas Cowboys at Busch. "Most of the football games were played in the outfield area," grounds superintendent Barney Rogers said. "They didn't dig up around the pitcher's mound or home plate too much."

To the Cardinals' surprise, Northrup's liner soared past the Cardinals' center fielder and bounced against the wall for a triple. Cash and Horton came around to score. Two runs that at that point seemed to Gibson "like two thousand." Reeling from the blow, Gibson gave up a double to Bill Freehan. When the inning ended, the defending champions trailed Lolich and the Tigers, 3–0.

Back in the Cardinals' dugout, Flood apologized to Gibson.

"I'm sorry," he said. "It was my fault."

"Like hell," Gibson told him. "It was nobody's fault."

Years later, Gibson added, "What is often forgotten about that play is the fact that Northrup hit the damn ball four hundred feet."

For his part, Northrup absolutely agreed. "I hit the crap out of it," he said years later. "Everybody wants to talk about Flood and how he should have played it. But I know I hit that fastball of Gibson's a ton."

Whether the play would be remembered as a miscue or a solid shot depended on whom you were rooting for. The fact was the Cardinals now trailed by three runs with only three innings left. And despite pitching on short rest, Lolich didn't show any signs of letting St. Louis off the hook.

The great Cardinals' teams of the 1960s were built upon pitching, defense, and speed. What they lacked was an abundance of power. Now trailing 3–0 to Detroit, the St. Louis offense desperately sought any break it could get. With one out in the bottom of the seventh, Northrup did his best to accommodate them when he booted a ball, putting Shannon on first base. The Cardinals were unable to take advantage, however, as Tim McCarver flied out and then Roger Maris popped out to shortstop.

After Gibson made quick work of the Tigers in the top of the eighth, he expected that his day would be over. Manager Red Schoendienst would look to his bench to generate some kind of attack. Indeed, Phil Gagliano pinch-hit for shortstop Dal Maxvill (who to that point in the Series had gone 0–22 and whose overall World Series batting record is a record low for a position player) to start the inning. In the on-deck circle, Gibson watched Gagliano ground out. At this point, the Cardinals' ace expected to be called back to the dugout, with Dick Schofield or Bobby Tolan taking his turn at the plate. Yet in a surprise move, perhaps an indication of how well Lolich was pitching on this day, but also surely a nod to how effective Gibson had been in the Cardinals' epic championship run, Schoendienst gestured for the pitcher to bat. Gibson went down swinging, taking a big cut on a Lolich fastball.

"I remain grateful to Schoendienst for sticking with me," Gibson wrote. "The obvious thing would have been to pinch-hit for me in the eighth inning, and Red's decision to leave me in the game had more to do with consideration than strategy, which is a rare thing in baseball."

Lou Brock followed with a walk but was left stranded when Julian Javier grounded out. With one inning left in Game Seven, the visiting Tigers led, 3–0.

Although Lolich didn't really need the support, the Tigers gave him another run in the top of the ninth inning. Willie Horton, Jim Northrup, and Don Wert each singled off Gibson to make it 4–0. One last time Detroit manager Mayo Smith went with his late-inning alignment, what St. Louis writers now sarcastically called his Maginot Line. Horton exited the game, Stanley moved to center field, and Ray Oyler once again manned shortstop. Even though the bullpen was loose and ready, Lolich took the mound for the bottom of the ninth, determined to end it.

"I didn't know how long I could go," Lolich said. "After the fifth inning, Mayo looked at me every inning and I would tell him I was OK. Then, when [they] got me some runs in the seventh, I told Mayo I would finish it."

When Oyler snared Curt Flood's liner for the first out (making Smith look like a genius) and Orlando Cepeda popped out in foul territory, it appeared the Cardinals would go gently into the night. But suddenly Shannon woke the hometown crowd and sent the Tigers' bullpen scrambling again when he homered into the left-field stands. The dinger assured that Shannon homered in the three World Series he played in (1964,

1967, and 1968). "The team's frustration from the past few days was manifested in one swing," wrote Doug Feldmann in *El Birdos*. "Since the first inning of Game Five, St. Louis had been shut out by the Tigers in twenty-four of the last twenty-six innings."

With that kind of history working against them, any rally for the ages simply wasn't to be. When Lolich got the next batter, McCarver, to pop out to Freehan, Game Seven was over. The contest had taken two hours, seven minutes to play, and when the ball dropped into Freehan's mitt, the Detroit Tigers were the 1968 World Series champions.

Lolich came off the mound and jumped into Freehan's arms. (He later said he did so to assure that Freehan didn't jump into his arms. "I couldn't have taken that," the pitcher said.) With his three complete game victories, Lolich was named the series MVP, and he received a new Dodge Charger for his efforts. "I hope it has a stick shift," he said. (It did.)

In the winning clubhouse, the Tigers were asked about Lolich's remarkable turnaround. In midseason, he had been banished to the bullpen, with a 7–7 record. He battled back to go 17–9 and became only the twelfth pitcher in major league history to win three games in the World Series. Cash claimed that the weeks working in relief helped Lolich. As a result, he threw only 220 innings in '68, compared to Gibson's nearly 305 innings and McLain's 336 for the same campaign.

"I guess I'm an unlikely hero," Lolich told the press. "Potbelly, big ears . . . just a steady guy who shows up every day and gets the job done as best he knows how."

Then in a dig at McLain and a nod to the crowds that were already forming at Detroit Metro Airport to welcome back their heroes, he added, "There's always somebody else making a big deal out of things, getting the ink, making the moves. But you know what? I knew all along I could do it. And I'm so thrilled that all those people are down there waiting for us. It's the biggest day of my life. . . .

"Mickey Lolich has never been a hero with the Tigers. Mickey Lolich has always been a number on a roster. Finally, somebody knows who I am."

While most of the Tigers agreed with their manager that Horton throwing out Brock at the plate in Game Five was the point when the Series turned, Cash felt the most decisive moment really occurred before a pitch was ever thrown. He maintained Smith moving Mickey Stanley to shortstop and putting Al Kaline in the everyday lineup was the key to everything. "Without (Stanley) playing shortstop," Cash said, "Al wouldn't have been in the Series."

And what a Fall Classic the sixteen-year veteran enjoyed. Kaline hit .379, with two home runs and eight runs batted in, and stood out defensively. In the victorious clubhouse, he cradled his own bottle of champagne to his chest. "I'd seen my other World Series in the country club, watching TV," Kaline said. "I considered people lucky to be in the Series. I knew all along I'd get into the Series someday, maybe as a pinch hitter. I never expected to have this good a Series. I was one of the lucky ones."

Even in victory, though, many of the Tigers reflected on the team and the pitcher they had just beaten.

"Gibson is the greatest pitcher I've ever faced," Kaline said at the time. It was an assessment he would repeat frequently in the years to come. "To beat him and win the World Series all in one game is really great. We just wanted to get into the seventh game real bad—for our pride after the way we played the first two games in Detroit."

In the home clubhouse, discussion centered on Flood's misplay of Northrup's line drive in the seventh inning, the triple to the wall that broke the game open. While Gibson told reporters that he thought his friend would catch the ball, he emphasized that he didn't think Flood should have caught the ball. "If Curt Flood can't catch that ball, nobody can," Gibson added. "I'm certainly not going to stand here and blame the best center fielder in the business. Why couldn't we score any runs off that left-hander? That's the reason we lost."

Waves of reporters stopped by Flood's locker, many of them asking the same questions.

When asked if he had lost the ball in the crowd, where so many were wearing white shirts, Flood simply replied, "Yes."

When asked if the field was sub-par, causing him to slip, the record-holder of 226 consecutive errorless games in the National League replied, "Yes."

When asked if he thought he could have made the play on a dry field, Flood said, "I think so. Look I don't want to make alibis. I should have made the play . . . but I didn't and that's all there is to it."

He added, "A ball hit right at me is the toughest play for me in this park. If the ball was up higher—over the edge of grandstand, I might have seen it in time."

Back in Detroit, the celebration began precisely at 4:06 p.m., moments after Freehan caught Tim McCarver's foul popup. Once again the populace crowded the Motor City's streets downtown and near Tiger Stadium, but this time nothing went up in smoke. "It was a great exuberant crowd," Detroit police commissioner told the *Sporting News*. "There were some opportunists, but no real looters."

People waded into the Kennedy Square pool downtown, several holding aloft beer bottles. Telephone books and IBM cards were shredded into confetti and thrown out the windows of the city's tallest buildings. The ticker tape rained down on the revelers below and many fans gathered up the celebratory fodder and tossed it again up into the air. While Detroit mayor Jerome Cavanaugh ordered fire and civil defense to be on alert, they weren't needed as more than 150,000 peacefully crowded the downtown sector. West of town, 35,000 fans swarmed the landing field at Detroit's Metropolitan Airport—so many of them in fact that the Tigers' charter from St. Louis couldn't land there. Thirteen departing flights and thirty-five other arrivals were delayed, and the ballclub's flight was diverted to nearby Willow Run Airport, where an estimated 1,500 more fans cheered the team's arrival.

"I was going home," Tigers reserve infielder Dick Tracewski said after the charter landed. "But I'm glad the baggage wasn't going to be taken to Tiger Stadium until tomorrow because I wouldn't miss this for the world."

A week or so after the Fall Classic concluded an old lady approached Gibson at the airport in St. Louis. The pitcher assumed she was going to ask for an autograph, perhaps congratulate him on another fine season, even his World Series record. Instead she stunned him by asking if he still spoke to Curt Flood.

"Lady, how can you ask that?" he replied.

In Detroit, senior baseball writer Joe Falls perhaps best summed up what the championship meant to his audience: "My town, as you know, had the worst riot in our nation's history in the summer of 1967, and it left scars which may never fully heal," he wrote. "And so, as 1968 dawned and we all started thinking ahead to the hot summer nights in Detroit, the mood of our city was taut. It was apprehensive. . . . But then something started happening in the middle of 1968. You could pull up to a light at the corner of Clairmount and 12th, which was the hub of last year's riot, and the guy in the next car would have his radio turned up: ' . . . McLain looks in for the sign, he's set—here's the pitch'. . . . It was a year when an entire community, an entire city, was caught up in a wild, wonderful frenzy."

FINAL SCORE: TIGERS 4, CARDINALS 1

Detroit wins the '68 World Series, four games to three.

Detroit	0	0	0	0	0	0	3	0	1	4	8	1
St. Louis	0	0	0	0	0	0	0	0	1	1	5	0

PART
VII

"Never the Same Again"

Official histories, news stories surround us daily, but the events of art reach us too late, travel languorously like messages in a bottle. Only the best art can order the chaotic tumble of events. Only the best can realign chaos to suggest both the chaos and order it will become.

—MICHAEL ONDAATJE

Unable to pitch winterball, ordered to stay home and rest his arm for next season by the Cleveland Indians, Luis Tiant did watch television, first the World Series and then the Olympics. He saw Mickey Lolich jump into Bill Freehan's arms after the final out in Game Seven, daydreaming of what it would be like to play in the World Series one day.

On October 14, 1968, Tiant's daughter, Isabel, turned one year old. The family planned a party for that evening at their home in Mexico City, and Tiant spent the afternoon watching the men's one-hundred meter Olympic trials with a friend. In a few days, U.S. sprinters Tommie Smith and John Carlos would raise black-gloved fists to the heavens, a demonstration that the *New York Times*'s columnist Robert Lipsyte would call "the mildest, most civil demonstration of the year," and one that would reverberate throughout sports for years to come.

Soon, however, Tiant's TV viewing was interrupted by his sister-in-law lugging a battered suitcase into the family living room.

"Hey," she asked, "do you remember this?"

Tiant glanced at the old valise and shook his head.

"You sure?" Tiant's sister-in-law Concepcion said.

Irritated by the interruption, Tiant got out of his chair and went over to better inspect the suitcase. That's when he saw his mother standing in the front hallway. After seven years apart, Senora Tiant had finally been allowed by the Castro government to leave Cuba and visit her only child.

Tiant took his mother in his arms—tears running down his cheeks. "Why are you crying?" she chided him. "I'm the one who should cry."

Years later Tiant said, "Everyone remembers different things from that year, '68. In the end, that's the time I'll never forget."

Only a few miles away from that joyful reunion, Jim Ryun prepared to run the most difficult race of his life. Just about everyone recognized Ryun once he reached Mexico City. After all, he was the favorite in the 1,500 meters. But the American miler had run only one real race at altitude—the final Olympic trial at Lake Tahoe, California—before arriving at the Games. He had worked hard in training, but would it be enough?

Such doubts only grew after Australian Ron Clarke's collapse in the 10,000 meters. A bronze medalist in the same event in 1964, Clarke set seventeen world records during his storied career. Yet in the thin air of Mexico City, he never had a chance.

Six runners in the 10,000 meters' thirty-six field dropped out that day, one after only two laps. Three others fell unconscious as the race soon whittled itself down to a small group, most of them from higher elevations, including Naftali Temu from Kenya and Mamo Wolde of Ethiopia. Clarke did his best to hang with the leaders. But the math didn't add up.

As Richard Hoffer later explained in *Something in the Air: American Passion and Defiance in the 1968 Mexico City Olympics,* high altitude can destroy the best of athletes. "Runners at shorter distances burn up ready glycogen and can repay the debt later at their leisure," he wrote. "Long-distance racers must use oxygen from the air they're breathing during the race to break down sugar, financing the debt as they go."

Clarke became the first favorite who couldn't pay the debt that Mexico City's altitude required. Even though the winning time in the 10,000 meters was 29:27.4, the slowest time for a winner in the event since 1948, the Aussie veteran keeled over at the line, finishing a distant sixth. Afterward he underwent electrocardiograms and eventually it was determined that his heart suffered permanent damage in the race. For the rest of his life, he took daily medication for a heart murmur.

"I did not win the Olympic gold medal," Clarke told *Sports Illustrated* in 1973, "and that has given rise to the idiotic idea that I was not good in real competition. My only contention, and I'm leaning over backward to be fair, is that because of the altitude at Mexico City I had no chance against the Africans, and therefore the critics' point that I was incapable of winning remains unproved. Personally, I have no doubt at all that I was the best 10,000-meter runner in the world in 1968. At sea level, I would have won easily."

For the record, Kenya's Temu won the 10,000-meter gold, with his countryman Kip Keino in contention until he suffered stomach cramps. Temu's gold was the first ever for Kenya, which seems remarkable considering the running legacy the nation now enjoys. "This feels like Africa," Temu said of the conditions in Mexico City. "We will be at home here."

Meanwhile, that meant trouble for Ryun, who was scheduled to go against Keino and the Kenyans in track's showcase event, the men's 1,500 meters. He was entering the contest as a favorite, but so had Clarke heading into the 10,000 meters.

The night before the 1,500 meters, Kenyan officials told Ben Jipcho to go out hard from the opening gun. Keino, who had taken a bronze medal in the 5,000 meters, would trail him and later charge to the finish. The fast pace from the outset, they proposed, would take care of Ryun. The Kenyans' plan almost didn't have a chance to work, however, as their team bus got waylaid in traffic leading to the Olympic stadium. Both Keino and Jipcho were forced to jog nearly three miles and barely made the event. ("They had to warm up before the race anyway," said a team official.) Yet when the gun went off, Jipcho moved out in a fast 56-second first lap, hoping to lure Ryun to come with him.

"So what do you do when you have never gone faster than a 61-second opening pace per 400 and your competition goes out in 56?" asked Dr. Jack Daniels, the U.S. team's expert about altitude training. "Do you go with them not knowing if everyone will die together or let him go hoping he will come back?"

Ryun correctly determined that Keino, not Jipcho, was the guy to beat. So he hung back. It also crossed Ryun's mind that "I've never tried this at altitude and I better be careful so I don't completely die."

In the second lap, Keino began to pull away from Ryun and the American was forced to let him go. By the third lap, the field had split into two groups. Keino led the first pack, with Ryun leading the other. By that point, any chance of gold had disappeared for Ryun.

By the bell lap the American was forty meters behind the Kenyan as he gamely continued to fight his way from tenth place up to second. In the end, though, he finished a long ways behind Keino. The race can still be found on YouTube and by the final stretch the Kenyan champion is the only runner in the frame. "That much ground was simply impossible to recover," Richard Hoffer wrote, "and the greatest miler of his day finished in second, a full twenty meters behind Keino. It was the largest margin of victory, or rather defeat, ever."

While Keino and Jipcho took a victory lap, a fatigued Ryun told a bystander, "God, it hurts." Afterward Jipcho apologized to the American for the team tactics by the Kenyans. Ryun told him it was the Olympics and not to feel guilty about anything. Even though Ryun's silver-medal finish was vilified back home, U.S. distance runners and coaches came away with valuable lessons about how to compete at altitude. Despite the conditions, all three U.S. entrants in the 1,500 meters—Ryun, Tom Von Ruden, and Marty Liquori—reached the final.

In the end, Roone Arledge's gamble paid off. Thanks to Ryun's heroic race, Bob Beamon's stunning record leap in the long jump, Tommie Smith's and John Carlos's fist-raised protest atop the podium after the two-hundred meters, the Olympics became must-see television and remain so to this day.

Closer to home, following the Tigers' World Series victory, Denny McLain and Bob Gibson were each named both the Cy Young winners and Most Valuable Players for their respective leagues. New York Yankees pitcher Stan Bahnsen was selected as the top rookie in the American League, with Cincinnati Reds catcher Johnny Bench edging out New York Mets pitcher Jerry Koosman for the honor in the National League.

Tigers manager Mayo Smith was named manager of the year, with Detroit general manager Jim Campbell selected as baseball's top executive.

The fourth game of the World Series, the one played in a downpour in Detroit, became the highest-rated sports event in television history at the time. The Nielsen Television Index indicated that more than 78.5 million people tuned in that afternoon. World Series games continued to outpace other sporting events, including Super Bowl II and the NFL championship, holding an overall seven-to-three edge in the TV's top ten. "From the rankings, it is easy to conclude that the World Series is still America's No. 1 sports event," baseball commissioner William Eckert said in a statement.

Just a Hail Mary pass off Interstate 295 in southern New Jersey, stands a two-story, space-age-style office building that serves as the home of NFL

Films. Even though baseball was atop the sports heap as the '68 World Series began, the soothsayers in the sports industry recognized that a sea change was coming. That's why I'm here, in the far corner of the NFL Films library, hard by the stacks that bolster every *Sports Illustrated* ever printed, staring at a Trinitron television rigged up to a DVC Pro Slow Motion tape machine. The idea is if we can conjure up time, slow it down frame by frame, perhaps we can glimpse the moments where baseball slips into second place and football becomes king.

Certainly there were hints of such a reversal back in 1968. The year began with O. J. Simpson, then the top running back for Southern Cal, on the cover of *Sports Illustrated*. But while other sporting events—such as the Super Bowl, select boxing matches, and some Olympiads—occasionally managed to escape baseball's shadow to draw plenty of media coverage and public attention of their own, one could argue such upheavals in the sporting landscape were temporary at best, distractions before things returned to baseball. With its dog days building up to the Fall Classic followed by the renewed countdown to spring training, the national pastime still set the tone and the calendar for sports in America. By '68, though—as with so much else—the stage was set for change. Of all things, it would take a miscue in television scheduling for the powers that be in football, especially those in the upstart American Football League, to realize how swiftly the winds of change were shifting, and just how popular the new kid on the block had become.

After cueing up on the Trinitron, I watch the final minutes of a regular-season game held on November 17, 1968, between the New York Jets and the host Oakland Raiders. Both teams have gunslingers at quarterback—Joe Namath for the Jets and Daryle Lamonica for the Raiders. Although each team boasted quality personnel on both sides of the ball, it was still widely regarded that the best teams resided in the more established National Football League, where they had been playing since the early 1940s when George Halas's "Monsters of the Midway" in Chicago first made headlines. Of course, that thinking had been further solidified by Vince Lombardi's Green Packers, which had won the first two Super Bowls handily over AFL teams (the Kansas City Chiefs and the Oakland Raiders).

Yet after Lombardi stepped down as coach the champion Packers fell to a 6–7–1 record in '68, and despite such household names as Bart Starr and Ray Nitschke, they didn't come close to defending their division. Instead, the Cleveland Browns and Baltimore Colts were NFL's top teams that season, and they were regarded as the best in any league.

Studying the film of the Jets-Raiders game, channeling my inner Ron Jaworski, I realize it doesn't take a genius to be impressed by what's flashing by on the screen. Of course, I'm watching the game for reasons that go beyond any ability I may have to grade the top running backs on these teams (Matt Snell and Charlie Smith) or be enthralled by how both quarterbacks can throw the long ball with regularity. For this was the infamous "Heidi Game," a contest that not only rewrote how sports was broadcast in this country, but reassured followers of the rival AFL that they had plenty of company and rabid fans.

With sixty-five seconds left, the Jets held a 32–29 lead. Both squads were considered among the best in the ten-team AFL, entering the game with 7–2 records. Even though the game was still close, NBC ended the broadcast early in the Eastern and Central time zones. The network schedule called for a made-for-TV movie, *Heidi*, to start at 7 p.m. sharp. As soon as the switch was made, calls began to pour into the NBC switchboard. Network executives tried to reach broadcast operations, telling them to keep the game on, but those calls didn't go through until the game was well over. And what a game it was. The Raiders stormed back in the final minutes, scoring two touchdowns, to win 43–32. The programming switch was so abrupt that announcers Curt Gowdy and Al DeRogatis didn't know. In fact, Gowdy's call of the winning touchdown ("Lamonica to Charlie Smith . . . Smith is heading . . . and he scores. What a game!") remains old-school classic.

For the record, the Raiders went ahead on that pass from Lamonica to Smith, and then salted the game away by recovering the ensuing kickoff in the end zone when the Jets fumbled.

While the action on the field was great, the reaction off the field was even better. When Jets' coach Weeb Ewbank, still fuming about what happened, reached the visiting locker room he was told he had a phone call. It was his wife, eager to congratulate him on the victory. She, and a lot of other fans, thought the Jets had won because they were ahead when NBC cut away.

"Win?" Ewbank replied. "Hell, we got beat."

With that he slammed down the receiver.

John Madden, who went on to greater fame as a broadcaster and product pitchman, was the Raiders' coach that day. "We knew we won the game," he said, "but people across the country thought the Jets had won and we had lost."

New York quarterback Joe Namath had the best line about the fiasco: "I didn't get a chance to see it, but I heard it was great."

Back in New York, the switchboard at NBC shut down due to the large volume of calls. Like it or not, America was watching *Heidi*, starring Jennifer Edwards, the stepdaughter of Julie Andrews, in the title role, along with Maximillian Schell, Jean Simmons, and Michael Redgrave.

Unbelievably, NFL Films also has *Heidi* available to researchers. So after seeing the end of the game, I figured it's only fitting that I check out what so many TV viewers were forced to endure. The made-for-TV movie opens in Frankfurt, at the turn of the last century, with a horse-drawn carriage pulling up in front of a stately mansion. The going is slow, slow, slow, with plenty of German accents.

"Don't make me stay here," Heidi says, and most football fans would wholeheartedly agree. They wanted to be back at the game, listening to Gowdy and DeRogatis.

Unable to find a home in Frankfurt, Heidi is sent off to the Swiss Alps to live with her hermitlike grandfather. "There was a considerable amount of plot information in the first reel," director Delbert Mann explained. "If you'd come into the show in progress you wouldn't know what was going on."

Due to its exclusive contract with sponsor Timex, the movie was required to begin at 7 p.m. sharp. And that's what Dick Cline, the network's broadcast operations supervisor, made sure happened. Too late, network president Julian Goodman got through to Cline, telling him to put the game back on the air. By then the game was over and the video link to the Oakland-Alameda County Coliseum already cut.

NBC scrambled to make amends, and the network's timing couldn't have been worse.

At 8:40 p.m. EST, NBC aired an ominous-looking alert that crawled along the bottom third of the screen with the final score. Unfortunately, it appeared during one of the film's crucial scenes. Heidi's cousin, Clara, who is paralyzed and living out her days in a wheelchair, has summoned up the courage to try to walk again. With the backdrop of snow-capped peaks, she falls, begging for help. Mann, *Heidi's* director, nearly fell out of his chair when he saw the NBC crawler appear at that very moment.

Everything came together at a "disastrous point in terms of the picture," Mann said decades later. "The little girl cousin, who has been crippled, is trying desperately to crawl and stand and start to walk, and the wheelchair rolls away. It was really quite a tense moment."

So tense that Mann began to jump up and down in front of the television, cursing his own production. He wasn't the only unhappy camper. By this point, the switchboard at NBC had ceased to function. Instead, irate viewers called NBC affiliates, local radio stations, and newspapers. In fact, the *New York Times* and NYPD absorbed so many calls in protest that the phone grid in Manhattan nearly went down. "Ten years before it wouldn't have caused such an uproar," NBC executive Scott Connell said. "[But] that's how important football and televised sports had become."

Soon after the film ended, NBC president Goodman issued a statement, calling the incident "a forgivable error committed by humans who were concerned about children expecting to see Heidi at 7 p.m."

He added, "I missed the game as much as anyone else."

Of course, back in '68, television ratings weren't as detailed as they are today. What the football moguls, especially those with the AFL, discovered was that their game was more popular with the general public than they even realized. Television executive Dick Ebersol said that the "Heidi

Game" occurred "when the public was making the major leap from having baseball as the American pastime to making a full-body decision that football was the national game."

The bottom line was that football was "a better match for TV than baseball," said Robert Thompson, the founding director of the Bleier Center for Television and Popular Culture at Syracuse University. "People had been realizing that since they got their first television back in the late 1940s and into the 1950s. By the time we get to 1968, it's really becoming clear that baseball may be America's pastime, but football is television's sport.

"It's not like the 'Heidi Game' caused any of that. But what the game really symbolized was now that a television programming story, a mess-up in how the networks aired a program, could make the front page of *The New York Times*. . . . That was a big symbolic moment. The one thing that the story seems to be telling us is that you don't take away our football. Maybe the 'Heidi Game' underscores that symbolic moment when football became, in the eyes of America, an inalienable right."

That afternoon, as I drove home on Interstate 95, I tried to determine why football surpassed baseball as the most popular game in America. On sports-talk radio out of Philadelphia, the hubbub of the day was about Derek Jeter. The night before, in a game against the Tampa Bay Rays, an inside pitch had struck the knob end of Jeter's bat. Looking for an edge, the Yankees' shortstop jumped back, appearing to be in pain, pretending that the ball had hit him on the wrist or hand. For his Academy Award performance, Jeter was awarded first base and later came around to score. The following day the debate raged about Jeter's actions. Was it cheating or simply smart baseball?

As I listened to the comments, I realized how rarely this happens in baseball. The grand old game still hasn't fully embraced instant replay. In comparison, football long ago made the camera and slow-motion replay part of its game. Much of that process took place at NFL Films. In the time frame of the late 1960s, the replays of Bart Starr's quarterback sneak in the Ice Bowl or Joe Namath signaling his team was number one while running off the field would be played over and over again—shown until they became ingrained into our sports consciousness.

In Super Bowl III, Namath's Jets shocked the world, upsetting the Baltimore Colts, 16–7. Overnight, talk of play-in games, a postseason bracket that favored the more established teams from the National Football League, all but disappeared.

The epic upset solidified "the thinking of the public that football is football," New York Jets guard Bob Talamini said in the victorious locker room, "and the NFL and AFL can be mentioned in the same breath."

Back in the 1960s, the Hickok Belt was among the most prestigious awards an athlete could win. Given annually by the Hickok Manufacturing Company of Rochester, New York, a leading manufacturer of men's belts and accessories, the prize itself was a wonder to behold, made of alligator skin with a five-pound solid gold buckle and encrusted with diamonds, rubies and sapphires. The gems were so valuable that some winners had them removed from the glittering cummerbunds and redone into necklaces and earring for wives and girlfriends. First awarded in 1950 to Phil Rizzuto, subsequent Hickok winners included Willie Mays, Arnold Palmer, Mickey Mantle, Jim Brown, Sandy Koufax, Brooks Robinson and Muhammad Ali, with Kenny Stabler receiving the final Hickok Belt in 1977 after the company suffered financial difficulties. Chosen by a panel of three hundred national sportswriters and sportscasters, the award was "an Oscar, a Tony and an Emmy all rolled into one," said Scott Pitoniak, whose book *Jewel of the Sports World* details the history of the Hickok Belt.

After the 1968 season, New York Jets quarterback Joe Namath was named the Hickok Award winner. The decision proved to be controversial in more ways than one. Many believed Bill Russell should have won, and indeed *Sports Illustrated* named the Boston Celtics player-coach its

"Sportsman of the Year." And of course such accolades overlooked the impressive parade of baseball stars that made '68 the "Year of the Pitcher"—Bob Gibson, Luis Tiant, Don Drysdale, Mickey Lolich, and Denny McLain.

That off-season Namath was on a USO tour of Southeast Asia and couldn't attend the Hickok dinner. Yet Lolich and McLain were there and the Tigers' duo made sure the evening made headlines.

"When Lolich took the microphone, he began blistering the voters who chose, in his words, 'a one-game wonder over a thirty-one game winner,'" Pitoniak said. "This went on for a few minutes as the dinner organizers began sinking down in their seats. When Lolich finished his tirade, many in the audience applauded."

Smooth as ever, McLain congratulated Namath when it was his turn at the podium, saying the decision was a good one. Afterward McLain told the organizers to donate his appearance fee to charity.

Years later, the Hickok family wondered if Lolich's criticism was really all a ruse, whether Lolich may have felt he should have won the Hickok Belt based upon his three victories in the 1968 World Series.

After the 1968 season, baseball's powers that be lowered the pitcher's mound by five inches and shrunk the strike zone, with the area from the armpits to the top of the batter's knee now being deemed a called strike.

This was done to generate more offense. Perhaps baseball should have simply let expansion and the new divisional playoff format do the heavy lifting instead. Before the 1969 season, four new teams were added—in Seattle and Kansas City in the American League, and Montreal and San Diego in the National League. Fifty players were parceled out to the new ballclubs, weakening several of the impressive pitching staffs of that era.

"Things were never the same again," Bob Gibson wrote. "As soon as the 1968 season was over the great thinkers of baseball, in their infinite wisdom, started screwing around with the game on the premise that the only way to fix it—the implication being that good pitching, as demonstrated so conspicuously in 1968, was inherently a problem—was to manipulate conditions in a way that would offer new hope to hitters. Some have called these changes the Gibson Rules in light of the fact that it was my 1.12 ERA that caused so much of the panic."

In 1970, Willie Horton made the American League All-Star Team for the third time. Before the game, while sitting in the visitor's clubhouse at Cincinnati's old Riverfront Stadium, Horton looked across the field at where the National League Squad was gathering and decided to try again. He knew that Bob Gibson had been selected, too. The Cardinals' pitcher would be in uniform for his sixth consecutive Midsummer Classic.

"I'm not one who gives up that easily," Horton said. "So I got ahold of another ball. But this time I was going to be a bit smarter about everything. I got one of the clubhouse kids to take it over to get Gibson to sign."

Later, the kid returned with the ball, which now had Gibson's signature between the looping in the laces. Years later, when both were out of uniform, Horton would get to know Gibson well enough to personally ask for and receive an autograph from the famous pitcher. But such times were still to come.

For now, in the shadow of 1968, the two of them remained rivals, seemingly always going against one another. That's why Horton couldn't help but smile as he studied the autographed ball, so appreciative of what he now held in his hand.

Aftermath

*When you're successful, like we were last year, it
changes your life. In a lot of respects, failure is easier to
cope with. You're all finding that out because your lives
are completely different than they were last year at this
time. You've had a lot of things come your way, a lot of
good things, and a lot of new pressures.*

—DETROIT TIGERS OWNER JOHN FETZER

THE DETROIT TIGERS

After taking the 1968 World Series, the Tigers appear ready for a long run
as the premier team in the American League. It isn't to be.

The Baltimore Orioles, with new manager Earl Weaver firmly in
charge, run away from the rest of the league in the first year of divisional
play, finishing nineteen games ahead of second-place Detroit. After
sweeping the Minnesota Twins, the Orioles are favored to take the Fall
Classic. But they are upset by the Amazin' Mets in five games.

The Tigers don't return to the postseason until 1972, where they lose
three games to two to the Oakland Athletics in the American League

Championship Series. Led by Catfish Hunter, Blue Moon Odom, and Rollie Fingers, the Athletics become the preeminent team in the junior circuit, winning three consecutive World Series.

Detroit doesn't win another championship until 1984.

Mickey Lolich

After winning three complete games in the 1968 World Series, the last pitcher to accomplish the feat, Mickey Lolich appears poised to be recognized as one of the top pitchers in the game. But the transformation to elite status doesn't quite take hold. In 1971, he goes 25–14, leading the American League in victories, games started, innings pitched, and strikeouts, only to finish second to Oakland Athletics' phenom Vida Blue in Cy Young balloting. In 1976, Lolich is traded to the New York Mets and then finishes his career with the San Diego Padres. While his career winning percentage is a pedestrian .532 (217–191), he ends his career undefeated in World Series play.

If anything, he becomes just as beloved for running a donut shop in the Detroit suburbs. He eventually sells the business and retires to his homes in Oregon and Michigan. He often coaches at the Tiger Fantasy Camp in Lakeland, Florida.

Denny McLain

Six days after the World Series ends, Denny McLain plays the Riviera Hotel in Las Vegas. The marquee sign reads Denny "31" McLain and he's booked for a two-week engagement in the hotel's lounge, which is also home to comedian Shecky Green. Other headliners within a few blocks include Alan King, Harry James, and Mama Cass.

A row of baseballs top McLain's organ and he certainly looks the part, dressed in a Nehru jacket and gold-chain medallion. His joke that he "wouldn't trade Bob Gibson for twelve Mickey Lolichs" brings down the house, but overall the act doesn't have legs. Standup comic Marty Allen, who is appearing in the main showroom at the Riviera, pays a visit along with singer Phyllis McGuire to help spice things up. McLain's Vegas debut is called "less than smashing" by critics and his two-week engagement isn't extended. The right-hander claims it doesn't matter. He has plenty of other gigs, several in Detroit, so many in fact that he expects to clear $250,000 in his first off-season after winning thirty-one games.

As well as McLain pitched in '68 while becoming the first pitcher in three decades to reach the thirty-victory plateau, many believe he threw even better the following season. While he drops to just twenty-four victories, McLain leads the American League with nine shutouts. But his career is closer to the end than anybody realizes.

Cortisone shots and innings pitched have taken their toll. In addition, new commissioner Bowie Kuhn suspends him for his involvement with gambling. McLain wins only three games in fourteen starts and is traded to the lowly Washington Senators after the 1970 season in a blockbuster deal that sends Tigers McLain, Don Wert, Norm McRae, and Elliott Maddox to the nation's capital for Joe Coleman, Ed Brinkman, Jim Hannan, and Aurelio Rodriguez. Senators manager Ted Williams, a critic of the trade, doesn't really want the right-hander. McLain splits the 1972 season between the Oakland Athletics and Atlanta Braves (this last deal involving Orlando Cepeda) before retiring from the game.

Outside the lines, McLain's life dissolves into equal parts soap opera and Greek tragedy. After becoming a popular radio talk-show host in Detroit, he's charged with racketeering, extortion and cocaine trafficking in 1984. Sentenced to twenty-three years in prison, he serves less than three after an appeals court throws out his conviction. The government decides not to retry the case.

A decade later, he's back in prison after he and a business partner purchase the Peet Packing Company in Chesaning, Michigan, and then rob almost $2.5 million from the employee pension fund. They are convicted of embezzlement, money laundering, and mail fraud. McLain does time at a federal prison camp for nonviolent offenders and later performs work release at a 7-Eleven store in Sterling Heights, Michigan. "It was packed in there, but I was very lonely," McLain says of his time behind bars. "The boredom in prison just kills you."

"I believe in forgiveness," retired Tigers' announcer Ernie Harwell says after McLain's release in 2003. "Denny's had a lot of lives. He's come back and then fallen again, so we'll have to wait and see."

Willie Horton

By hitting thirty-six home runs in 1968, Willie Horton establishes himself as one of the outfield stars for the Tigers. He plays for Detroit until 1977 when he is traded to the Texas Rangers. From there he plays for the Cleveland Indians, Oakland Athletics, Toronto Blue Jays, and Seattle Mariners in short order. He goes on to play two more years in the Pacific Coast League and another season in Mexican baseball. Through it all, he still wears the same batting helmet from his Tigers' days, which he repaints at each stop.

In July 2000, a statue to Willie "the Wonder" Horton is unveiled behind the center-field fence at Comerica Park, the Tigers' new home in Detroit. By then Horton has returned to the fold as a special assistant to Tigers president Dave Dombrowski. Horton still prides himself on knowing somebody wherever his travels may take him.

Al Kaline

If it wasn't for Mickey Lolich's heroics, Al Kaline could have been named the 1968 World Series Most Valuable Player. He hit .379 in his first and only Fall Classic appearance in his twenty-two-year career, with two home runs and eight runs batted in. By the time he retires in 1974, he has played in 2,834 games, fifth-best in baseball history at the time. Elected to baseball's Hall of Fame in Cooperstown in 1980, he is named a special assistant to the Tigers. Decades later, he would say his biggest thrill in baseball was winning the 1968 World Series. His biggest disappointment? Losing the pennant on the last day of the season in 1967.

Gates Brown

With his eighteen pinch-hits, Gates Brown will be remembered as one of the few hitters to have success in the "Year of the Pitcher." In 1974, he again demonstrates why he is one of the top clutch hitters ever to wear a Detroit uniform as he picks up a league-high sixteen pinch-hits in fifty-three at-bats.

Brown retires after the 1975 season, all of them with the Tigers, ranking tenth on the American League all-time pinch-hitting list. Decades later, he can still be found at the ballpark in Detroit, signing autographs and talking with the fans.

Dick McAuliffe

After leading the American League in runs scored in 1968, Dick McAuliffe is limited to seventy-four games the following season due to a serious knee injury. Even though he will play another four seasons in Detroit, he will never be the threat he was in 1968.

After the 1973 season, the Tigers trade McAuliffe to Boston for outfielder Ben Oglivie. Expected to challenge Doug Griffin for the Red Sox's second base job, McAuliffe hits only .210 and retires after playing just seven games the following season. "I never should have left Detroit," he says. "That's where I was the most comfortable. That's where I should have finished up."

Jon Warden

Despite being the only player on either roster in the 1968 World Series (fifty players in total), not to appear in a single game, the future appears bright for the hard-throwing left-hander. With baseball expanding by two teams in the American League and National League, Warden is left unprotected by the Tigers and selected by the Kansas City Royals. Soon after reporting to camp in the spring of 1969, though, Warden becomes sidelined with a sore shoulder. Instead of going north with the big-league club, he is sent down to the minors. While Warden struggles to find the prowess he exhibited early in the '68 season, he discovers he has a knack for making people laugh. In Oklahoma City, where the hometown team has a cowboy fire blanks to the sky after an 89ers' home run, Warden decides the visiting Omaha Royals could do just as well. He brings a blank-shooting pistol to the ballpark and teammate Steve Boros helps him tape on a fake mustache. When his team hits a long ball, Warden comes bounding out of the visiting dugout, firing away. Jack McKeon, then the Omaha manager, calls Warden the team's cheerleader and appreciates his ability to keep his teammates loose.

While clowning comes naturally to Warden, making it back to the majors proves to be much more difficult. After the Royals release him, Warden signs on with Evansville and the St. Louis Cardinals' team in the Texas League. After that he tries out with the Cleveland Indians before retiring. His will be a single line in *The Baseball Encyclopedia*: four victories, one loss and an ERA of 3.62.

After making a name for himself on ESPN's *Cold Pizza* as a wisecracking baseball analyst, Warden travels the country for the Major League Baseball Players Alumni Association, making appearances at golf outings and old-timers games across the country. In addition, he begins auditioning for stage shows on both coasts.

"What's the old saying? 'You've got to laugh instead of cry sometimes?'" he says. "I guess I'm an ambassador for baseball. I wouldn't be here if it weren't for that year with the Tigers. I've gotten more mileage out of that one year in the big leagues. I'm very thankful for it. I would never trade that one year."

THE ST. LOUIS CARDINALS

Roster changes begin soon after the final out in Game Seven in St. Louis, as the Cardinals trade outfielder Bobby Tolan and pitcher Wayne Granger, two players they probably would have lost in the upcoming expansion draft anyway, to the Cincinnati Reds for outfielder Vada Pinson. Pinson replaces the retiring Roger Maris in right field. While the ballclub appears ready to make a run at another championship, management then sends first baseman Orlando Cepeda to Atlanta for catcher-first baseman Joe Torre. (Three years later, Cepeda will be traded from the Braves for Denny McLain.)

"Trading Cepeda signaled to us, loud and clear, that things would no longer be the same around the Cardinal clubhouse," Gibson writes in his autobiography. "The front office apparently had very little regard for what the players considered to be the special character of the ballclub."

The New York Mets, led by pitchers Tom Seaver, Jerry Koosman, and Gary Gentry, out-duel the Chicago Cubs down the stretch to take the new National League East Division. The Cardinals fall to fourth place and the front office decides more changes are needed. Tim McCarver, Curt Flood, Joe Hoerner, and Byron Browne are sent to Philadelphia in a seven-player trade. Flood refuses to report and St. Louis eventually sends Willie Montanez and Bob Browning to the City of Brotherly Love to complete the blockbuster deal. But what the remaining Cardinals realize is that Gibson has called it: the era when the ballclub won two, almost three championships in five seasons has come to an end.

St. Louis doesn't return to the World Series until 1982, when it defeats the Milwaukee Brewers in seven games.

Bob Gibson

While much of the ballclub is dismantled around him, Bob Gibson re-mains—once again pushing back against the heartache the world offers. A critic of lowering the mound, because he contends it will give hitters too much of an advantage, the intimidating right-hander nonetheless car-ries on, winning twenty games in 1969, with a league-high twenty-eight complete games, and the following season he notches a league-leading twenty-three victories.

By the mid-1970s, Gibson's best performances are behind him and he retires after the 1975 season. With 251 victories and 3,117 strikeouts, the second-highest total ever in baseball history at the time, Gibson enters the Hall of Fame in 1981.

"I'm glad I had the opportunity of playing against a person of Bob's cal-iber," Hank Aaron says. "I feel that he was one of the best pitchers I faced in baseball."

Rusty Staub adds, "In my thirteen years in the big leagues, for consis-tency of performance, competitiveness, desire and plain old guts, Bob Gibson was my idea of what it takes to be a true champion. I wish I could have played on the same team with him."

Of all the lofty statistics of his seventeen-year career, none stand out more than his three World Series campaigns: a cumulative record of seven and two, eight complete games and ninety-two strikeouts. Unfortunately for the pitcher, and perhaps the game itself, he doesn't appear in the Fall Classic again after the '68 season.

Lou Brock

If the Cardinals had captured the 1968 World Series, Lou Brock certainly would have given Bob Gibson a run for MVP honors. His .464 batting average raises his career mark in postseason play to .391, breaking the record of .363 set by J. Franklin (Home Run) Baker.

After '68, Brock leads the league in stolen bases five more times, establishing the career thefts mark of 938, which stands until Rickey Henderson surpasses him in 1991. His goal of being remembered as something more than a base stealer, somebody mentioned in the same breath with the all-time greats, becomes reality as Brock is elected to the Hall of Fame in 1985.

"He sometimes doesn't get the general credit that Babe Ruth or Lou Gehrig or Reggie Jackson get, but you talk about Mr. October," says Bob Broeg, the longtime sportswriter with the *St. Louis Post-Dispatch*. "His last two Series were fabulous. In those games, he would combine power and speed."

Orlando Cepeda

Throughout much of his career, behind the smile and ability to rally his teammates, Orlando Cepeda worried about his balky knee. He initially hurt it after the 1962 season—a secret he kept hidden from nearly everybody. By 1968, however, it becomes apparent that he's playing on borrowed time.

The Cardinals trade him for Joe Torre after the 1968 season and he'll play in Atlanta until 1972 when he moves on to Oakland in the deal involving Denny McLain. From there, Cepeda does brief stints in Boston and Kansas City before retiring in 1974. His seventeen-year career includes nine .300 seasons and eight seasons of twenty-five or more homers. Along with Roberto Clemente and Orestes (Minnie) Minoso, he's recognized as one of the Latino pioneers in the game.

Soon after his playing days end, Cepeda is arrested trying to pick up 160 pounds of marijuana. Sentenced to five years in prison, he serves only ten months. But the incident certainly delays his entrance into the Hall of Fame in Cooperstown. In 1993, Cepeda is inducted into the Puerto Rico Sports Hall of Fame and misses being voted into Cooperstown by just seven votes—the fifth-narrowest margin a player has ever missed being inducted by in baseball history.

He is finally elected into the Hall in 1999, with a class that includes Nolan Ryan, Robin Yount, and George Brett.

Mike Shannon

With close ties to the Busch family, Mike Shannon is one of the few regulars from the 1967–1968 teams to remain in St. Louis. But he begins to suffer from a serious kidney infection. He plays only fifty-five games in 1970, batting .213 with no home runs. Shannon continues to try to play until the ballclub takes away his uniform, permanently sidelining him.

"Mike reminds me of Eddie Mathews," Joe Torre says. "He couldn't be hurt bad enough to keep him out of the lineup. The only way they could take Mike out of the lineup is to do what they did. Take him out of uniform."

Shannon retires at the end of the season, taking a position in the Cardinals' front office. Soon he finds his second calling, behind a microphone. Even though he doesn't know how to keep score at the time, he joins the legendary Jack Buck in the KMOX broadcast booth. The guy with the no-bones-about-it baritone soon gains a following among Cardinals' fans. He isn't especially smooth behind the mike—one of his best malaprops comes after St. Louis catcher Ted Simmons homers against the Dodgers. "That's the kinda pitch that's bread on Simmons' butter," Shannon tells listeners.

Shannon's misadventures aren't limited to calling games, either. He loses and finds his 1964 World Series ring an amazing four different times. The precious bauble falls out a car window along Interstate 70, drops from a coat pocket while at the barbershop, and survives being eaten and passed by the family's pet goat. "That ring has got nine lives," Shannon says.

Roger Maris

Memories of the stoic, strong-armed outfielder invariably go back to his 1961 season with the New York Yankees when he hit sixty-one home runs, breaking Babe Ruth's single-season record. But Maris never liked the bright lights, big city, and was much more at home in St. Louis.

"I was born surly," he tells the *New York Times*, "and I'm going to stay that way. Everything in life is tough."

After retiring in 1968, his career line reads: 275 home runs, 850 runs batted in, and an average of .260. Perhaps most impressively, he hit six home runs in seven World Series.

Once Maris hangs up his uniform, he avoids old-timers games and only begins to attend team reunions late in life. He moves to Gainesville, Florida, where he owns a beer distributorship. After a two-year battle with cancer, he dies in 1985. He is only fifty-one years old.

In 1998, slugger Mark McGwire, playing for the St. Louis Cardinals, breaks Maris's single-season mark. Mike Shannon, who once roomed with Maris, calls the game on the radio. "And somewhere up there Roger is looking down at all this and cheering for McGwire, too," Shannon tells the Cardinal nation.

Nellie Briles

In July 1967, Bob Gibson suffered a broken leg when struck by a line drive off the bat of the Pirates' Roberto Clemente. Nellie Briles took his place in the St. Louis rotation and closed the season with nine consecutive victories. A year later, in 1968, Briles posted a 19–11 record, helping the Cardinals repeat as National League champions.

After 1968, Briles survives the first round of housecleaning in St. Louis. Still, he struggles, in large part due to the lower mound, and in 1970 his ERA soars to 6.24. Before the 1971 season, he's sent along with infielder/pinch-hitter Vic Davalillo to the Pittsburgh Pirates for outfielder Matty Alou and journeyman pitcher George Brunet. Briles plays a key role in the Pirates' title run that season, pitching a two-hit shutout in Game Five of the World Series against Earl Weaver's Baltimore Orioles. Thanks in large part to Briles's pitching gem, the Pirates become only the sixth team in baseball history to win the World Series after losing the first two games. A year later, Briles falls one hit shy of hurling a perfect game against the San Francisco Giants.

Off the field, Briles proves to be a better entertainer than Denny McLain or any of the other ballplayers to take a star turn after the 1968 season. An accomplished singer, Briles also does a great impersonation of President Richard Nixon. In 1974, with Hank Aaron on the verge of breaking Babe Ruth's all-time home-run record, Briles releases a single for Capitol Records called "Hey Hank." At three-plus minutes, the song's chorus is a lament by big-league pitchers everywhere: "Hey Hank, I've got a reputation. And I've got a family. . . . So please don't hit it off me."

After fourteen years in the majors with five different teams, Briles returns to Pittsburgh. He's in the broadcast booth in 1979 when the Pirates again defeat Baltimore in seven games to take the World Series. Soon he moves into the front office as the ballclub's corporate vice president and head of their alumni association. Briles dies of a heart attack while playing golf in 2005. Pallbearers at his funeral include Manny Sanguillen, Jim Leyland, and Roberto Clemente's son, Luis.

Steve Carlton

After the 1968 World Series, the Cardinals travel to Japan for a series of exhibition games. There left-hander Steve Carlton begins to experiment with a slider—a pitch that will soon become his signature offering. Thrown nearly as hard as his fastball, the slider breaks down and in, with great late action, against right-handed batters. In 1969, his first year with the pitch, Carlton's ERA drops to 2.17. In addition, he strikes out nineteen batters in a close loss to the New York Mets.

The left-hander wins twenty games for the first time in 1971 and holds out for a $5,000 raise. In response, the Cardinals' front office trades him to Philadelphia for right-hander Rick Wise. With the Phillies, Carlton becomes only the sixth pitcher to win twenty games for a last-place ballclub, going a league-leading 27–10. That season includes a fifteen-game winning streak, eight shutouts, and thirty complete games. In addition, he wins pitching's equivalent of the Triple Crown, leading the National League in victories, ERA, and strikeouts.

In 1980, Carlton leads the Phillies to their first-ever world championship. Two years later, Carlton wins his fourth and final Cy Young Award. Recognized as the best pitcher in Phillies' history, he is elected into the Hall of Fame in Cooperstown, New York, in 1994, his first year of eligibility.

The night before the induction ceremony, at a banquet in the Otesaga Hotel in Cooperstown, New York, Tim McCarver tells the crowd, "If Carl Hubbell will be known as having the best screwball in the history of the game and Sandy Koufax the best curveball, Steve Carlton will go down as having the best slider in the history of the game."

Afterward Bob Gibson corners McCarver and says his long-time catcher made a mistake. He should have said that Carlton had the best *left-handed* slider in the game. Of course, Gibson, a right-hander, believes his slider was the best.

Tim McCarver

Every great team needs a Boswell, somebody to sing its praises to the heavens, and nobody has done a better job over the years than Tim Mc-Carver. In addition, he is remembered as a confidant, even a soul mate to many of the pitchers he caught. After being the starting catcher on the Cardinals' three World Series teams, he is part of the stunning blockbuster trade with Philadelphia. There he catches Rick Wise's no-hitter in 1971. After that season, Wise is traded to St. Louis for Steve Carlton and there McCarver helps the left-hander to his best season in the majors (27–10). But in the 1972 season, McCarver is dealt to Montreal, where he catches the second of Bill Stoneman's two career no-hitters. The next season Mc-Carver returns to St. Louis for almost two seasons before being traded to Boston and he returns to Philadelphia, where he plays four more seasons and again is reunited with Carlton. In fact, Carlton is so comfortable pitching to McCarver, rather than Bob Boone, the Phillies' regular catcher, the joke becomes that the Carlton and McCarver will be buried sixty feet, six inches apart. McCarver retires in 1980, one of the few players who can claim that he played in four different decades.

After hanging up the tools of ignorance, McCarver gains a following on television, where he will be a central player in the baseball telecasts for all four major U.S. television networks. His partners in the broadcast booth include Don Drysdale, Al Michaels, Jim Palmer, Jack Buck, and Buck's son, Joe. In the offseason, McCarver turns his attention to the Olympics and cohosts the primetime coverage with Paula Zahn in 1992. In addition, he releases an album of jazz standards (*Tim McCarver Sings Songs from the Great American Songbook*) in 2009.

Through it all, nobody can doubt McCarver's allegiance and love of those great Cardinals teams of the 1960s. When appearing with good friend and former batterymate Bob Gibson on a *Major League Baseball Network* special about the 1968 World Series, McCarver still plays the role of the good catcher, the trusted sidekick. When Gibson appears reluctant to field queries from host Bob Costas about Curt Flood misplaying Jim Northup's line drive in Game Seven, and the heartbreak of losing a contest that would have ranked the Cardinals among the best teams of all time, McCarver steps in, effortlessly answering for his good friend.

Studio 42 host Bob Costas adds that McCarver once said, "Bob Gibson was the kind of player that teammates didn't just respect, they revered."

"I still feel that way," McCarver replies, "I'm happy to say."

Curt Flood

Some trades and transactions shake up teams. A rare few remake the game itself. At first the seven-player deal between the St. Louis Cardinals and the Philadelphia Phillies including outfielder Curt Flood appears a far cry from Babe Ruth coming to the Yankees or Jackie Robinson signing with the Dodgers. But Flood has no interest in playing in Philadelphia, a city experiencing strong racial tensions at the time. Flood calls Philadelphia "the nation's northernmost southern city." In addition, he objects to being treated like a piece of property. Flood asks new commissioner Bowie Kuhn, who has taken over for William Eckert, to make him a free agent. When that request is denied, Flood decides to take the matter to court.

In January 1970, he files a lawsuit stating that Major League Baseball has violated the nation's antitrust laws. With the backing of the Players Association, Flood's case rises from the district and circuit levels, reaching the Supreme Court in the summer of 1972. Although the highest court in the land eventually rules against Flood, the case sets the stage for the 1975 Andy Messersmith-Dave McNally rulings and ultimately opens the door to free agency in the national pastime.

While professional ballplayers coming after those court decisions reap the rewards, the battle comes at a huge cost to Flood. He returns to the field in 1971, signing for $110,000 with the Washington Senators, but the game has passed him by. Flood plays only thirteen games and then retires. He spends a year in the Oakland Athletics' broadcast booth and then moves to Europe, where he spends much of his time painting and writing.

Marvin Miller, the Players Association's former executive director, points out that when Flood decided to fight baseball's reserve clause, "he was perhaps the sport's premier center fielder. And yet he chose to fight an injustice, knowing that even if by some miracle he won, his career as a professional player would be over. At no time did he waver in his commitment and determination. He had experienced something that was inherently unfair and was determined to right the wrong, not so much for himself, but for those who would come after him. Few praised him for this, then or now. There is no Hall of Fame for people like Curt."

Bob Gibson, Flood's best friend in the game, adds, "The modern player has gotten fat from the efforts of Curt Flood and has returned him no gratitude or any other form of appreciation. I've often thought of what an appropriate and decent thing it would be if every player in the major leagues turned over one percent of his paycheck just one time to Curt Flood."

Flood dies in 1997 of throat cancer at the age of 59.

OTHERS

Catfish Hunter

In 1974, Oakland Athletics owner Charlie Finley fails to pay an annuity clause in Catfish Hunter's contract. Eventually that makes the right-hander a free agent—and among the first to take advantage of the sea change Curt Flood's case has ushered in. Hunter signs a five-year contract worth $3.75 million—a princely sum at the time—with the New York Yankees. With Hunter as their staff ace, the Yankees reach the World Series three consecutive years, winning twice. Upon his retirement, Hunter can look back on having started nine games in the Fall Classic, tying him with Bob Gibson.

In 1999, Hunter dies of amyotrophic lateral sclerosis (ALS), Lou Gehrig's disease, only a year after being diagnosed. Elected to the Hall of Fame in Cooperstown, his plaque reads, "The bigger the game, the better he pitched."

Luis Tiant

The right-hander's fears about what will happen to his pitching arm without an offseason of winterball prove to be astute. In 1969, Luis Tiant loses a league-worst twenty games, issues a league-worst 129 walks, and is traded from Cleveland to Minnesota before the next season. He gets off to good start with the Twins, winning six games, but then breaks his right scapula. Tiant is released in 1971 and many believe his baseball career is over. But the Cuban right-hander signs a minor-league contract with the Boston Red Sox and goes 15–6 in 1972. He averages more than seventeen victories a season between 1973 and 1978, and stars in the 1975 World Series, when Boston loses in seven games to Cincinnati.

"You can talk about anybody else on that team (1975 Boston Red Sox) you want to, but when the chips are on the line, Luis Tiant is the greatest competitor I've ever seen," says Baltimore Orioles pitcher Jim Palmer.

Tiant finishes his nineteen-year career with the Yankees, Pirates, and Angels.

Frank Howard

"The Capital Punisher" follows up his forty-four home runs in 1968 with forty-eight the following season and forty-four again in 1970. But when the Washington Senators move to Texas, becoming the Rangers, Howard's best days at the plate prove to be behind him. Near the end of the 1972 season, he is traded to Detroit, where he finishes his major-league career, retiring in 1973.

Larry Dierker

After winning a dozen games in 1968, Larry Dierker reaches the twenty-victory plateau for the first and only time in his fourteen-year career the following year. He plays all but one of those seasons with the Houston Astros, firing a no-hitter in 1976 against the Montreal Expos. After retiring in 1977, he works for eighteen years as a radio and television analyst. He then manages the Astros for five seasons, winning four Central Division titles.

Nolan Ryan

After finishing the '68 season, his first full year in the majors, with a record of 6–9, Nolan Ryan nearly quits the game. That's how frustrated he is with his inability to throw strikes and win consistently. In the end, Ryan decides to tough it out with the New York Mets, winning a key game in relief during the team's amazing 1969 World Series run. Before the 1972 season, Ryan is traded along with pitcher Don Rose, outfielder Leroy Stanton, and catching prospect Francisco Estrada to the California Angels for in-fielder Jim Fregosi. "That deal was the best thing that ever happened to me," Ryan says. "In Anaheim, I got a chance to pitch on a regular basis and to develop my game."

On the West Coast, "The Express" smoothes out his delivery and goes on to win 324 games in the majors, including seven no-hitters. He is elected to the Hall of Fame in 1999, with 98.79 percent of the vote, second-highest all-time to Tom Seaver (98.84 percent in 1992).

Milt Pappas

The right-hander goes 10–8 for Atlanta after his trade from Cincinnati, which many believe was initiated due to his protest regarding the Reds' decision to play while other teams mourned Robert Kennedy's assassi-nation. Pappas retires after the 1973 season, with a career record of 209–164, including a no-hitter, in seventeen seasons.

But many in the game remember Pappas more for the curious disap-pearance of his wife, Carole, than any achievement on the mound. On a summer day in September 1982, she takes the car to do some errands and disappears without a trace. Pappas makes a national appeal for any infor-mation about her whereabouts and the family even consults a psychic, but to no avail. Five years later, Carole Pappas and her 1980 Buick are found in the deepest part of a small pond blocks away from the family home in the Chicago suburbs.

"How she got there," Pappas writes in his memoir, *Out at Home*, "no-body knows for sure because nobody saw her go in. It was a mystery in 1982, a mystery in 1987, and it's still a mystery."

Bill Russell

The 1968–69 season marks Russell's third year as player-coach for the Boston Celtics. After limping into the playoffs, the Celtics once again catch fire, defeating the Los Angeles Lakers and newly acquired Wilt Chamberlain in seven games. Afterward Russell retires, having guided Boston to eleven championships in thirteen years. Decades later, Russell is considered one of the best centers ever to have played the game.

Roone Arledge

After putting the Olympics on the TV map, Arledge transforms professional football into primetime viewing with ABC's *Monday Night Football*. In 1994, *Sports Illustrated* magazine ranks Arledge third, behind Muhammad Ali and Michael Jordan, in its list of forty individuals who have had the greatest impact on the world of sports in the last four decades.

Jim Ryun

Before the 1968 Summer Games in Mexico City, Jim Ryun and Dr. Jack Daniels believed a time of 3:39 or so would be good enough to win 1,500 meters. But Ryun's 3:37.8 at altitude proves to be well behind Kip Keino's 3:34.9. In 1981, Ryun tells *The Runner* magazine, "We had thought that 3:39 would win and I ran under that. I considered it like winning a gold medal; I had done my very best and I still believe I would have won at sea level." Ryun will compete again four years later in the 1972 Olympics in Munich, Germany. But he is tripped and falls during a 1,500-meter qualifying heat. Despite protests by the U.S. team, the International Olympic Committee refuses to reinstate him for the event final. His best Olympic showing will remain the silver medal in 1968.

Joe Namath

The AFL Player of the Year caps off the 1968 season with MVP honors in Super Bowl III. Namath backs up his pregame "guarantee" of victory with a 206-yard passing production in New York's 16–7 victory over Baltimore, assuring the competitive viability of the AFL-NFL Super Bowl series. Despite knee injuries, Namath plays thirteen years at the professional level.

Tom Hayden

The political activist remembers having little time for baseball or his hometown team in 1968. "Sure, I was aware of the irony that it was the Tigers' year, and that my high school friend (Bill) Freehan was having his greatest year," he says, "but it was like being on two different planets."

Hayden goes on to become "the single greatest figure of the 1960s student movement," according a *New York Times* book review. He serves eighteen years in the California legislature, writes nineteen books, and teaches at Harvard. In addition, he marries actress-activist Jane Fonda. He's often considered to be the basis for the Kris Kristofferson song line "partly truth and partly fiction, a walking contradiction." Through it all, Hayden never forgets his love of baseball.

In the 1980s, he begins playing again and attends the Dodgers' fantasy camp in Vero Beach, Florida. Despite being out of shape, he sticks with it and is MVP and batting champion the next spring. He still plays and coaches in the Los Angeles area.

"All at once the desire grabbed me," Hayden says. "I wasn't finished with baseball.... Right now, I am seventy-one and play first base in a dirt league, hitting .300 and slipping. With good weather, I play all year."

ACKNOWLEDGMENTS

It is one thing to have a notion creep into your mind while watching television one evening. It is quite another to turn it into a book. For that to happen, you need a lot of people in your corner.

Jonathan Crowe, my editor at Da Capo, heard me out from the beginning and offered guidance and enthusiasm throughout this project. He's a delight to work with.

Special thanks to Chris Park, my agent, and the folks at Foundry Media. Chris was with me every step of the way and she always has my back.

Kärstin Painter and Anais Scott at Perseus Books helped in the final stages, making sure that *Summer of '68* became a reality, while Lissa Warren championed it in the marketplace.

When I'm working on a new book, I become a big believer in omens—constantly keeping an eye out for signs that this will really play out. On an early trip to Detroit, my good friend Tom Stanton took me on a tour of the Motor City and I saw that it was true: that sports, politics, race, culture, and music can connect in ways that we seldom acknowledge.

Months and months later, with deadlines fast approaching, I took a trip to Memphis at the urging of a new friend, David Waters. It was a roll of the dice really. So little was set up when it came to appointment times and the like. But twenty minutes after my plane landed, my cell rang and it was Erica Cunningham with the Monumental Baptist Church. If I could be there within the hour, Rev. Billy Kyles would see me. Rev. Kyles was a member of Dr. Martin Luther King's inner circle, and after talking with him I saw that that's where things truly went over the edge in 1968. For King's assassination was followed by Robert Kennedy's shooting, the riots in Chicago, and so on. Just as importantly, what happened in Memphis couldn't be ignored. Whether we liked it or not, everybody in America, even athletes, were buffeted by what was going down.

I'm grateful for interviews and conversations over the years with Hank Aaron, Bud Anzalone, Budd Bailey, David Black, Erik Brady, Nellie Briles, Lou Brock, Gates Brown, Gary Brozek, Orlando Cepeda, Thurston Clarke, Dr. Jack Daniels, Paul Dickson, Larry Dierker, Greg Downs, Dave Duncan, Tim Gay, David Granger, Phil Grisdela, Ken Harrelson, Tom Hayden, Hugh Hefner, Willie Horton, Frank Howard, Tommy John, Tony La Russa, Mickey Lolich, Howard Mansfield, Juan Marichal, Bill Mead, Dick McAuliffe, Tim McCarver, Jack McKeon, Tim McQuay, William Mead, Jim Palmer, Gaylord Perry, Annie Phillips, Scott Pitoniak, John Pietrunti, Phil Pote, Scott Price, Dick Rhoads, David Rowell, Nolan Ryan, Tom Stanton, Robert Thompson, Luis Tiant, Joe Torre, Jon Warden, David Waters, Lonnie Wheeler, and Paul White.

Dave Raglin and his fellow members of the Mayo Smith Society are a treasure trove of information about the old Tigers. Sam Moore of the Major League Baseball Players Alumni Association always takes the time to talk with me. Thomas Mann and David Kelly at the Library of Congress in Washington put things in perspective for me. Special thanks to Chris Willis, who opened the vaults at NFL Films so I could view the end of the "Heidi Game."

In looking back at things, I realize that much of this book took root when I was involved with an amazing group of advisors—Milton Jamail, Rob Ruck, Adrian Burgos, and Alan Klein—as we were involved with "Viva Baseball," an exhibit about Latinos in baseball for the National Hall of Fame in Cooperstown, New York. There we worked with Erik Strohl,

John Odell, Ted Spencer, Tom Schieber, Brad Horn, Lenny DiFranza, Mary Quinn, Tim Wiles, and Jeff Idelson. Hang with those people for a while and you start to see things in a different light.

In addition, a special nod to the Hall of Fame's Bill Francis, who is one of the best researchers in the business. Also, with the final deadline looming, Jim Gates located several vintage interviews from the Cooperstown archives and Freddy Berowski sent them along. Pat Kelly of the Hall of Fame helped me locate many of the iconic images in these pages that bring the year 1968 to life—several at the eleventh hour.

Special thanks to Charles Eisendrath and the Knight-Wallace Fellowship at the University of Michigan. That 1995–96 school year in Ann Arbor started me in a new direction.

The Writing Department at Johns Hopkins University has been my base camp for a decade now and it's no coincidence that I've produced some of my best work while with them. Thanks to David Everett, my students, and the faculty.

And, finally here's to Jacqueline Salmon, Sarah Wendel, and Chris Wendel—my wife and children. They are the ones who insist I keep swinging for the fences.

NOTES

PREFACE

xi **Vince Lombardi's second Super Bowl victory:** www.nfl.com.

xi **short view:** Bill Russell and Taylor Branch, *Second Win: The Memoirs of an Opinionated Man,* 96–97.

PART I

1 **Asking for autograph:** Willie Horton, author's interview, September 9, 2010.

2 **"basis of intimidation":** Bob Gibson, with Lonnie Wheeler, *Stranger to the Game,* 153–157.

2 **color of the afternoon:** "St. Louis Turn Off, Tunes In on Series Opener," *St. Louis Globe-Democrat,* October 3, 1968; "Conventional View Is Taken of Game," *New York Times,* October 3, 1968.

3 **643 batters at major-league level in 1968:** Baseball Hall of Fame research department. Figure supplied by the HOF Library in Cooperstown, N.Y.

3 **Seasonal statistics:** *The Baseball Encyclopedia: The Complete and Definitive Record of Major League Baseball,* Macmillan, 1993.

3 **"No hitter had an easy time":** Orlando Cepeda, author interview, August 31, 2010.

3 **Bob Gibson/Denny McLain statistics:** *Baseball Encyclopedia.*

4 **approaching a crossroads:** *Sports Illustrated,* "One Hundred and One," April 14, 1969.

4 **"People forget how honest":** Horton interview.

5 **Gibson was in rare form:** *St. Louis Globe-Democrat*; author interview with Tim McCarver, October 3, 1968.

5 **top arms in 1968:** Allan Roth, *Who's Who in Baseball,* published by Who's Who in Baseball Magazine Co., Inc., 1969.

5 **"Against studs like Gibson":** Don Drysdale and Bob Verdi, *Once a Bum, Always a Dodger,* 168.

6 **"You could see":** Gates Brown, author interview, September 9, 2010.

6 **Start of season:** Baseball Hall of Fame research department.

7 **"Strikeouts weren't the problem":** Nolan Ryan, author interview, June 16, 2009.

7 **"The evidence":** William Mead, author interview, October 15, 2010.

7 **Catfish Hunter's perfect game:** "Catfish Makes Perfecto Look Easy," *Sporting News,* May 25, 1968; "Catfish as Excited About His Hitting as Perfect Game," *Los Angeles Times,* May 9, 1968; "No runs, No Hits, No Errors," *New York Times,* May 14, 1968.

8 **Hunter background and signing:** "Finley Gifts Hunter with $5,000 Bonus for Perfect Game," *Los Angeles Times,* May 9, 1968; "In the Wake of the News . . . ," *Chicago Tribune,* May 10, 1968; "The Catfish Enigma," *New York Times Magazine,* September 7, 1975.

9 **"It was the times":** Jon Warden, author interview, May 11, 2010, and May 17, 2010.

10 **Vietnam War/Tet Offensive:** Mark Kurlansky, *1968: The Year That Rocked the World,"* 50–53.

10 **Walter Cronkite trip/televised remarks:** Daniel Hallin, "Vietnam on Television," online at Museum of Broadcast Communications, http://www.museum.tv/eotvsection.php?entrycode=vietnamonte

11 **"I experienced":** Ryan interview.

12 **"Let's just say":** Mickey Lolich, author interview, August 16, 2010.

12 **Detroit scene:** Mead interview.

12 **Red light:** Lolich interview.

12 **Detroit burned in 1967:** "The Great Rebellion," http://www.detroits-great-rebellion.com/.

13 **"There was no getting around it":** Frank Howard, author interview, September 15, 2010.

13 **Howard background and home-run streak:** "Howard Becomes Monster," *Washington Post,* May 19, 1968; "Howard Breaks 2 Home Run Records," *Chicago Tribune,* May 19, 1968; "Howard Set Record," *Los Angeles Times,* May 18, 1968; "Howard, Platooned and Dropped by

Dodgers, Thrives as Regular," *Los Angeles Times,* May 19, 1968; Bob Gibson and Reggie Jackson, *Sixty Feet, Six Inches: A Hall of Fame Pitcher & A Hall of Fame Hitter Talk About How the Game Is Played.*

PART II

17 **"best baseball town":** Tony La Russa, author interview, August 1999.

17 **St. Louis Cardinals *Sports Illustrated* cover:** http://sportsillustrated .cnn.com/vault/cover/featured/8096/index.htm

18 **"complete shock":** Cepeda interview.

19 **The "El Birdos" routine** was mentioned by several players and arguably the best description can be read in Gibson's *Stranger to the Game,* 131–132. It is also detailed in Doug Feldmann's *El Birdos: The 1967 and 1968 St. Louis Cardinals.*

20 **"no problem fitting in":** Nellie Briles, author interview, June 2003.

20 **"my reputation":** Gibson, 133–135.

21 **Reds brawl:** Cepeda interview.

21 **"rainbow coalition":** Gibson, 148.

22 **"I'll never forget":** *Sporting News,* January 15, 1968.

22 **"in the other man's shoes":** Gibson, 165.

23 **Busch Stadium:** Gary Gillette and Eric Enders, *Big League Ballpark: The Complete Illustrated History,* 290–298.

24 **Jim Ryun's struggles:** Richard Hoffer, *Something in the Air,* 41–43; Dr. Jack Daniels, author interview, July 14, 2010.

24 **three times the amount:** Roone Arledge, Museum of Broadcast Communications, http://www.museum.tv/.

26 **"changing events":** Daniels interview.

26 **"plain of Lethe":** James Hillman, *The Soul's Code: In Search of Character and Calling,* 46–47.

27 **"to be a ballplayer:"** Gibson, 15.

27 **Monarchs:** Ibid., 19.

28 **Globetrotters:** Ibid., 46–48.

28 **Passing Martin Luther King:** Ibid., 184.

28 **"Martin enjoyed sports":** Rev. Billy Kyles, author interview, June 15, 2011.

30 **"greatly admired":** Gibson, 124.

30 **King and Jackie Robinson:** SI.com, Dave Zirin, January 18, 2010, http://sportsillustrated.cnn.com/2010/writers/dave_zirin/01/18/mlk /index.html

30 **King meeting with Olympic athletes:** Ibid.

30 **"I agree with them":** "Bob Gibson: Black Man Nobody Wanted—Until He Was a Hero," Dwight Chapin, *Los Angeles Times,* July 5, 1968.

31 **John Carlos speechless:** Hoffer, 156.

31 **Sirens and lightning:** Kyles interview.

31 **Mason Temple:** http://www.nps.gov/nr/travel/civilrights/tn1.htm

32 **Martin Luther King's last speech** is chronicled in many places but none surpasses Hampton Sides' *Hellhound on his Trail,* 139–141.

32 **Elvis Presley film at State Theater:** Photo by Ernest C. Withers, exhibited at Memphis International Airport, June 17, 2011.

33 **"after you make a touchdown":** Andrew Young interview, audio for exhibit outside Room 306 of the Lorraine Hotel, National Civil Rights Museum.

33 **King assassination:** Kyles interview; Sides, 168–170; "An Assassination Remembered," *Time,* March 31, 2008.

34 **Bobby Kennedy in Indianapolis:** Thurston Clarke, *The Last Campaign: Robert F. Kennedy and 82 Days That Inspired America,* 91–98; audio available on YouTube, http://www.youtube.com/watch?v=3Zb9EjHXyJc

35 **"you can kill the dreamer, but you cannot kill the dream":** Kyles interview; *The Witness: From the Balcony of Room 306,* a film by Adam Pertofsky (dir.), Rock Paper Scissors with the National Civil Rights Museum, 2008. I'd also highly recommend a visit to the National Civil Rights Museum in Memphis, which has been built around the Lorraine Hotel. The tour includes the apartment building from across the street, where James Earl Ray fired his shots. I was also struck by how a wreath was put on the balcony railing outside Room 306 a few days after King's assassination and one has been maintained ever since.

35 **peanut butter and jelly sandwich:** Kyles interview.

36 **in St. Petersburg:** Gibson, 184–185.

36 **Boston Celtics:** http://www.hoophall.com/hall-of-famers/tag/william-f-bill-russell; "Sportsman of the Year: Bill Russell," *Sports Illustrated,* December 23, 1968; John Gardella, *2010–2011 Official NBA Guide;* Russell and Branch, 148–149.

39 **Drysdale's scoreless streak:** Drysdale and Verdi, 163–178; Jeff Torborg, author interview, March 9, 2009.

42 **Green Bay Packers:** David Maraniss, *When Pride Still Mattered: A Life of Vince Lombardi,* 410–415; Russell and Branch, 111.

43 **"a different direction":** Lamar Hunt, author interview, December 2000.

45 **Kennedy assassination:** Clarke, 271–273; YouTube, http://www.you tube.com/watch?v=vXuHcQlMrqs; "The Teammates," *New York Times*, June 8, 1968.

46 **"From here on":** "the Aftermath—Baseball Takes a Beating," *Sporting News*, June 22, 1968.

46 **Three . . . took matters:** "Compounding a Felony," *New York Times*, June 12, 1969; "Ballplayers Urge Day of Mourning," *Chicago Tribune*, June 8, 1968.

46 **"Among all the mealy-mouthed statements":** "Baseball's Brass Further Tarnished," Red Smith, *Washington Post*, June 11, 1968.

46 **Mets refuse to play:** "Giants Yield to Mets and Postpone Today's Game out of Respect for Kennedy," *New York Times*, June 8, 1968.

47 **"You guys are wrong":** *Sporting News*, June 22, 1968; Robert Lipsyte, "The Rebellion," *New York Times*, June 15, 1968.

47 **Pappas-Wagner confrontation:** Milt Pappas with Wayne Mausser and Larry Names, *Out at Home: Triumph and Tragedy in the Life of a Major Leaguer*, 189–190.

47 **Frank Mankiewicz sent telegrams:** Associated Press, "Kennedy Aide Applauds Stand of Mets, 4 Players," June 12, 1968.

47 **"We had been working on a trade":** "Atlanta Gets Pappas in 6-Player Deal," Richard Dozer, *Chicago Tribune*, June 12, 1968.

48 **"Baseball again returned to normalcy–confusion.":** *Sporting News*, June 22, 1968.

48 **"disorganized, illogical and thoroughly shabby":** Ibid.

48 **"This is the portrait of a commissioner trying to please everyone":** "Soft Generals Never Last, Eckert Warned," *New York Daily News*, June 9, 1968.

48 **Dodgers armbands:** National Baseball Hall of Fame research; Tom Shieber, author interview, Hall of Fame, May 15, 2011.

49 **End of Drysdale's streak:** Drysdale and Verdi, 171–174.

49 **"there was no escaping the pervasive realities of 1968":** Gibson, 187.

50 **"hogging the headlines":** Ibid., 187.

50 **"infuriated":** Ibid.

50 **"such intensity":** Briles interview.

50 **Gibson's shutout streak:** National Baseball Hall of Fame research; Bill Francis, author interview, Hall of Fame, July 5, 2011.

52 **"You saw it."** Gibson, 189.

PART III

53 **"have it slip away"**: Dick McAuliffe, author interview, July 15, 2011.

55 **"In '67, we were really"**: Ibid.

55 **"The team really grew up last year"**: *Sporting News*, March 23, 1968.

55 **Lakeland and Tigertown**: http://springtrainingonline.com/teams /detroit-tigers.htm

55 **one of the last big-league teams to integrate**: George Cantor, *The Tigers of '68: Baseball's Last Real Champions*, 26.

55 **Team breakdown**: Ibid., 14.

56 **"The door was open"**: Jon Warden interview.

56 **Denny McLain incident**: Cantor, 16–17; Mark Pattison and David Raglin, *Sock It to 'Em Tigers*, 111–112; Denny McLain with Eli Zaret, *I told You I Wasn't Perfect*, 81–82; "Baseball's Big Scandal," *Sports Illustrated*, February 23, 1970.

57 **orange hair**: Cantor, 17.

57 **contacts, Hammond organ, bowling**: "Never Touch a Superstar," Bill Freehan with Steve Gelman and Dick Shaap, *Sports Illustrated*, March 2, 1970; McLain, 83, 105.

58 **"Me? Revel in the media"**: McLain, 168.

58 **cortisone shots**: Mead interview; McLain, 127.

59 **McLain's background**: McLain, 13–21; Pattison and Raglin, 109–110.

59 **Tom McLain's death:** "He'd done a lot for baseball, and he'll be the first to let you know it," *Chicago Tribune*, David Condon, October 27, 1968.

60 **"clobbered pretty good"**: Lolich interview.

61 **Return to Portland**: Lolich interview; "Lolich Tops Premier Win," *(Portland) Oregonian*, May 31, 1962.

62 **Gerry Staley's instruction**: Lolich interview.

62 **Riding motorcycles**: Lolich interview; "Mickey Lolich: Out From Behind McLain's Shadow," *Super Sports*, March 1969.

62 **"Denny McLain was Denny McLain"**: McAuliffe interview.

63 **"Nobody cared"**: *The Wild Ride to Super Bowl I*, NFL Films, directors Ray Didinger, Jeff Hillegass, 2004.

63 **Super Bowl name**: www.superbowl.com.

64 **No footage exists**: Patrick Pano, NFL Films, author interview, January 11, 2006.

64 **"hooked on football"**: Hugh Hefner, author interview, January 14, 2006.

64 **"too predictable to be memorable"**: Michael MacCambridge, author interview, January 15, 2006.

64 **"bigger, grander":** MacCambridge interview.

65 **Tigers in camp:** Warden interview.

67 **"a graduate course in capturing the magic":** Gillette and Enders, 133.

68 **Detroit under curfew:** Warden interview.

68 **Riots in Detroit:** http://www.67riots.rutgers.edu/d_index.htm; Todd Gitlin, *The Sixties: Years of Hope, Days of Rage,* 245; Kurlansky, 8.

68 **Detroit riots:** Horton interview.

69 **philosophy of coaching:** Russell, 100.

70 **"If we can rebound":** Roland Lazenby, *Jerry West: The Life and Legend of a Basketball Icon,* 262.

70 **"Track is really psychic":** *Sports Illustrated,* December 23, 1968.

71 **"a fantastic athlete":** Ibid.

71 **"He is an unbelievable man":** Lazenby, 263.

72 **"hated anything (Celtic) green":** Ibid., 246.

72 **Wilt Chamberlain trade:** http://www.hoophall.com/hall-of-famers/tag/wilton-n-wilt-chamberlain

72 **"Don't be shy":** Gates Brown interview; Pattison and Raglin, 3–7.

76 **"Don't worry, Skip":** Bill Freehan with Steve Gelman and Dick Schaap, *Behind the Mask,* 16.

76 **"still in the worst way":** Warden interview.

PART IV

79 **road map:** Horton interview.

80 **tour of Detroit:** On the Road with Tom Stanton, September 9, 2010.

80 **"follow us on the radio":** Lolich interview.

80 **"best go home":** Horton interview.

80 **Detroit's shrinking population:** http://blog.mlive.com/chronicle/2008/04/report_detroits_population_to.html; http://mapscroll.blogspot.com/2009/06/shrinking-of-detroit.html; http://www.forbes.com/2007/06/11/ghost-cities-future-biz-cx_21cities_ee_0611ghostcities.html

81 **Henry Ford's old neighborhood:** "Henry Ford's Detroit Neighborhood Tries Hard to Keep Up Appearances," *Wall Street Journal,* September 11, 2008.

83 **"never really felt any pressure":** Horton interview.

83 **every port of call home:** Ibid.

85 **Walking the rails:** Ibid; Grant Eldridge and Karen Elizabeth Bush, *Willie Horton: Detroit's Own Willie the Wonder,* 18–24.

86 **"worst in the league":** McLain, 84–85, 91–92.

86 **"that was Denny McLain":** Brown interview.

87 **Key victory:** Jerry Green, *Year of the Tiger: A Diary of Detroit's World Champions*, 123–124.

87 **Fans tune in Harwell:** Lolich interview.

87 **"ridiculous divisive gossip":** Freehan, 94.

88 **The Lost Son of Havana:** Luis Tiant, author interview, June 12, 2002.

88 **Tiant's background:** Luis Tiant, with Joe Fitzgerald, *El Tiante: The Luis Tiant Story*, 22–25; http://www.baseball-almanac.com/players/player .php?p=tiantlu01

89 **"I didn't want him to come to America":** Rob Ruck, *Raceball: How the Major Leagues Colonized the Black and Latin Game*, 71.

90 **"still have nightmares":** Howard interview.

90 **"the ball last":** Bob Dolgan, *Baseball Digest*, July 2002.

90 **"finish what you started":** Ryan interview.

90 **"It's the amount of money":** Dick Bosman, author interview, June 22, 2009.

91 **the Robinsons . . . complained:** Dolgan.

91 **"never seen a fastball thrown so hard":** Ibid.

91 **"He's a great pitcher":** Tiant, 67.

92 **McLain serenades Tiger Stadium crowd:** Green, 117.

92 **Astrodome conditions:** "Tiant Claims Throw to 1st 'Moved Away,'" July 10, 1968.

93 **"No better example":** "National League Wins All-Star Game, 1–0, on Mays's Unearned Run in First," Leonard Koppett, *New York Times*, July 10, 1968.

93 **"I watched you on television":** Tiant, 73.

94 **"The Orioles are not winning":** "Ousted Bauer Blasts Choice of Successor," *Los Angeles Times*, July 12, 1968.

95 **"a pennant contender":** "Orioles Name Earl Weaver," *Chicago Tribune*, July 1968.

95 **Home run club:** Hank Aaron, author interview, October 2, 2000.

95 **"huge block 'S'":** "Aaron, r.f.—Story of Superman in Flannels," Jim Murray, *Los Angeles Times*, July 23, 1968.

96 **"not sure I've mastered it yet":** "Record Looms for Wilhelm By Birthday," *Washington Post*, July 24, 1968.

96 **Hansen triple play:** Associated Press, "Hansen in Triple Play Unassisted," July 31, 1968.

97 **"fighting for thirty wins":** Tiant, 67.

97 **"If Luis played for us":** Ibid, 68.

97 **"So all I want is twenty wins":** Ibid.

97 **"never have an easy inning":** Tiant interview.

97 **"hurt his arm":** Tiant, 70.

98 **Alvin Dark legacy:** Cepeda interview; Ruck, 164–165.

99 **"It's a different race":** Daniels interview.

99 **Balke's involvement:** Ibid.

100 **"No you're not":** Ibid.

100 **"Chemistry":** Horton interview.

101 **Plane in Pool:** Cantor, 137–140; Lolich interview; Brown interview.

102 **"patient at plate":** Tim McCarver, with Phil Pepe, *Few and Chosen: Defining Greatness Across the Eras*, 98.

103 **Flood background:** Brad Snyder, *A Well-Paid Slave: Curt Flood's Fight for Free Agency in Professional Sports*. This remains the definitive work for anyone wishing to read more about Flood and his epic court battle.

103 **"child of the Sixties":** Ken Burns, *Baseball* (PBS, 1996).

104 **Following in Lombardi's footsteps:** If Snyder's biography is the one to read about Flood, then certainly David Maraniss's *When Pride Still Mattered* remains the standard on the football coaching legend.

104 **"new regime":** Maraniss, 443.

105 **"not dead":** Ibid., 444.

106 **Chicago:** Tom Hayden, author interview, February 28, 2011, and May 28, 2011.

106 **Lombardi VP choice:** Maraniss, 445.

106 **Nixon then Kennedy:** Ibid, 446.

106 **Kennedy telegram:** Ibid. Also cited in several other publications.

107 **Harrelson at Tiger Stadium:** Ken Harrelson, author interview, August 16, 2011; Green, 94–95; McLain, 88.

108 **"whole world gone crazy":** Green, 74.

108 **"doesn't need . . . basic training":** Ibid., 96.

108 **No permits in Chicago:** Hayden interview; Kurlansky, 281.

108 **16 million watched on television:** www.nielsenwire.com; also available on http://www.youtube.com/watch?v=KvebyWqLXeo&feature=related.

108 **Tigers-White Sox game rescheduled for Milwaukee:** Cantor, 136.

109 **"pro-war stances":** Kurlansky, 281.

109 **"We flew into Chicago":** Larry Dierker, author interview, July 13, 2011.

110 **"clubbing anyone they could find":** Kurlansky, 282.

110 **"amazed by what was going on":** Dierker interview.

111 **"guy who made us go":** Brown interview.

111 **"hard as I've ever been hit"**: McAuliffe interview.

112 **"I'm dead"**: Green, 163.

112 **McLain missed fight**: Ibid., 165.

113 **McAuliffe suspended**: McAuliffe interview; Green, 166.

114 **"I feel so funky"**: Cantor, 109.

114 **blackboard in Yankee Stadium**: Green, 170; Cantor, 110.

115 **Showdown with Dark**: Tiant interview; Tiant, 71.

PART V

117 **"pins and needles"**: Hayden interview.

118 **"a little guy, always arguing"**: Freehan, 22.

118 **"good memory"**: Hayden interview.

118 **"some of the best amateur baseball"**: Freehan, 21.

118 **"Wouldn't it be funny?"**: Green, 173.

119 **"It took a lot"**: McAuliffe interview.

119 **"only four games ahead"**: Green, 174.

120 **"it will just about be over"**: Ibid, 177.

120 **"If we beat them tomorrow"**: Ibid, 179.

120 **"It's first goddamn inning"**: McLain, 99.

121 **"Fastball's coming"**: Ibid, 100.

121 **"flair for showmanship"**: Green, 179.

122 **Ed Sullivan**: McLain, 102–103; Green, 187; Cantor, 144.

122 **Winning No. 30**: McLain, 104–106; Green, 189–196; Cantor, 145–148.

122 **"How could I be a thirty-game winner?"**: Green, 189–190.

124 **Children's Crusade**: Cantor, 145.

125 **Gibson's closing run**: "Gibson was great in '68," Bill Deane, Baseball Analysts, http://baseballanalysts.com/archives/2005/06/gibson_was _grea_1.php

126 **"I mastered my craft"**: Gibson, 1. Ironically, this is the opening line, his "Call me, Ishmael," of his second memoir.

126 **"always gave you a ball to hit"**: Gibson and Jackson (this is Jackson's opinion), 147.

127 **Grooving one to Mickey Mantle**: McLain, 111–113; Green, 210, Cantor, 154–157.

129 **Gibson's reaction**: Gibson, 200.

129 **"a nice guy like Roger"**: Pappas, 84.

130 **Only fastballs to Maris**: Ibid., 84–85.

130 **"To have any hope"**: Ryan interview.

131 **Perry's no-hitter:** Associated Press, "Perry Hurls No-Hitter," September 18, 1968; United Press International, "Mom Misses No-Hitter by Perry," September 19, 1968; United Press International, "'My Biggest Thrill,' Says Veteran Perry," September 18, 1968; Gaylord Perry, author interview, August 2001.

131 **"They are not":** Shirley Povich, *Washington Post*, September 20, 1968.

131 **Washburn's no hitter:** Associated Press, "Cards' Washburn Hurls No-Hitter, Second Successive One at Giants' Park," September 19, 1968; Harry Jupiter, "Gay, Ray Play No-Hit Tit for Tat," *Sporting News*, October 5, 1968.

132 **"kind of summed that up":** Perry interview.

132 **Candlestick Park:** Gillette and Enders, 222–229.

133 **"Prayer":** Brett Butler, author interview, September 1990.

134 **"culture of the new league":** MacCambridge, 250.

135 **Zimmerman on Namath:** Ibid., 251.

135 **"It was redundant":** Ibid., 262.

136 **"meant to . . . pitch":** Tiant interview.

136 **"flared like a bull":** Tiant, 69.

137 **"bowing the neck":** Ibid.

137 **"watch TV":** Tiant interview.

137 **"end of an era":** Mead interview.

138 **"I would not trade places with anyone":** Associated Press, "Rose Doesn't Walk, He Always Hustles," June 30, 1968.

138 **Look out for Lolich:** McCarver interview.

139 **Smith retools lineup for World Series:** Green, 211–213; Cantor, 166–170; Pattison and Raglin, 159–163, 193–196.

140 **"Smith was really ahead of his time":** Dave Raglin, author interview, July 6, 2011.

141 **"asleep at the switch":** Ibid.

141 **Other World Series gambles:** Bill Francis, National Baseball Hall of Fame, author interview, September 10, 2011.

142 **"started to practice":** Horton interview.

PART VI

145 **End of year statistics for 1968:** National Baseball Hall of Fame research.

146 **"big heart":** Steve Jacobson, "Perfect Match? Gibson vs. McLain," *Newsday*, September 28, 1968.

146 **"influence of champagne":** *Sporting News*, October 19, 1968.

146 **at Gas House Lounge:** McLain, 116; Green, 215–216; Cantor, 183.

148 **"Our guys were charged up":** *Sporting News*, October 19, 1968.

148 **Gibson Message to Tigers:** Ibid.

148 **"just be adequate":** Ibid; Cantor, 171–175.

149 **"lay off his high stuff":** Associated Press, "Cards' Plan," October 3, 1968.

149 **"Surprised?":** "McLain Stunned at Being Lifted," *St. Louis Post-Dispatch*, October 3, 1968.

150 **Crowd:** "Sinatra Won Crowd, Gibson the Game," *St. Louis Globe-Democrat*, October 3, 1968.

150 **"I read it on the board":** "Gibson Overwhelms Tigers," *St. Louis Globe-Democrat*, October 3, 1968.

151 **Gibson strikes out Kaline, Cash and then Horton:** Perhaps the best description of this record-breaking sequence belongs to David Halberstam. "Could We Be Friends?" *Parade Magazine*, July 24, 1994.

151 **"the toughest pitcher":** Horton interview.

152 **"we can't beat him":** "Tigers Impressed," *St. Louis Globe-Democrat*, October 3, 1968.

152 **"wonderful pitcher":** *Sporting News*, October 19, 1968.

152 **"guys who swing for home runs":** "Gibson's Pitches Slide by Tiger Batters, *St. Louis Post-Dispatch*, October 3, 1968.

152 **back at Gas House:** Green, 217.

154 **McCarthy roamed the field:** "This time Sen. McCarthy Won't be Shut Out," Stan Isaacs, *Newsday*, October 4, 1968; "McCarthy Plays No Favorites," *St. Louis Globe-Democrat*, October 4, 1968; Special thanks to former scout Phil Pote for the tutorial on fungo bats.

154 **"the problem and the attraction":** Hayden interview.

154 **"a little groggy":** Lolich interview.

155 **"until I see a replay":** *Sports Illustrated*, October 19, 1968.

155 **"wasn't my day":** "Briles Bemoans Home-run Habit," *St. Louis Globe-Democrat*, October 4, 1968.

156 **"we had some fun":** Brown interview.

156 **"my best three arms":** Green, 220–221.

156 **"self glory":** *Sporting News*, October 19, 1968.

156 **in the Detroit bullpen:** Warden interview.

157 **"None of the Cardinals' six hits":** *Sporting News*, October 19, 1968.

157 **"enjoy days like this":** Feldmann, 339.

157 **"in good shape":** "Reflecting Tigers Find Themselves, *Newsday*, October 4, 1968.

157 **Smith/Horton meeting:** Horton interview; Green 221–222.

158 **Curtis LeMay:** "LeMay Joins Wallace," *St. Louis Globe-Democrat*, October 4, 1968.

158 **Riots in Mexico City:** *The National Security Archive*, October 10, 2003; Kurlansky, 321–344. I highly recommend both sources for those looking to read more about the student demonstrations on the eve of the Mexico City Games.

159 **Detroit preps:** "Detroit Fever High," *Sporting News*, October 19, 1968.

159 **"Whoever wins today":** Ibid.

160 **"Speed":** Lou Brock, author interview, July 1999.

161 **"play without bases":** *Sporting News*, October 19, 1968.

161 **"That's how quickly":** Mead interview.

161 **Washburn:** Feldmann, 341.

162 **"When it all came together for us":** Cepeda interview.

162 **"cooked":** *Sporting News*, October 19, 1968.

162 **Rain:** Brown interview.

163 **On . . . campaign trail:** "Nixon Helped," *Newsday*, October 7, 1968.

163 **"they take it away from us":** "No Authority in Rain Game, Umps Say," *Sporting News*, October 19, 1968.

164 **"I'm not a mudder":** McLain, 117.

165 **"toast is burnt":** Gibson, 146.

165 **Flowers:** Ibid., 203.

166 **Sparma:** Pattison and Raglin, 153–157.

166 **Rain:** "Fair Weather Fans Dampened: Rain and Tears," *Detroit Free Press*, October 7, 1968.

167 **"trying to stall":** *Sporting News*, October 19, 1968.

167 **"In rain or shine":** "A Clay-Tongued McCarver Immortalizes His Pal Gibson," *Newsday*, October 7, 1968.

167 **"become a farce":** Green, 226–227.

167 **Eckert and steroids:** *www.steroidsinbaseball.net*.

168 **Brock steals:** *Sporting News*, October 19, 1968.

168 **"I almost got in":** Warden interview.

170 **"And we aren't":** Green, 227.

170 **"grasping at straws":** Horton interview.

171 **"The guy on either side of you":** Lolich interview.

171 **Jose Feliciano's rendition of the national anthem:** "Fans Irate Over 'Desecrated' Anthem," Barbara Stanton, *Detroit Free Press*, which later was republished in *Sporting News*, October 19, 1968; McLain, 118–119; Lolich interview.

172   **"we would wrap it up"**: Cepeda interview.

172   **"I was in control"**: Briles interview.

173   **"wasn't the game plan"**: Lolich interview.

174   **"He's not Carl Yastrzemski or Reggie Jackson"**: Feldmann, 351.

174   **Play at the plate**: Horton interview; *Sporting News*, October 19, 1968;
        Green, 229–231; Cantor, 197–198; Feldmann, 351; Gibson, 203–204;
        Bob Broeg, author interview, August 2, 1996; National Baseball Hall of
        Fame, archived interview. As you can see, everyone weighs in on this cru-
        cial play, the one on which the 1968 Series turned.

175   **"Some superstitions die hard"**: Horton interview.

176   **Feliciano backlash**: Cantor, 196–197; Feldmann, 349; Green, 229;
        McLain, 118–119.

177   **"What made this wait so acute"**: Ibid, 149–150,

178   **McLain's preparation**: *Sporting News*, October 19, 1968; McLain, 119–
        120; Mead interview.

178   **"The rules for Denny"**: Freehan, 35.

179   **"lie and lie"**: Brown interview.

181   **Jack McKeon/Josh Beckett**: "McKeon, Beckett: Old Man & The
        MVP," *Hartford Courant*, October 26, 2003.

182   **"just like college to us"**: Horton interview.

182   **"Cheeseburger, fries, vanilla shake"**: Lolich interview.

182   **Northrup's grand slam**: *Sporting News*, October 19, 1968.

183   **"He was the emotional backbone"**: *Detroit Free Press*, June 12, 2011.

184   **"better pitcher with a lead"**: Gibson, 205.

185   **"I didn't hate Denny, no"**: Cantor, 188; McLain 120–121.

185   **"Lolich was so miserable"**: McLain, 121.

186   **"There wasn't a lot of love lost"**: Warden interview.

186   **"the last guy"**: McLain 98–99.

186   **"We battled back"**: *Sporting News*, October 19, 1968.

187   **"didn't have to prove a goddamn thing"**: Green, 236.

188   **Tigers clubhouse**: Feldmann, 356.

188   **"comedy act"**: Green, 240.

188   **"not a good psychologist"**: Ibid.

188   **"down to me and Lolich"**: Gibson, 205.

188   **"I felt fine"**: Lolich interview.

189   **shock-wave machine**: "Add a Machine to Tiger Heroes," *Newsday*, Oc-
        tober 11, 1968.

189   **"get to Lolich"**: Gibson, 205.

189 **"I wasn't feeling good really":** Lolich interview.

190 **Hamburger conversation:** Freehan, 77–78.

191 **Picking off Brock, then Flood:** Feldman, 356–357; Green, 240–241; *Sporting News*, October 19, 1968.

191 **"had to navigate":** Gibson, 205.

191 **"in my ear":** Horton interview.

192 **two pedestrian singles:** "'68 wasn't for the Bird," *St. Louis Post-Dispatch*, October 21, 2005.

192 **Flood's play/Northrup's triple:** "It's My Fault . . . " *Detroit Free Press*, October 11, 1968; Gibson, 205–207; Feldmann, 357–358; Green, 240–241; Cantor, 202–204; McCarver interview; Horton interview; McAuliffe interview.

193 **"absolutely agreed":** "Jim Northrup, hero of 1968 champion Tigers, dies at 71," *Detroit Free Press*, June 8, 2011.

194 **"I remain grateful to Schoendienst":** Gibson, 206.

195 **Tigers champions:** Lolich interview; Horton interview; *Sporting News*, October 26, 1968; "Tigers On Top of World!" *Detroit Free Press*, October 11, 1968; "Lolich Can't Find Room to Celebrate," *Detroit Free Press*, October 11, 1968.

197 **Motown celebration:** " . . . When Our Tigers Came Through for Us!" *Detroit Free Press*, October, 11 1968; "Win Puts Detroit in High Gear," *Newsday*, October 11, 1968; "The Night Detroit Went Wild Over Its World Champs," *Sporting News*, October 26, 1968; "We Win!," *Detroit Free Press*, October 11, 1968; Cantor, 205–210; Green, 243–248; Feldmann, 359.

198 **Lady at the airport:** Gibson, 207.

PART VII

200 **Tiant's mother visits:** Tiant interview; Tiant, 73–75.

201 **"idiotic idea":** "But Only On Sunday," Kenny Moore, *Sports Illustrated*, February 26, 1973.

202 **Ryun's race:** Daniels interview; Hoffer, 199–202.

204 **Visit to NFL Films Library:** September 18, 2010.

209 **Hickok Belt:** Q&A with Scott Pitoniak, *USA Today*, Sports section, January 18, 2011. Scott Pitoniak is the author of *Jewel of the Sports World*.

210 **"Things were never the same":** Gibson, 208–209.

211 **Horton lands Gibson's autograph:** Horton interview.

AFTERMATH

213 **ready for long run**: National Baseball Hall of Fame research department.

213 **elite status:** Lolich interview; Pattison and Raglin, 83–89.

214 **Las Vegas gig:** McLain, 167–208, 261–348; Pattison and Raglin, 109–115; "Denny's Vegas Debut Called 'Less Than Smashing,'" *Detroit News*, December 14, 1968; "His Idol is Sinatra," *Time*, September 13, 1968; "Never Touch a Superstar," *Look*, March 2, 1970.

216 **same batting helmet:** Horton interview; Pattison and Raglin, 67–72.

216 **only Fall Classic appearance:** http://www.thebaseballpage.com/players/kalinal01; Pattison and Raglin, 73–78; Hal Butler, *Al Kaline and the Detroit Tigers*, Henry Regnery, 1973; Seth Swirsky, *Baseball Letters*, Three Rivers Press, 88–89.

217 **one of the few:** Brown interview; Pattison and Raglin, 3–8.

217 **serious knee injury:** McAuliffe interview; Pattison and Raglin, 101–108.

218 **future appears bright:** Warden interview; Pattison and Raglin, 169–172.

219 **Roster changes:** Cardinals' postscript, National Baseball Hall of Fame research department, Bill Francis interview, July 5, 2011.

219 **"Trading Cepeda":** Gibson, 211.

220 **critic of lowering the mound:** Gibson, 222–247; http://www.baseball library.com/ballplayers/player.php?name=Bob_Gibson_1935

220 **"Bob's caliber":** Aaron interview.

220 **"I wish I could have played on the same team with him":** National Baseball Hall of Fame research department, material gathered for Gibson's Hall of Fame induction in 1981.

220 **"the opportunity":** *Baseball Digest*, March 1972.

220 **"plain old guts":** Ibid.

220 **MVP candidate:** Brock interview; http://www.baseballlibrary.com/ballplayers/player.php?name=Lou_Brock_1939

221 **rally his teammates:** Cepeda interview; http://www.baseballlibrary.com/ballplayers/player.php?name=Orlando_Cepeda_1937

222 **"reminds me of Eddie Mathews":** "Cards' Shannon Fights Nephritis," Joe Donnelly, *Newsday*, May 4, 1971; "Sunny Side Up: Mike Shannon Like to Embrace Life Fully," *St. Louis Post-Dispatch*, August 11, 1996; "Woman, Barber, Goat Have Story with a Familiar Ring–Shannon's," *St. Louis Post-Dispatch*, June 15, 1995.

223 **"born surly"**: "Roger Maris Is Dead at 51," *New York Times*, December 15, 1985; "Broadcaster friend says Maris would tune in," *USA Today*, September 1, 1998.

224 **better entertainer:** Briles interview; http://www.baseballlibrary.com /ballplayers/player.php?name=Nellie_Briles_1943

224 **signature offering:** Feldmann, 370–371; www.carlton32.com; Tim McCarver with Danny Peary. *Tim McCarver's Baseball for Brain Surgeons and Other Fans*, 51.

226 **gains a following:** McCarver interview; Feldmann, 370–371. http://www .baseballlibrary.com/ballplayers/player.php?name=Tim_McCarver_1941

226 **shake up teams:** Feldman, 372–373; Snyder, 1–16; Gibson, 218–221. http://www.baseballlibrary.com/ballplayers/player.php?name=Curt _Flood_1938

228 **princely sum:** "Catfish Hunter Dead, CNN/SI, http://sportsillustrated .cnn.com/baseball/mlb/news/1999/09/09/hunter_obit_ap/index.html

228 **league-worst twenty games:** Tiant interview; http://www.latino sportslegends.com/Tiant_Luis-bio.htm; http://bioproj.sabr.org/bioproj .cfm?a=v&v=l&bid=645&pid=14207

229 **"The Capitol Punisher":** Howard interview; http://www.thebaseball page.com/players/howarfr01

229 **reaches the twenty-victory plateau:** Dierker interview; http://www .larrydierker.com

229 **decides to tough it out:** Ryan interview; http://mlb.mlb.com/tex /community/executives/ryan.html

230 **curious disappearance of his wife:** Pappas, 326–337; "Body Found in Submerged Car Is Identified as Wife of Milt Pappas," *Los Angeles Times*, August 9, 1987.

231 **once again catch fire:** http://www.nba.com/history/players/russell _bio.html

231 **third, behind Muhammad Ali and Michael Jordan:** http://www .museum.tv/eotvsection.php?entrycode=arledgeroon

231 **good enough to win:** Daniels interview; Hoffer, 200–202; http://www .distancerunning.com/inductees/2003/ryun.html; http://www.you tube.com/watch?v=jZ8OieCDOk8

231 **caps off the 1968 season:** http://www.profootballhof.com/hof /member.aspx?player_id=161

232 **"partly truth and partly fiction, a walking contradiction":** Hayden interview; http://tomhayden.com/biography/

BIBLIOGRAPHY

Baseball Encyclopedia: The Complete and Definitive Record of Major League Baseball. Macmillan, 1993.

Brennan, Christine. *Best Seat In The House: A Father, A Daughter, A Journey Through Sports.* Lisa Drew/Scribner, 2006.

Brokaw, Tom. *Boom! Talking About the Sixties.* Random House, 2007.

Bulter, Hall. *Al Kaline and the Detroit Tigers.* Henry Regnery, 1973.

Cantor, George. *The Tigers of '68: Baseball's Last Real Champions.* Taylor, 1997.

Charters, Ann. *The Portable Sixties Reader.* Penguin, 2003.

Clarke, Thurston. *The Last Campaign: Robert F. Kennedy and 82 Days That Inspired America.* Henry Holt, 2008.

Drysdale, Don, and Bob Verdi. *Once A Bum, Always A Dodger: My Life in Baseball from Brooklyn to Los Angeles.* St. Martin's Press, 1990.

Eldridge, Grant, and Karen Elizabeth Bush. *Willie Horton: Detroit's Own Willie the Wonder.* Wayne State University Press, 2001.

Enders, Eric. *Baseball's Greatest Games.* MLB Insiders Club, 2008.

Feldman, Doug. *El Birdos: The 1967 and 1968 St. Louis Cardinals.* McFarland, 2007.

Freehan, Bill, with Steve Geldman and Dick Schaap. *Behind the Mask.* Maddick Manuscripts, 1970.

Gardella, John. *Official NBA Guide, 2010–2011 Edition.* NBA Properties, 2010.

Gibson, Bob, with Lonnie Wheeler. *Stranger to the Game: The Autobiography of Bob Gibson.* Viking, 1994.

Gibson, Bob, and Reggie Jackson, with Lonnie Wheeler. *Sixty Feet, Six Inches: A Hall of Fame Pitcher and A Hall of Famer Hitter Talk About How the Game Is Played.* Doubleday, 2009.

Gillette, Gary, and Eric Enders, with Stuart Shea and Matthew Silverman. *Big League Ballparks: The Complete Illustrated History.* Metro Books, 2009.

Gitlin, Todd. *The Sixties: Years of Hope, Days of Rage.* Bantam, 1987.

Green, Jerry. *Year of the Tiger: The Diary of Detroit's World Champions.* Coward-McCann, 1969.

Greene, Graham. *Ways of Escape.* Lester & Orphen Dennys, 1980.

Halberstam, David. *October 1964.* Ballantine, 1994.

Hoffer, Richard. *Something in the Air: American Passion and Defiance in the 1968 Mexico City Olympics.* Free Press, 2009.

Hillman, James. *The Soul's Code: In Search of Character and Calling.* Random House, 1996.

Kaiser, Charles. *1968 in America: Music, Politics, Chaos, Counterculture and the Shaping of a Generation.* Grove, 1988.

Kurlansky, Mark. *1968: The Year That Rocked the World.* Random House, 2004.

Lazenby, Roland. *Jerry West: The Life and Legend of a Basketball Icon.* Ballantine, 2009.

Lipsyte, Robert. *An Accidental Sportswriter.* Ecco, 2011.

MacCambridge, Michael. *America's Game: The Epic Story of How Pro Football Captured a Nation.* Anchor, 2004.

Maraniss, David. *When Pride Still Mattered: A Life of Vince Lombardi.* Simon & Schuster, 1999.

McCarthy, Eugene. *The Year of the People.* Doubleday, 1969.

McCarver, Tim, with Danny Peary. *Tim McCarver's Baseball for Brain Surgeons and Other Fans.* Random House, 1998.

McCarver, Tim, with Phil Pepe. *Few and Chosen: Defining Cardinal Greatness Across the Eras.* Triumph, 2003.

McCarver, Tim, with Ray Robinson. *Oh, Baby, I Love It!* Villard, 1987.

McLain, Denny, with Eli Zaret. *I Told You I Wasn't Perfect.* Triumph, 2007.

Mead, William. *Two Spectacular Seasons: 1930 The Year the Hitters Ran Wild, 1968 the Year the Pitchers Took Revenge.* Macmillan, 1990.

Norman, Philip. *Shout! The Beatles in Their Generation.* MJF Books, 1981.

Pappas, Milt, with Wayne Mausser and Larry Names. *Out At Home: Triumph and Tragedy in the Life of a Major Leaguer.* LKP Group, 2000.

Pattison, Mark, and David Raglin. *Sock it to 'Em Tigers.* Maple Street Press, 2008.

Risen, Clay. *A Nation on Fire: America in the Wake of the King Assassination.* John Wiley & Songs, 2009.

Pitoniak, Scott. *Jewel of the Sports World: The Story of the Hickok Belt.* RIT Cary Press, 2010.

Price, Reynolds. *Letter to a Man In the Fire: Does God Exist and Does He Care?* Scribner, 1999.

Ruck, Rob. *Raceball: How the Major Leagues Colorized the Black and Latin Game.* Beacon Press, 2010.

Russell, Bill, and Taylor Branch. *Second Wind: The Memoirs of an Opinionate Man.* Random House, 1979.

Schlesinger Jr., Arthur M. *Robert Kennedy and His Times, Volume II.* Houghton Mifflin, 1978.

Sides, Hampton. *Hellhound on His Trail: The Talking of Martin Luther King Jr. and the International Hunt for His Assassin.* Doubleday, 2010.

Snyder, Brad. *A Well-Paid Slave: Curt Flood's Fight for Free Agency in Professional Sports.* Plume, 2007.

Stanton, Tom. *The Final Season: Fathers, Sons, and One Last Season in a Classic American Ballpark.* Thomas Dunne, 2001.

———. *The Detroit Tigers Reader.* University of Michigan Press, 2005.

Swirsky, Seth. *Baseball Letters: A Fan's Correspondence with His Heroes.* Three Rivers Press, 1996.

Tiant, Luis, with Joe Fitzgerald. *El Tiante: The Luis Tiant Story.* Doubleday, 1976.

Ward, Geoffrey, and Ken Burns. *Baseball: An Illustrated History.* Alfred Knopf, 1994.

INDEX